WHY TRUST MATTERS

WHY TRUST MATTERS

An Economist's Guide to the Ties That Bind Us

BENJAMIN HO

Columbia University Press   *New York*

Columbia University Press
Publishers Since 1893
New York   Chichester, West Sussex
cup.columbia.edu

Library of Congress Cataloging-in-Publication Data
Names: Ho, Benjamin Tseng author.
Title: Why trust matters : an economist's guide to the ties that bind
us / Benjamin Ho.
Description: New York City : Columbia University Press, 2021. |
Includes index.
Identifiers: LCCN 2020051482 (print) | LCCN 2020051483 (ebook) |
ISBN 9780231189606 (hardback) | ISBN 9780231548427 (ebook)
Subjects: LCSH: Trust–Economic aspects. |
Economics–Psychological aspects. | Game theory.
Classification: LCC HB72 .H596 2021 (print) |
LCC HB72 (ebook) | DDC 330.01/9–dc23
LC record available at https://lccn.loc.gov/2020051482
LC ebook record available at https://lccn.loc.gov/2020051483

Columbia University Press books are printed on permanent and
durable acid-free paper.

Printed in the United States of America

Cover design: Milenda Nan Ok Lee
Cover image: kadirkaba © iStock

BRIEF CONTENTS

ACKNOWLEDGMENTS

THANK you to all the many readers, students, and former students who gave comments and feedback of early drafts along the way. Writing a book is daunting, and you worry that nothing you write makes any sense. Comments and suggestions provided helpful reassurance that at least some parts of the book now make some sense to at least some people.

Thank you all of my former students, and in particular to Ivy Teng, Stephanie Coons, Zoey Chopra, Eric Heydorn, and Sanaya Shikari for their detailed comments.

Thank you to my research assistant, Diana Henry, whom I hired because she never hesitated to challenge my ideas. She helped greatly in thinking through the structure and themes of the book. Thank you also to my line editor, Sara Streett, whose careful and critical reading did much to clarify my prose and my thinking. Thank you to Seth Stephens-Davidovitz for his guidance. Thank you to my friend Reza Hasmath for our long discussions about trust that helped inspire this book.

Thank you to my great and supportive editors at Columbia University Press, Bridget Flannery-McCoy, Eric Schwartz, and Christian Winting.

Thank you to my PhD advisor Edward Lazear, who passed away shortly before this book came to print. While I was still a student, he told me to always sign and dedicate every gift copy of the book that he was sure I would one day write. I was excited to dedicate the first copy to him. His influence is everywhere in this book, particularly his unwavering faith in the ability of economics to uncover universal truths. He will be greatly missed.

Thank you to all my professors, friends, and colleagues who have shaped my intellectual journey, challenged my ideas and forced to refine my thinking.

Thank you to my mom, Lan Ho, for making me the person I am today, and my brother Andy Schlesinger, for always keeping me honest.

Finally, thank you to my wife, Romina Wahab, who has supported me every step of the way, and to my children for their inspiration and for always reminding me about what is most important.

WHY TRUST MATTERS

1

ECONOMICS OF TRUST

HAVE you ever thought about how amazing it is that we tend to trust one another and about what it took to get us here? Not long ago, life, as the philosopher Thomas Hobbes characterized it in the 1690s, was "nasty, brutish, and short," "a war of all against all," but today, we can walk down the street feeling relatively safe, buying things from anonymous strangers, like the book you are reading now.

Just think about all the little leaps of trust that brought you here, reading my book about trust. You had to trust the bookseller to give you a book in exchange for your money and not just take the money and run. Or if you made the purchase online, you had to trust your bank or Visa or Mastercard to accurately keep track of your money or credit and transfer the proper amount to the bookseller's account. You had to trust the bookseller's website to not steal your account information. Alhough you may not have thought about it, you also had to trust the central bank that issued the currency that you used to pay for the book to maintain the value of the money you used. We don't always think about this, but every action that we take in our complex, interdependent society—buying a book, driving to work, dropping the kids off at school, picking up groceries—requires the combined efforts of countless numbers of people working in concert to enable that thing to happen. It seems risky when you do stop to think about it: people can be unreliable, and the more people we depend on, the greater the risk.

How, then, did our society (particularly our global society) grow so complex and interdependent? Economic historians could tell a long and interesting story about the growth of trade, the development of technology and the advantages of specialization, and the role of capital investment in fueling innovation—but this story ultimately rests on a deeper one. This is the story of the "it factor" that enables trade and specialization and investment and innovation. It is a story that goes all the way back to the beginning of human civilization and all the way down to the bedrock of our relationships with one another. It is the story of how we learned to rely on one another in spite of the risks.

It is the story (the history) of *trust*.

As I see it, the story of human civilization is the story of how we learned to trust one another. In the beginning, humanity lived in small tribes. We learned that we could accomplish more together than alone. Members of a group could hunt larger prey and better defend themselves from predators. But working with others involves relying on others, and trust becomes more difficult as the number of others increases. As civilization grew and became more complex, people moved to cities and organized themselves into guilds and city-states and nations. Living with more people required learning to trust in new ways, and institutions developed—through religion, markets, and the rule of law—that enabled the development of ever-more-complex societies and the coordination of ever-larger networks of people. This is the process that brought us to the modern economies and societies of the twenty-first century, even as our premodern tribal instincts continue to structure modern life.

This book will examine how trust structures our religions and our workplaces, how trust informs how we apologize and why we laugh. The brands we buy and the politicians who run our democracies all seek to win our trust. Every time we interact with another person under conditions of uncertainty, we are engaging in an act of trust.

If you're surprised to learn that trust is something economists care about, I'm *not* surprised. Perhaps you see trust as falling within the purview of other social sciences—psychology, anthropology, or sociology, or perhaps even philosophy. You would be right, and part of the goal of this book is to see what economics can learn from those other disciplines. But trust is deeply important to economics as well. Even the word "trust" is deeply entwined with how we think about the economy. A bank is sometimes called a trust; many corporations are managed by trustees; money saved for our children can be placed in a trust.

At the introductory level, economics professors like me tend to portray economic actors as faceless and impersonal, but this is merely a useful fiction (in the same way that physicists assume frictionless surfaces) that we eventually relax as our economic concepts and principles mature. These days, economics recognizes that only "rational fools" would neglect the importance of relationships in structuring interactions within the modern economy.[1] Trust is essential to structuring our workplace relationships, our relationships with brands, our investment relationships—right down to our relationship with national currencies and the institutions that guarantee their value. Many of the most recent innovations in the online economy are about trust, from how we connect on social networks to the platforms that power the sharing economies of Uber and Airbnb. Blockchain is a technology designed to digitize trust.

In recent decades, however, we have also begun to see trust fraying at the edges. Trust in the media, politicians, doctors, government—in expertise generally—has eroded. Patterns of trust have been mixed, with some ups and some downs, but the negatives are noticeable and significant. This book looks at the causes of these trends and what economics could do to help mitigate them.

WHY READ AN ECONOMICS BOOK ABOUT TRUST?

Trust is so fundamental to the human experience that philosophers, sociologists, psychologists, and anthropologists have all devoted a lot of attention to its study. So why should you care what an economist has to say about it? After all, just because trust is fundamental to the functioning of the economy doesn't mean that economists are best able to explain trust. You may even think that economics is especially ill suited to the task of understanding trust: economics is about transactions and money, numbers and figures and rates. It makes sense that your first instinct might be to distrust people who seem to care only about money.

To an economist, however, economic science is about more than just making money. It is about making choices. You may have read or heard that economics is about *scarcity*: economists use this term to remind us that every choice we make requires trade-offs. (At least all the interesting ones do.) If we lived in an Edenic paradise where all our desires were taken care of, then we could all have everything we wanted; scarcity reminds us that resources are finite and that choices must be made. Even if we had unlimited money, we have limited time, so we must make trade-offs. Choices that require trade-offs require us to understand the pros and cons of each choice in order to assess the costs and benefits and balance the potential rewards against the possible risks.

At its heart, trust is about making a choice: *Do I rely on this person, or do I not?* Having trust means that you are willing to enter into a risky situation with another person because you believe in them. Trust is needed in situations where working with someone is better than working alone. But working with someone brings risks: what if this person lets me down, or what if they prove to be unreliable? Trust matters when the choice to rely on someone is difficult, when trusting someone means taking a risk. Economists have spent a lot of time studying how people make decisions under uncertainty, when pros and cons have to be evaluated, and when the benefits have to be weighed against the costs. The same tools that economists use to evaluate the riskiness of investing in the stock market can be applied to the choice we make to invest our trust in one another.

Economics is also about picking apart the complex, rich tapestry of life into its individual threads. This is often accomplished through the use of math, which forces us to be more precise about what we are measuring and what we are assuming about how things work and how things interact. In the past two decades, economists have become obsessed with the problem of *identification*: how do we identify what specific feature is responsible for an outcome we see in the world? We care about this problem because we want to be able to tell policy makers which thread they should tug on to make the world a better place. This is true for all the sciences, but in economics, more than other social sciences, we are focused on precisely identifying how just a few mechanisms come to interact in rich and complicated ways.[2] Economics is about finding ways to understand human society without including so many details that we succumb to irreducible complexity.

I believe that drawing from a multitude of perspectives is the best way to achieve understanding of any topic.[3] To gain a full appreciation of the concept of trust, it would be best to read broadly, covering a range of different disciplines, so I invite you to explore the many valuable works listed in the notes to this chapter. But as I am an economist, my book will be about economics, so while I will draw from other disciplines, the underlying theories and data motivating the book will be economic.

WHY I WROTE AN ECONOMICS BOOK ABOUT TRUST

I've been thinking about trust for a long time: I wrote my dissertation on the economics of apologies. We use apologies when we need to repair relationships and restore trust. As microeconomists, we focus on how two parties interact with each other. But understudied is how those relationships rely on trust, and largely unstudied by economists is how people repair their relationships when trust is broken—namely, they apologize.

The study of economics is largely divided between the micro and the macro. Roughly speaking, the microeconomist studies individual transactions between two parties, such as the purchase of a car within an economy, the hiring of a worker to fill a job, or the contract between a company and its supplier. The macroeconomist studies aggregate quantities, such as the gross domestic product (GDP) of an entire country, the country's level of unemployment, or the trade that flows between two countries.

Of course, there is overlap, but those outside the profession are often surprised at how separate the two worlds are.

A macroeconomic view of trust focuses on the aggregate amount of trust in the entire economy. Social scientists call this *social capital*, which is somewhat imprecisely defined but typically includes some combination of how likely people are to trust strangers on the street, how many friends people have, and how often people go bowling alone, as opposed to bowling as part of a league. The Harvard sociologist Robert Putnam famously described this latter trend in his book *Bowling Alone*. This social capital approach is also championed by the Stanford political scientist Francis Fukuyama, who articulates the importance of trust to a country's prosperity.

My perspective, however, is decidedly micro, and therefore this book is primarily about the microeconomic foundations of trust. Instead of thinking about the aggregate amount of trust in a population, we are interested in the nature of interactions between two individuals. The first person we call the *trustor*, who places their trust in another, whom we call the *trustee*. As microeconomists, we are interested in the beliefs of the parties involved and the underlying motivations of the choices made by each party. Macroeconomics emphasizes aggregate patterns of behavior; the microeconomic approach focuses on understanding the rules and mechanisms that govern individual choices.

I was lucky to be attending graduate school just as behavioral economics was beginning to take off within the discipline. I had never even heard the term in my undergraduate studies, despite majoring in economics; it wasn't until midway through graduate school that I realized that the questions I was interested in could be classified as behavioral economics.

Modern behavioral economics was founded by Daniel Kahneman and Amos Tversky and is still heavily influenced by their work.

Kahneman won the Nobel Memorial Prize in Economic Sciences in 2002; Tversky unfortunately passed away before he would have assuredly received the same honor. The two were psychologists, and in the late 1980s, along with the economist Richard Thaler (who also would go on to win the Nobel, in 2017), they introduced ideas and methods from the field of psychology to the study of economics; thus, they established behavioral economics as a field of study. Psychologists focus on human cognition. They have tended to look at how individuals make choices in controlled lab settings, and as a consequence, much of behavioral economics since then has focused on questions that can be asked of and about individuals: why do we procrastinate, how do we perceive risk, and how do we form and hold mistaken beliefs about the world around us? Open any textbook on behavioral economics, and you will see that it is likely to be organized around these three topics. The advances in these areas have been genuinely amazing, and they have led to real policy changes in a wide range of areas, from retirement savings, to health insurance, to consumer finance regulation.

However, my interests have diverged a bit from those of other behavioral economists. The focus on what economics can learn from psychology has meant that less attention has been paid to what economics can learn from other social sciences like sociology, where the study of identity and relationships and institutions is much more at the forefront. The focus on psychology has led to a relatively greater focus on the beliefs and motivations of the individual, as opposed to the beliefs and motivations of an individual in relation to others. The study of trust is about understanding how we relate to others in our community.

In particular, the study of trust is a study about institutions, and one of the organizing principles of this book is to follow the development of the institutions that make trust possible at ever-greater scales.

HOW DO ECONOMISTS THINK ABOUT TRUST?

Recognition of the importance of trust goes way back in modern economics. As long as half a century ago, Kenneth Arrow, one of the founders of modern economics, noted:

> I want, however, to conclude by calling attention to a less visible form of social action: norms of social behavior, including ethical and moral codes. I suggest as one possible interpretation that they are reactions of society to compensate for market failures. It is useful for individuals to have some trust in each other's word. In the absence of trust it would become very costly to arrange for alternative sanctions and guarantees, and many opportunities for mutually beneficial cooperation would have to be foregone.[4]

Arrow was prescient about many things, including the recognition of the importance of moral codes and trust in markets. The rest of the profession began to catch up only in the 1990s, as the study of trust within the economics discipline began to emerge. This does not, however, explain how or why economics should attempt to give an account of the concept of trust. Why not leave such accounting to others? What can economics add?

Arrow later goes on to say in *The Limits of Organization*, "Trust is an important lubricant of a social system. It is extremely efficient; it saves a lot of trouble to have a fair degree of reliance on other people's word. Unfortunately this is not a commodity which can be bought very easily. If you have to buy it, you already have some doubts about what you have bought."[5]

The main takeaway from Arrow is that those who care about economics should also care about trust. But this perspective also suggests that those who care about trust can learn and benefit from the tools employed by economists—tools that offer a different perspective from those employed by other social sciences. As noted in the introduction to this chapter, trust is a fundamental human concept that has been studied across the social sciences— so what makes the economist's approach to trust different?

Part of what makes economics different is its insistence on the translation of everything humans do into mathematical formalism. While other social sciences use mathematical (or logical) formalism at times and in their own ways, none do so as pervasively as economics. By privileging mathematical rigor in determining what we can study, economists intentionally limit the scope of inquiry to what can be expressed precisely, using symbols. We also gain the advantages of expressing ideas and information using mathematics: namely, more clarity about the underlying assumptions and mechanisms that drive our models and greater ease in collaborating and communicating with other economists.

However, the commitment to mathematical formalism does not define economic inquiry by itself. Probably more fundamental is our focus on identifying cause and effect, instead of mere associations, because we are interested in guiding policy. We will explore the way that economists think about trust in two steps: First, we will compare the ways that economists define trust using definitions provided by other disciplines, in order to better understand the kinds of things that economists value and how we attempt to quantify them. Second, we will examine the tools of behavioral economists—a mixture of theory, experiments, and empirical methods—and see how these tools help us achieve depth and precision, though at the expense of comprehensiveness and breadth. I will show how our tools help us identify cause and effect, not just correlation.

Defining Trust

We sat in a coffee shop in Melbourne. I had flown halfway around the world to meet my friend, a sociology professor, to talk about running an experiment on how trust functions in the office. The trouble was that we couldn't agree on what trust was.

Sociologists can spend hours (as we did, day after day, in the coffee shop) coming up with various definitions of trust. In a recent paper on the subject, the New York University sociologist Blaine Robbins notes that "despite decades of interdisciplinary research on trust, the literature remains fragmented and balkanized with little consensus regarding its origins."[6] He agrees that trust promotes cooperation, but beyond that, "conceptualizations of trust differ to a great extent. In fact, no single psychological or social element—besides the notion that trust emerges under conditions of unknown outcomes—is shared by the various conceptualizations of trust."

While anthropology, biology, philosophy, psychology, and sociology have all wrestled with the definition of trust, they have largely had the same problem of coming up with a consensus.

The following definition, taken from Carolyn McLeod's entry on trust in the *Stanford Encyclopedia of Philosophy*, comes closest to how economists view trust, but then she goes on to add a dozen pages of qualifiers and addenda:

> Trust is an attitude that we have towards people whom we hope will be trustworthy, where trustworthiness is a property, not an attitude. Trust and trustworthiness are therefore distinct although, ideally, those whom we trust will be trustworthy, and those who are trustworthy will be trusted. For trust to be warranted (i.e. plausible) in a relationship, the parties to that relationship must

have attitudes toward one another that permit trust. Moreover, for trust to be warranted (i.e. well-grounded), both parties must be trustworthy.

Trusting requires that we can, 1) be vulnerable to others (vulnerable to betrayal in particular); 2) think well of others, at least in certain domains; and 3) be optimistic that they are, or at least will be, competent in certain respects. Each of these conditions for trust is relatively uncontroversial. . . . There is a further condition which is controversial, however: that the trustor is optimistic that the trustee will have a certain kind of motive for acting. Controversy surrounds this last criterion, because it is unclear what, if any, sort of motive we expect from people we trust.

Likewise, it is unclear what, if any, sort of motive a trustworthy person must have. Clear conditions for trustworthiness are that the trustworthy person is competent and committed to do what s/he is trusted to do. But this person may also have to be committed in a certain way or for a certain reason (e.g. s/he cares about the trustor).[7]

Economists, on the other hand, like simple, concrete definitions, and the model of trust we use is simple. For most economists, trust is simply anything that looks like the behavior in the "trust game" designed in 1995 by the researchers Joyce Berg, John Dickhaut, and Kevin McCabe for a set of laboratory experiments. The experiment that they designed was framed as a game between an "investor" and an "entrepreneur." The investor starts with some money (typically around ten dollars), and the other player, the entrepreneur, has a way to grow that investment. The investor can play it safe and keep the money or take a risk and entrust the money to the entrepreneur, who is able to generate some return on the investment (typically tripling its value, so a ten-dollar investment becomes thirty dollars). The entrepreneur then decides whether to do the trustworthy thing and share the returns with the investor or to demonstrate untrustworthiness by taking the money and running.

The trust game highlights the key properties that economists see as essential to understanding how trust works in relationships generally. This game can be used to help us understand relationships between two parties, where each can get some kind of material gain from participating in the relationship, but some level of risk entails in the transaction. The investor (or "trustor") bears the risk in the relationship and chooses to rely on the entrepreneur (the "trustee"), assuming the risk of material loss. The trustor makes the decision based on the trustee's reputation, which gives the trustee reason to want to signal that they are a trustworthy type—someone who shares values with the trustor and is likely to contribute to a successful, mutually beneficial venture.

The parsimony of the trust game model is one of the strengths of economics, but it is also one of its weaknesses. We distill our definitions into something concrete that we can all agree on, but that also means that we lose some of the complexities that other fields contend with.[8] That consensus means that new research on trust can more easily build on the old, allowing deeper investigation of how trust works in this specific context, at the expense of some of the nuance that other fields seek to capture.

Of course, trust isn't just about monetary transactions. Trust can be found in any risky situation where you need to rely on another person. We place our trust in someone when we believe that their intentions will lead them to act in a beneficial way.

As an example, consider the "trust fall"—the team-building activity where one person stands up (often blindfolded) on a high ledge and falls backward into the arms of their teammates. The situation is inherently risky. This is typically done by new teams during orientation events. We are uncertain about the intentions of our new teammates or whatever distractions they may encounter when the time comes to fall. But most of us wind up doing it, trusting our teammates to catch us to keep us from having a painful encounter with the ground.

When my younger son was two years old, he delighted in trust falls—he would climb atop beds, sofas, playground ladders, what have you, and blithely fall backward, with no attempt to catch himself, giggling all the way, confident that his mom or I would be there to catch him. His older brother (age four) thought that looked fun and tried to fall backward also, but he was already old enough to have doubts. He (like most of us) would invariably look back or throw his arms back to catch himself just in case. That pure blind trust in the infallibility of his parents to keep him safe was over—he had aged out of it. We can think of the trust fall as just another kind of trust game. The faller is like the investor who puts themself into a position of risk, placing their trust in the catcher (the entrepreneur) to keep them safe. The simplicity of using the trust game to think about all of these trust interactions allows us to represent trust interactions mathematically and take advantage of the rigor and precision that mathematics gives us.

The world is undoubtedly more complex than the mathematical models used by economics normally presume, but economists tend to favor parsimonious definitions over complex ones. Economists tend to give preference to definitions and models that can be quantified with math, replicated in laboratory settings, and readily tested from available data. An oft-told parable is useful here: It is late, and after a long night of drinking, an inebriated man is in a parking lot. There is only one working streetlight, illuminating just a small portion of the large lot. The unfortunate man is crawling around on his hands and knees beneath the light, searching for keys that he has lost. A police officer passes by and offers to help. The officer begins to conduct a systematic search across the whole parking lot. After a while, the police officer notes that the inebriated man never left the area around the streetlight. She asks the man why he hasn't started looking elsewhere, since the keys could be anywhere in the lot. The inebriated man replies, "This is where the light is."

The story is meant to make the inebriated man look foolish, but economists are not so sure. We can think of economics as being focused on where the light is while fields like sociology are searching the parking lot as a whole. Although the truth may be anywhere in the dark parking lot, economists prefer to focus on answering questions that can be illuminated by the bright light of economic tools like experiments, econometrics, and mathematical game theory. Ed Lazear, author of the manifesto "Economic Imperialism," about the relationship between economics and other social sciences, often used to say to me: "Sociologists are better at asking questions. Economists are better at finding answers."[9]

The lighted area that economists focus on—that is, the questions we ask and the answers we provide—can best be described by three features:

- Economic questions and answers can be studied using statistical and experimental empirical tools;
- they can be modeled using mathematical models; and
- they are focused on inferring causality.

All three of these points are interrelated. While economics was once dominated by the second feature, adherence to theory, economic research today is primarily empirical.[10] The questions that economists ask are most often driven by the data that are available. However, theory remains critical because it gives meaning to empirical relationships. Data alone (Big or otherwise) can only show that two patterns are related. They can never explain why something happened or how best to improve things. Statistics can show that two phenomena are correlated, but theory is necessary to ascertain the direction of causality (if any even exists).[11] Theory, in other words, allows us to derive meaning from empirical tests, extrapolating empirical results from one context to a new one.

For example, a well-established statistical pattern is that countries in which people report higher levels of trust in their neighbors are also wealthier. However, to give that information meaning (and to provide well-founded policy recommendations), we need theory: do higher levels of trust among citizens cause countries to get richer, or do people start to trust one another more as their country gains wealth? Or maybe some third, unrelated factor causes increases in both trust and wealth. Established theories can suggest mechanisms that link trust and wealth, which then can inspire the data-oriented people to seek out new statistical tests.

This points to another advantage of restricting the scope of economics to a relatively small number of common mathematical and statistical tools: it increases the ability of members of the economics profession to work together. Simple definitions act as interfaces, allowing studies and research designs to talk to one another in a shared language. Theories beget testable implications, which lead to new empirical studies, which suggest new theories. And the cycle of "normal science" repeats itself.[12]

Throughout this book, we will discuss the interplay between theory and experimental data. Over time, the experimental process allows economics to expand the scope of the tools it uses—brightening the streetlight and enlarging its circle of illumination.

THE ECONOMIC THEORY OF TRUST

My favorite series of books growing up was the Foundation series, by Isaac Asimov. In it, a mathematician uncovers the equations that govern human interactions. He called his discovery "psychohistory." I was amazed to learn in college that economics had similar ambitions. Economics wasn't just about stocks and bonds and interest rates; it was about understanding how we make choices when there are trade-offs to be made. In other words, economists have the ambition of uncovering pretty much everything humans do and how human society might unfurl.

I began my career studying economic theory in order to model the totality of human behavior, much as Hari Seldon, the protagonist of the Foundation books, does. I have since expanded my research toolkit to the more empirical side of economics, following the general trend in the profession, but I still love the aesthetic beauty of theoretical modeling.

Most of us deal with trust all the time in our daily lives, from trusting your kids' teachers to take good care of them, to trusting your friends to show up on time when you're going out, to trusting your neighbors with your house keys when you're on vacation, to trusting your taxi or Uber driver to take you where you want to go, to trusting Amazon to send you your correct order, to trusting your company to pay your paycheck. However, we probably don't think about the mechanisms that allow this trust. The goal of the economic theorist is to use math to bring to light the relationships that structure our daily interactions.

In this section, I will give an overview of three key insights from economic theory that help us understand the mechanisms underlying trust:

- Bilateral relationships are modeled by what economists call the *trust game*, a type of principal-agent scenario where all the key economic features of trust—*risk, shared values, sacrifice,* and *reputation*—can be observed through various iterations of the game.
- Trust occurs in the context of a cooperative relationship with *repeated interactions* over time. How we act today depends on how those actions will affect cooperation in the future. At the same time, how we behave today is determined by the cooperative behavior in the past.
- We are uncertain about what other people value. Taking *costly actions* tends to signal more about us than cheap talk.

The Trust Game

As noted in the previous section, economists largely define trust as any behavior that looks like the behavior in the experimental trust game. Broadly, this is any game between two parties where both will be made better off by working together. Situations involving trust are characterized by risk. One player, the trustor, invites the potential for cooperation by putting herself in a position of risk, while the other player, the trustee, can either reciprocate that act of vulnerability or violate it. If the trustee reciprocates, then both players are made better off, but if the trustee violates the trust put in him, he gains a personal benefit at the expense of the trustor. Knowing that this might happen, the trustor might not initiate the interaction to begin with. Making herself vulnerable requires trust.

The trust game experiment described previously, where an investor makes a decision about whether to invest and the entrepreneur makes a decision about whether to pay back the investor, is an example of a broader class of games called "principal-agent games." These are games in which the principal (the investor, in this case) has to rely on someone else, the agent (the entrepreneur, in this case), to accomplish a task. These games are fundamentally about the risk that the principal (the person we have been calling the trustor) faces in trusting the agent (the person we have been calling the trustee). However, we typically can accomplish more together than alone. Therefore, these games offer insights into the kinds of systems that we put into place to mitigate the risks that come from relying on others.

We can visualize this interaction using a game tree (see figure 1.1). At the beginning of the game tree, the trustor chooses a path—whether to Trust or not. If she chooses Not Trust, then she keeps her ten dollars and the trustee has zero. However, if she chooses Trust, then the trustee gets to make a decision. The act

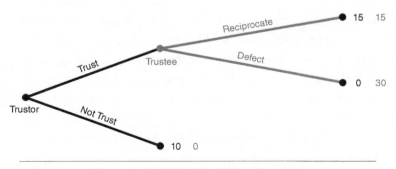

FIGURE 1.1 A game tree of the Berg et al. trust game.

of Trust has tripled the value of the investment, so now there is thirty dollars to divide. The trustee can choose to Reciprocate and share the money with the trustor, so each gets fifteen dollars, or to Defect and take all the money for himself (thirty dollars for trustee and zero for the trustor).

To analyze how people behave in the trust game, we turn to game theory. In game theory, we expect players to have perfect foresight into how others will act in response to their own actions, so in order to analyze what happens in the game, we start at the end, with the trustee's choice, where the situation is simplest, and move back to the beginning.

When the trustee is asked to make a decision, he will simply compare his payoff from reciprocating (fifteen dollars) with his payoff from defecting (thirty dollars) and choose Defect because thirty dollars is more than fifteen dollars.

We then move backward to the beginning of the game and ask what the trustor would do, given her accurate prediction that the trustee will defect. That is, she knows that Trust will lead to a payoff of zero, while Not Trust will at least get her a payoff of ten dollars. Therefore, the trustor chooses Not Trust.

The traditional economic analysis of the trust game predicts a breakdown in trust: why should the trustor trust and risk getting nothing when she could not trust and guarantee ten dollars? Even though both players would be better off if they trusted each other, earning fifteen dollars each, it seems reasonable to expect the trustor to try to avoid the big goose egg. And yet—both in experiments and in their real-world counterparts, *trust happens all the time*. So . . . what gives?

Explaining this phenomenon has been the subject of intense research by behavioral economists for decades. Many experiments have shown that thinking about the moral values on the part of the trustee—values like reciprocity, altruism, or guilt—can lead to more accurate models of human behavior.

We can describe the economic model of how people behave in the trust game according to the following four key variables:

1. *Trust (Reputation).* The trustee's reputation in this game informs the belief that the trustor has in the trustee's trustworthiness. The trustee knows what they value and whether they are trustworthy, but the trustor has to rely on inferences based on the trustee's past actions and the trustor's prior beliefs on general trustworthiness when encountering somebody new.

2. *Trustworthiness (Values).* The trustee's trustworthiness depends on their values, or what economists refer to as "preferences." The kinds of values that make somebody trustworthy will depend on the task and relationship at hand, but we generally think of trustworthy people as those who share our values and are more likely to help us succeed at the task at hand when we place our trust in them.

3. *Act of Trust (Vulnerability).* The trustor has a choice to make— one that entails risk. If they choose to trust the trustee they are risking loss for the possibility of greater gain. If they choose not to trust, they reduce their exposure to risk, but at the expense of missing out on the potential gains from cooperation. Whether the trustor chooses to trust depends on the reputation that the trustee has coming into the game.

4. *Act of Trustworthiness (Sacrifice).* What the trustee chooses to do with trust that has been given them often involves some cost or tangible sacrifice. By acting in a trustworthy manner, they reward the trust that was placed in them, which enhances their reputation and increases future trust.

These four components of trust form a cycle (see figure 1.2 and table 1.1), with the reputation earned from an act of trustworthiness setting the groundwork for the trust between the two parties, the next time they meet. In this basic formulation of the trust game, trust is asymmetric. The principal is the trustor, and the agent the trustee. Of course, in most relationships, trust often goes both ways. Sometimes I have to trust you, and other times you have to trust me. The basic trust game only considers one side of the trust equation but we will come back to examples and experiments involving mutual trust throughout the book.

The Cycle of Trust Model

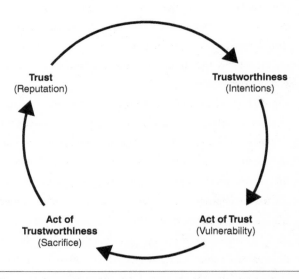

FIGURE 1.2 Trust has four stages. It is a belief by the trustor in the trustworthiness of the person they are interacting with. If that trust is high enough, it leads to an act of trust, where the trustor takes a risk and makes herself vulnerable by relying on the trustworthiness of the trustee. The trustee demonstrates his trustworthiness by reciprocating that act of trust, usually through some act that involves cost or personal sacrifice. The trustee's actions update the reputation he has with the trustor, which sets the stage for their next interaction.

TABLE 1.1 TRUST IN ECONOMICS

	Trust	Trustworthiness	Act of trust	Act of trustworthiness
Main idea	Reputation	Values	Vulnerability	Sacrifice
Economic idea	Beliefs	Preferences	Action	Reciprocity
Economic jargon	Bayesian updating	Surplus from cooperation	Principal-agent problem	Costly signaling

Trust/Reputation/Beliefs

First, we are going to separate the state of trusting someone (trust as a noun) from the act of trust (trust as a verb). Trust is a belief; an act of trust is an action. In economics, actions stem from a combination of what you care about and what you believe. Your beliefs about another's trustworthiness determine whether you trust them, and these beliefs depend on your understanding of their reputation.

Trust is needed only in risky situations. If we had perfect information about how others are going to act, then we wouldn't need trust. Trust by one person in a particular other person is the belief that that person will act in a way that will be beneficial to the person doing the trusting.

When we trust someone, our trust is based on our belief that they have good intentions. We believe that it is worth the risk to take a chance on them. We trust them if they've taken costly actions in the past to demonstrate their trustworthiness. Trust can be built as I acquire evidence of somebody's trustworthiness. This is in contrast to faith, which is often defined as trust in the absence of, or without the need for, evidence.

In the mathematical trust game, trust is your belief regarding the probability that the trustee will choose to share the payoffs of the game instead of taking it for themself.

When interacting with someone for the first time, we rely on our prior instincts. These priors depend on stereotypes and our general trust of strangers.[13] How we form stereotypes, as well as humanity's journey from trusting only those we know to people in general, will structure our path through history for the first section of the book.

Stereotypes exist because the primary mechanism for building trust through much of history was trusting those with whom you shared similarities and trusting members of your in-group. Group norms and rules have been powerful tools for building trust and cooperation throughout the development of human civilization, but they also have significant costs. When we rely on stereotypes and instincts, we fall prey to untrustworthy con artists who subvert our stereotypes for their own gain. We can also wind up excluding people that we might benefit from interacting with, violating their dignity and preventing society from reaching its full potential. We will return to these trade-offs later in this book.

Trustworthiness/Values/Preferences

Just as we separated the state of trust from the act of trust, we will separate the state of being trustworthy from actions that reflect trustworthiness. A trustworthy person may sometimes do things that decrease or damage their trustworthiness, and an untrustworthy person may sometimes act trustworthy given the right incentives. However, on average, a trustworthy person is someone who has good intentions, meaning that a person would trust them if they knew those intentions. A person's intentions derives from their values.[14] In economics, we think about someone's values in terms of their preferences.

People often associate economics with the idea of perfect information, where all parties know everything about everybody. In fact, a lot of economic game theory for the past half-century has been about asymmetric information, where one party knows something that the other doesn't. In this case, the trustee knows how trustworthy they are, but the trustor has to guess. A trustworthy person will take trustworthy actions that justify the risk that someone takes when they trust them. In the case of the trust game, that action is to choose the more equitable payoff rather than the one that keeps all the profits for themself. In the case of trusting a bookseller to sell you a good book, it is the cost of making a good book rather than a bad one.

Recall that actions depend on beliefs and preferences. Because the setup of the simple trust game means that all the uncertainty falls on the trustor side, beliefs don't matter as much for the trustor as they do for the trustee. What determines a person's trustworthiness, therefore, is their own set of preferences. Those preferences reflect what they value and determine their intentions.

What specific qualities define trustworthiness depend on the people involved and the task at hand. The traits that make somebody trustworthy are the traits that lead to good outcomes for the trustor and make the trustor want to interact more with that person again in the future.

Traits that define a trustworthy person include:

- Competence
- Altruism
- EmpathyConscientiousness
- Sense of fairness

- Sense of reciprocity
- Respect
- Interest in my well-being
- Knowledge of and understanding about what I value

In the mathematical trust game, a self-interested, rational trustee will always keep all the money for themselves and not share. However, a trustor who feels guilt when not sharing, empathy toward the other person, or altruism would choose to share. Those qualities that induce somebody to share in the trust game define what it means to be trustworthy in that situation.

Acts of Trust/Vulnerability/Risk

An act of trust requires an opportunity for cooperation and then the taking of a risk. People are willing to take a risk on someone when they have sufficient trust in them. That trust is based on an assessment of the other person's trustworthiness.

The idea that we can accomplish more together than we can individually lies at the heart of economics. Adam Smith's *Wealth of Nations*, the 1776 book that we typically think of as the progenitor of economics, famously begins with a discussion of a pin factory, where each person's specialization means that a team of workers laboring together can produce much more than the same number of workers each making the whole pin individually. He then carries that analysis into a discussion of the gains of trade: when a buyer and a seller agree to a sale, both sides are made better off. Both of these are examples of how the total product is increased when people cooperate. We often think of economic interactions as zero-sum, requiring us to compete to figure out how to divide a fixed-size pie of resources. However, economists tend to think of most interactions as positive-sum: that is, cooperation can increase the size of the pie for all.

However, cooperation is often risky. In situations where there is no risk, no trust is needed. But when it is necessary for people to work together, there is often a question of whether they will all work conscientiously or some (or all) of the participants will shirk. When a buyer and seller agree to a transaction, there is the risk that the seller might sell a defective product, or that the buyer might not pay.

The other key determinant of whether the risk of cooperation is worth it is what game theorists call the "outside option," and what we teach MBA students to call the "best alternative to a negotiated agreement" aka BATNA. In economics, a choice is always considered in light of what the BATNA would be (this is called the "opportunity cost"). Therefore, the risk of trusting someone is always measured relative to the risk of trusting somebody else. In the mathematical trust game, the act of trust is the first decision the trustor makes. The outside option is what she could get if she chose Not Trust (in this case, ten dollars). The risk comes from not knowing for sure how the trustee might respond. A coldly self-interested trustee would take the selfish option, but an altruistic trustee would share. Not knowing how the trustor might behave is the risk that the trustee is taking.

Although we generally think that risk is a bad thing, sometimes a little risk is helpful (or even necessary) in a relationship. Trust often goes both ways, and sometimes the best way to earn the trust of others is to trust them first. Reciprocity is often at the heart of cooperative behavior, and the trustor can't earn a reciprocal response unless they are willing to take a risk themselves. We will see later in this book that sometimes contracts in business work better when we allow a little more risk— when we allow ourselves to be vulnerable.

Perhaps the most evocative metaphor for this need for vulnerability comes from a paper published in 2000 called "The Kiss of the Porcupines." In it, the psychologist Frank Fincham argues that human relationships are like the love of two porcupines: full of affection but always with the chance of pricking the other.

Acts of Trustworthiness/Reciprocity/Costs

The point of placing your trust in someone is that you expect the trustee to take some action that will make you better off. The risk that you take with them is based on the expectation that there could be a mutually beneficial gain from cooperation. How the trustee responds to your act of trust depends on their values. Those values define a person's trustworthiness.

Trustworthy behavior generally comes with a cost. If doing the right thing were easy, then everybody would do it, and there wouldn't be any uncertainty about how the trustee would behave. There wouldn't even be a trustee because there would be no need for trust.

Demonstrating trustworthiness requires someone to pay a cost.

In the trust game experiment, the act of trustworthiness is the decision the trustee makes. The cost of choosing the trustworthy action (sharing the payoff with the trustor) is the money that he would have gained had he acted selfishly (i.e., the trustee would get thirty dollars for being selfish and fifteen dollars for sharing, so there is an opportunity cost of fifteen dollars for trustworthy behavior in the game).

Sometimes acting in a trustworthy way comes from a sense of guilt: the guilty party *feels* a cost when acting selfishly. If the cost of feeling the guilt outweighs the cost of cooperation, then the person will act cooperatively.

The importance of demonstrating trustworthiness in human society is great, so we have many institutions designed to enable such demonstrations. One of them is the institution of apologies. One of the paradoxes of apologies is that while we want people to apologize when they have wronged us and apologies are often the road to forgiveness and a rebuilding of trust, our first response to someone who apologizes is often to punish them further.[15] In the context of the trust game model, this is because we need to make apologizing costly. Only a costly apology can demonstrate trustworthiness and begin the rebuilding of trust (I actually proved this mathematically for my dissertation[16]).

How we balance the cost of sacrificing today for the benefit of your future reputation becomes an important question. In game theory, the practice of making costly choices to enhance one's reputation is called *signaling*.

A NOTE ON CAUSALITY AND THE METHODS OF EMPIRICAL ECONOMISTS

I was once asked by the chief executive officer of a company why he should hire an economist (me) over the statistician who had applied for the same consulting contract. He was looking for an academic with data science skills to help analyze the data that his company was generating. I told him that the reason he should hire me was simple: I was trained as a theorist. Statisticians use theory, too, but their theories are based on the abstract world of numbers and could be employed to count stars or amoebas as easily as people. Economics has a century of theory devoted to understanding how people behave. That gives us economists a crucial advantage.

Mathematical theory has always been under attack by social scientists outside of economics as being a waste of time. People don't behave like mathematical robots, and the obsession with math means that we miss out on lots of questions. Even within economics, the role of theory has been on the decline as the new availability of vast data sets and widely accessible computing tools has made empirical work more central.[17] At the same time, economics has been undergoing a "credibility revolution,"[18] where the focus of recent research has not been just on establishing statistical relationships between two phenomena (e.g., more educated people are more trusting), but also in trying to figure out causal relationships. For example, the fact that more educated people are more trusting could be because when you trust others more, you do better in school and go on to higher education. Or it could be because those who study more encounter more diverse people and learn to trust more widely. Or it could be just that the same kinds of parents who teach children good study habits also teach children to trust. The possibilities are endless, but understanding what causes what is crucial if we want to effect change. One might want to create a more educated populace by building trust, but that works only if trust leads to higher education. Or one might want to increase trust in society by putting more money into schools, but that works only if more education increases trust.

Thus, theory plays two crucial roles in helping us understand causality:

1. Theory helps us rule out some directions of causality.
2. Theory helps us design experiments to test causality.

How can theory help us rule out directions of causality? Imagine that every time I push a button, a light bulb turns on. There are two possible inferences:

1. Pushing the button turns on the lightbulb.
2. The light bulb turning on causes me to push the button.

We have a theory of how consciousness works that allows us to rule out explanation.[19] We can never prove the direction of causality for certain, but we can decide what is likely, given our view of the world. In the same way, economic theories that we generally accept about human behavior allows us to rule out possibilities about relationships like the one between education and trust.

The second way that economic theory helps us understand causality is that the theories simplify situations enough to enable us to run laboratory experiments to test them. Experimental economists often run experiments by bringing subjects (typically college students) into a room where they play economic games with each other, typically on a computer. Of course, a computer game will never fully simulate the kinds of choices we make in the real world. But economic theory does help researchers decide which features of the real world are most important to simulate.

In my own work, I have used lab experiments to show that people are more likely to mimic the untrustworthy patterns of behavior of those around them than to mimic trustworthy patterns. Also, first impressions matter more in determining whom you decide to mimic; apologies can help restore trust, but only when they are costly; and people are more likely to apologize early in relationships, when there is more uncertainty, rather than late in relationships, when trust has been well established.[20]

A lot of the evidence presented in this book will be based on findings derived from experimental iterations of the trust game.

Of course, lab evidence is only one form of evidence, and these results are grounded in mathematical theory and then confirmed in the field by looking at real-world data and experiments conducted in the field. A *lab experiment* in economics typically means one done in an artificial setting—one where students come into a computer lab on campus, or a randomly selected population logs in to a website—and the participants play an economic game like the trust game, designed to simulate something that happens in the real world. On the other hand, a *field experiment* is an experiment that takes place in the real world. For example, in the experiment that my coauthors and I ran to see how apologies restore trust, we identified 1.5 million Uber riders who had just experienced an unsatisfactory ride (e.g., they were dropped off late because of traffic), divided them into control and treatment groups, and sent a different e-mail message to each treatment group apologizing for the lateness. We then measured the impact of that message on their future use of Uber, which we took to be a proxy for trust.[21]

While field experiments are often more compelling because they are more realistic, they have a number of drawbacks. First, field experiments are logistically difficult to set up. Designing and implementing field experiments often require years of working with stakeholders and writing special software. Therefore, in the time it takes to run one field experiment, one could run many lab experiments. Second, field experiments are also often very specific to the circumstances of a particular company. Research is about coming up with generalized knowledge that can be broadly applied. While we assume that what Uber experienced could be generalized to other companies, Uber is so different than even their closest competitor (Lyft) that one might worry that the results for one company will not hold for another. Finally, field experiments have a lot less experimental control. In a lab, you have more control over the kind of people who participate in your experiment and the information they are exposed to. In the real world, exposure to other people or outside events could contaminate your results.

As a result, lab evidence about the trust game provides the most varied and nuanced data that economists have about how trust operates. For the trust game, students come to the lab in groups of two to twenty, though increasingly we are running more and more experiments online so that we can recruit subjects from across the country who participate from their own computers. We try to maintain anonymity so that they don't know whom they are playing against. Each participant sits at a separate computer terminal, and each is given instructions. Once we have made sure that everyone understands the rules, the participants begin to play. They are typically randomly matched with someone else in that session and play a version of the trust game either once or multiple times. One player in each pair plays the role of the investor, and the other plays the role of the entrepreneur. They are given real money for participating, which they use to play the game. For economists, it is important that the players' choices have real monetary consequences. We worry that people behave differently when the game is hypothetical. Therefore, all games in economics experiments use real money.

From that basic setup, we can start varying some of the rules of the game to see what happens. We could increase or decrease the monetary stakes. Experiments suggest that people behave surprisingly consistently in economic games like the trust game for stakes ranging as high as two weeks' income to as low as a few pennies.[22] We could have people repeat the game over and over with the same people to see how trust increases and decreases over time. In my own experiments, we see that trust declines as we approach the end of the game. We could vary the amount of information that people have about how others are behaving in the game. Doing so, we find that first impressions matter and that trust is contagious.[23] In this way, we can identify the mechanisms through which trust operates in the real world in contexts ranging from religion to monetary policy to scientific research, and we can use lab experiments to better understand how those mechanisms work and how they interact with each other.

Research works best when lab evidence is used in concert with mathematical theory that clarifies how all the different forces interact. Field evidence can then be used to make sure that what happens in the controlled confines of a lab also applies to the real world.

WHAT YOU'LL FIND IN THIS BOOK

Chapter 2 reframes the history of human civilization as a story about the expansion of trust. Trust is encoded in our DNA; we are born with instincts designed to promote trust and to demonstrate our trustworthiness to those around us. But these instincts initially extended that trust only to those in our family or tribe. Helping us to extend trust to more people and larger groups has been one of the central roles of civilization over the centuries. We have developed institutions like religions, markets, and courts to enable and support that extension—though the very same institutions that promote trust to those in our in-group can make it even harder to trust those on the outside. I will also explain why a relatively unassuming institution—gift-giving—is one of the most fundamental institutions that humans use to build cooperation and trust.

Chapter 3 looks at all the ways that trust functions in the institutions that constitute the modern economy, from its central role in money and banking to the sharing economy and blockchain. So much of the modern economy depends on trust that we take for granted, as we save our money in a trust and our organizations are run by trustees. We trust the central bank to manage the money supply, and indeed the concept of money itself requires us to place faith in the monetary system. This centrality of trust continues into the twenty-first century, where the biggest innovations in the past decade in e-commerce, the sharing economy, and blockchain are all fundamentally about creating new ways to overcome distrust.

Chapter 4 looks at our trust in modern institutions outside the market, ranging from our trust in medicine to our trust in the science behind climate change. While the story of this book is about how civilization and technology has moved hand in hand to advance our trust of each other, recent decades have seen an erosion of trust in some areas of expertise. We see this decline in trust in medicine, in the media, and in politics, where there is growing distrust in those who govern us. Trust in expertise has been affected by the ubiquity of access to information. Trust is a belief, and that belief is affected by the information that our institutions give us access to.

Chapter 5 looks at the role that trust plays in our daily lives and our own personal relationships, from its role in how we think about privacy and dignity, to how blame leads to breakdowns in trust and how apologies can repair it. We'll examine how sometimes we can't even trust ourselves, and our theories of trust can help us make better decisions. This chapter also offers a road map for restoring lost trust and continuing to expand. We talk about the baseline level of trust that we have toward strangers; how trusting ourselves is necessary for us to invest in our relationships; how we restore trust when relationships are frayed; and how principles of human dignity both impede and impel us toward the ultimate goal of strengthening the bonds of trust that connects the human race.

Chapter 6 concludes, retracing the path of trust across human history that we explore throughout the book and extending that line into the future. I try to ground the book in research and it's hard to research the future, so I can only speculate here, but I hope you walk away from this book with the same optimism that I have for what the future may bring in terms of trust.

2

THE HISTORY OF TRUST

THIS chapter tracks the history of trust as it evolved from our prehistoric ancestors all the way to modern times. One could tell the story of human civilization as a story of how we learned to trust one another. We learned first to share the spoils of a group hunt instead of hunting and eating (or not eating) alone. Working together, we could build cathedrals and pyramids. But working together means relying on others, and this creates opportunities for shirking—for some members of the group to take advantage of others. We needed to find ways to create trust. Over time, we developed governments and rules to help manage these dilemmas of cooperation, but those rules also need trust to function.

Moreover, we are going to look at each step of the evolution of human civilization by examining the evolution of the institutions that govern them. Still, to keep things concrete, I will use the economic definition supplied by Nobel laureate Douglass North—namely, that institutions are the beliefs and norms, the invisible rules, that constrain how we act. Every game has rules, and so does every society. Why do we follow them? Because of our expectations of what will happen if we do and what will happen to us if we don't. Those expectations create norms of behavior and rules that we can study through the lens of game theory. Those norms or rules are a large part of what we call *culture*.

The study of institutions is central to understanding trust, for two reasons. The first is that most human institutions rely on trust to function. Societies develop institutions to solve the problems they face, from the problems of collective action to the allocation of scarce resources. More specifically, modern institutions like markets and courts and democracies all rely on trust at many levels. Recall from Chapter 1 the trust needed to buy a book. Think of the trust needed to adjudicate a lawsuit or enforce a regulation.

More fundamentally, the second reason why institutions are central to trust is the fact that so many of our human institutions are designed around facilitating trust. The story of human civilization has been about building bigger and greater things by learning to cooperate on ever-larger scales. Sometimes I stand in the crush of a crowded New York City subway platform and marvel at the system that moves over five million people each and every day. While people complain about crowding and delays, I am amazed at the feat of human ingenuity that it represents— the coordinated effort of so many people and so many systems that does its job day after day.

We can think about the institutions supporting trust in terms of components of the trust game outlined in Chapter 1.

Institutions Supporting Trust

We have defined trust as a belief in trustworthiness of the person we interact with. Our beliefs are based on the information we receive, and many human institutions are about spreading and curating the flow of information. Examples that we will discuss include

- Gossip networks in premodern villages
- Brands that we look for when we go shopping
- Social networks in the age of the Internet

Institutions Supporting Trustworthiness

We have defined trustworthiness as a character trait of someone who acts in a manner that justifies the trust placed in them.
Trustworthiness could vary for different people in different
situations, and while they reflect some internal moral compass,
those internal values often originate from some outside institutional influence. Examples will include

- Our biologically evolved capacity for empathy and altruism
- Religious values that instill moral codes of behavior
- Codes of conduct, as in medicine

Institutions Supporting Acts of Trust

The act of trust is a leap of faith. We are taking a risk by relying on
somebody else to complete a task or take an action. We may have
strong beliefs (i.e., trust) that that person is trustworthy but we
will never know for sure. Institutions discussed in the book that
help allow people to take that leap include

- Norms of gift giving that encourage us to give gifts with no
  expectation of return
- Contracts that provide recourse if trust is broken
- A blockchain, which seeks to automate how deals and contracts are executed

Institutions Supporting Acts of Trustworthiness

Finally, once trust has been placed in the trustee, the trustee
decides whether or not to act in a trustworthy way. That choice

depends not only on their values, but also on the institutions that govern their behavior. Some of these institutions create sanctions for untrustworthy behavior. Other institutions provide added ways for people to signal their trustworthiness. Examples will include

- Courts and enforcement within the legal system
- Religious rituals, such as painful tattoos
- Apologies which serve as a way to restore broken trust

We will return to each of these examples throughout the course of the book, but for now we will begin at the beginning, by looking at the biological basis of human trust.

BIOLOGY

Have you ever stopped to wonder why babies smile or laugh?

Most mammalian newborns stagger to their feet and begin to walk within minutes of birth. It takes human babies months to accomplish this feat. But long before humans learn to walk, we smile and laugh. What is up with an animal that doesn't need to walk for the first year of its life but does need to start to *smile* in its first weeks of existence?

Evolution selects traits for a purpose, and these behaviors were programmed into our genes tens of thousands of years ago—but why? What is the purpose of laughter? What is the purpose of a smile? For that matter, why are humans the only animal that can blush? What other behaviors can we find in our genetic code that help to define us as social animals?

Like all living things, humans are driven to pass on our genes to the next generation. This biological imperative requires us to ensure the survival of our immediate family, particularly our offspring. Biology, therefore, impels us to trust a group of one to ten people (the size of our immediate family, give or take).

We will see how the social institutions that we have developed over the course of many centuries have taken those biological roots and expanded human groups into societies of millions and even billions.

The Economics Within our Passions

While emotional cues and responses are more the purview of psychology than economics, economists have studied human emotions because of their role in shaping economic transactions. In his book *Passions Within Reason*, economist Bob Frank argues that we can think of innate emotional responses as biological mechanisms that help us choose the optimal strategy in an economic game. These mechanisms operate automatically and shape our behavior, typically without our knowing why they exist or what game they are helping us play.

Economic games take a wide variety of shapes and forms, from firms deciding how to price their goods to workers choosing a company to work for—but the prototypical economic game (perhaps because it is the oldest) is about this question: when two people need to work together to complete a task, can they trust each other and work together?

Frank argues that certain behaviors, like crying or laughing or smiling, evolved to help us work together and thus produce better economic outcomes for ourselves. Evolution works by selecting traits that increase the chance for survival, but our understanding of evolution today recognizes that the most important traits aren't the ones that ensure the survival of the individual organism.[1] Instead, evolutionary theory suggests that we should think about how advantageous traits ensure the survival of the gene itself. That is, Darwin focused on the evolution of traits that would help an individual to survive—for instance, the shape of a finch's beak might help it to obtain more food. But contemporary biology recognizes that for at least some types of animals, the individual's chance of survival depends crucially on how well that individual's social group functions.[2]

This insight represents the solution to a longstanding puzzle in the theory of evolution: altruistic behavior. Why would evolution design bees to die when they sting an intruder? If evolution is about promoting survival of the fittest, why would it design mechanisms that lead to suicide, the exact opposite of survival? Today, we are largely comfortable with the idea that biology impels the survival of the fittest *genes* rather than the fittest *organisms*, but getting to that point required a conceptual revolution.[3] An individual bee's sacrifice helps ensure the survival of the hive, which helps ensure that that bee's genetic code is passed on to future generations even if that individual itself does not survive. Once biologists knew where to look, evidence of altruism in the animal kingdom became abundant, from vampire bats that regurgitate blood to feed other bats who are hungry, to vervet monkeys that sound an alarm to warn others, even as it increases the danger to themselves.[4] In humans, examples of selfless acts of sacrifice and altruism abound, from superhero stories on the silver screen to the canonization of saints like Mother Teresa by the Roman Catholic Church.

Behavioral economists measure altruism using simple games. The simplest of these is called the *dictator game*. Here, the subject gets complete control over the outcome of the game. Subjects in a lab are given, say, twenty dollars and asked to divide the money between themselves and an anonymous stranger. There are no strings attached, regardless of how the money is divided. A surprisingly high number of dictators (64 percent) choose to share the money with an anonymous stranger even though they could keep all the money for themselves with no consequences.[5] Economists call this innate altruism a "social preference" because they represent a preference for the well-being of others in society rather than just oneself.[6] The experiment has been repeated for large stakes, in different countries, and with different degrees of anonymity, to name just a few variables, and the results have consistently shown substantial levels of altruistic behavior.

The evidence provided by the dictator game alone does not tell us if this altruistic preference is learned or innate, although we can make some inferences. Psychologists look at the extremes of human behavior to gain insight into the ways the brain functions. Approximately 1 percent of the human population can be described as psychopathic.[7] In general, psychopaths can be high functioning and appear normal because they know what the norms of human behavior are and can mimic them, but they tend to lack innate empathy that prevents them from wanting to harm others. Lack of empathy implies the inability to understand or share the feelings of others. As a consequence, psychopaths often feel no guilt or remorse when they cause others harm. In recent years, twin and sibling studies have shown that psychopathic behavior is heritable; this suggests that at least part of our desire to feel what others feel is encoded in our genes. The fact that we can find genes for empathy suggests that altruism and empathy have evolutionary benefits and that these social preferences have been part of human behavior for evolutionary lengths of time.

So Why Do Babies Smile?

This brings us back to our original question: why do babies smile? Bob Frank's hypothesis was that evolution chooses traits that lead to better outcomes in economic games. Communities that perform better in such games (like sharing the food from a hunt) are more likely to survive and pass on these traits to their offspring. In the case of trust, the central dilemma is knowing whom to trust. Therefore, a useful evolutionary trait is one that helps people signal their trustworthiness.

Smiles can do just that. Most facial expressions tend to be autonomic—they happen automatically, without conscious thought.[8] Psychologist Paul Ekman has spent a lifetime documenting these facial expressions and can identify the emotional trigger associated with different configurations of facial movements. The smile is one of the most basic facial expressions: babies can start smiling even before they are born and smile in response to someone else smiling when they are as young as two months old.

Smiling serves many purposes, and genuine smiles are hard to fake convincingly. This is easy to see in, for instance, the fake smiles of toddlers posing for the camera, or the admonition that Tyra Banks used to give to aspiring models on her reality TV show that smiles can be seen as much in the eyes as in the mouth, even though most of us don't have conscious control over what our eyes are doing. A true smile is a window into the emotional state of the smiler. It automatically signals the true intentions of the smiler and gives a way for others to update their beliefs on whether the smiler is worthy of trust.[9] Trust game experiments show that we are more likely to trust someone who smiles.[10] Because smiles are difficult to fake, they are informative in helping us determine who to trust.

Smiles have another purpose: they serve as an invitation to smile back. They are one of the first forms of reciprocal behavior exhibited by babies, and in that sense, they serve as an entry point into the cycle of trust. Just as a smile acts as a way to signal trustworthiness, it serves to initiate an invitation to trust.

Shortly after babies begin to smile reciprocally, they begin to laugh. Just as smiling and other facial cues offer a window into someone's thoughts, laughter does the same. Whereas smiling represents happiness and amusement, unconscious laughter often signifies playful intent.[11] As noted in our theory of trust, intentions are the key component of determining trustworthiness. Beyond intent, however, laughter is associated with an even more sophisticated social behavior: joking.[12]

What is a joke? What makes something funny? Observing the laughter of small children gives us some clue. Peekaboo is a favorite pastime for the pretoddler set. For children in their first year of life, who do not yet understand object permanence, humor is about the unexpected. When a parent's face disappears behind their hands, the parent also disappears from the child's mental representation of the world. When the hands are removed, the parent has unexpectedly reappeared. Laughter ensues. Once a child starts to understand that objects that are hidden still exist, the humor of peekaboo disappears.

Similarly, one category of humor is sure to delight slightly older kids: "poo" jokes. Understanding poo jokes helps explain how jokes become a source of trust.[13] Despite a parent's best intentions, children quickly learn that talking about bathroom functions in certain contexts is taboo. Therefore, they find the unexpected discussion of such things to be outrageously funny. People laugh (sometimes nervously) when a norm is violated. In this case, the norm is that we do not talk about poo in polite company. As we get older, our jokes get more sophisticated, often referencing social roles and identities, but the basic premise remains: we laugh when norms are unexpectedly violated.

Next time you come across somebody new but are not quite sure whether to trust them, try telling a joke. If they laugh at the same humor as you (a genuine, autonomic laugh as opposed to a forced one), you can take that as a signal that they find the same things funny. Because we find norm violations to be funny, a shared sense of a humor indicates shared norms. Shared norms form a solid foundation for trust.

Profanity functions in much the same way. Michael Adams notes that the use of profanity also can build trust.[14] The use of profanity is a deliberate breaking of a taboo. By definition, those who break taboos are subject to social sanction as punishment. By deliberately breaking the taboo, the profaner places themself in a state of vulnerability, thus initiating an act of trust. A positive response to the expression of profanity reciprocates that act of trust, completing the cycle.

A Trust Hormone?

The ultimate evidence that trust is encoded in our genes can be seen in the research surrounding oxytocin, also known as the *trust hormone*. Just as endorphins are associated with pain and pleasure and adrenaline is associated with danger, oxytocin is associated with feelings of trust. Oxytocin is the hormone that is associated with long-term love after the initial feelings of infatuation more associated with testosterone and estrogen have passed. It is released during orgasm to promote human bonding after sex.[15] It is associated with new mothers, is produced during childbirth and lactation, and is thought to promote bonding with the new baby. Interestingly, oxytocin levels are also heightened in new fathers, mirroring the responses in new mothers even without the direct physiological stimuli associated with childbirth and breastfeeding.[16]

Researchers have taken the study of oxytocin a step beyond observing when we produce oxytocin. asking if we can control how people behave by manipulating the amount of oxytocin in their bodies. Observing a correlation between oxytocin and trusting behavior by itself doesn't show that oxytocin causes trust. Maybe oxytocin is simply a by-product of other biological processes that kick in when we experience trust. Or maybe trust causes the release of oxytocin. To show that oxytocin causes feelings of trust, we need to introduce extra oxytocin in an experimental setting.

Paul Zak and others did just that.[17] Starting with findings that the oxytocin levels produced in the brain by people playing in a trust game are correlated with how much they trusted the other player, Zak and his coauthors then conducted experiments in which they had participants inhale oxytocin. (Synthetic oxytocin is readily available, as it is given to mothers to help induce labor and to mothers who have trouble breastfeeding.) They found that inhaling oxytocin increased the amount of trust that a person exhibited in games like the trust game and changed their perceptions of someone else's intentions. They argued that increasing oxytocin levels affects trust because exposure to the hormone increases empathy, although some concerns have been raised about how well the oxytocin and trust research replicates.[18]

Other studies have looked at brain scans to discern the neurophysiological basis of trust.[19] Similar experiments have shown that other parts of the brain are associated with guilt and remorse—two important emotional responses integral to the trust cycle. Consistent with Frank's conjecture that our emotions are designed to facilitate social interaction, feelings of guilt are an inducement to us to restore broken trust and to signal future trustworthiness.

Still other research has looked at the connection between genes and trust. Twin studies comparing fraternal and identical twins show that our behavior in the trust game is heritable, although the role of the environment is found to be more important than the role of genetics.[20]

A recent strain of psychology known as *embodied intelligence* provides more physiological clues about how the brain processes social information. The literature in this area argues that because all the parts of the brain are connected, seemingly irrelevant sensory inputs can affect our perceptions and behavior. One experiment had test subjects meet a new person. In one treatment, they were given a cold beverage to hold in their hand, and in the other, they were given a warm beverage. People who held a warm beverage were more likely to rate a stranger as being trustworthy, perhaps because they unconsciously associated the new person with warmth.[21]

In sum, biology gives us ways to initiate trust and to demonstrate trustworthiness in order to solve the information problem of knowing whom to trust. From the way that a baby knows how to smile to the ways that we autonomically respond to profanity and taboo violations, we are born with certain social reflexes that encourage us to trust others and that act as credible signals of our own trustworthiness. We have a tendency to trust those who share our norms and values, so mechanisms that bring these norms to the surface and make them visible become important components for completing the cycle of trust.

We use jokes to identify others who share the same values. A common type of joke that is worth bringing attention to are jokes that deliberately put down the "other." We build cohesion around "us" by denigrating those we perceive to be "them." One pernicious feature of the mechanisms that we use to build trust is the way they often deliberately *otherize* the out-group. We will return to this pernicious feature of trust throughout the book.

GIFTS

I love Christmas. The music, the decorations, the general feeling of happiness, the presents! Growing up, I think that my mom made up for her childhood of relative deprivation in postwar Taiwan with an abundance of Christmas presents. The Christmas tree was always buried under brightly wrapped gift boxes. Some people express their love through words of affirmation, quality time, acts of service, or physical touch; my mom expressed it through gifts.[22]

Economists and pundits alike love to dump on the practice of Christmas gift giving. They say that it ruins the spirit of Christmas, which should be about family and togetherness. Economist Joel Waldfogel, in his book *Scroogenomics*, calculates that of the 66 billion dollars spent on gifts in the United States each year, about 18 percent (12 billion dollars) are probably spent on gifts that the recipients don't want.[23] Waldfogel argues that is money basically being flushed down the drain. He advocates gift cards instead, or better yet, cash. If you really want to show that you care, give a person cash and let them decide. In many cultures, giving cash is the standard (like the red packets stuffed with money given for Chinese New Year). Nevertheless, Waldfogel's argument contains a hole that you could drive a big, red sleigh through: it neglects the important role that gift giving plays in strengthening human relationships.

The institution of gift giving is actually an important way to build trust, precisely because it is a situation that entails risk. We risk buying the wrong gift—both a waste of money and an embarrassment. Why don't we just ask for cash and buy what we want for ourselves; why do we have a system where we rely on someone else to choose our gifts for us? As noted in our theoretical framework, one way in which trustworthiness can be measured is in terms of how well somebody knows what we value. If it became the norm to give only money for Christmas, there would be no way for somebody who knows us better to signal their trustworthiness by choosing a better gift. The choice of a gift can convey both the willingness to spend time to find a gift and intimate knowledge of the recipient. Economist Colin Camerer lays out the game theory underpinning gift exchange in one of my favorite research papers.[24] In his model, he fully acknowledges the inefficiency costs associated with gift giving but argues that those costs are useful precisely because they are costly. We need the risk of giving the wrong gift in order to strengthen relationships when we get it right.

Today, we think of gift giving as something childish, a frivolity that distracts from more grown-up activities. However, gift giving is perhaps one of the oldest human institutions and the basis of the modern economy.

The Economics of Gifts

Waldfogel argues that gift giving is wasteful because it doesn't take advantage of the allocative efficiency of the market system. An efficient market (as defined by economics) distributes the resources in society to those who value them the most. There is a lot of truth to Waldfogel's argument. Markets are incredibly efficient institutions for allocating the resources in a society.[25]

However, efficient markets haven't always existed; even today, markets are far from perfectly efficient. Economists dedicate their entire careers to identifying and finding ways to correct for market failures like asymmetric information and oligopolistic collusion. Things were worse in the past, though, when we didn't have institutions like courts and contracts, communication networks, and systems of accreditation, which are all necessary for properly functioning markets. Before there were institutions and markets, there were gifts.

Marco Polo and other medieval European merchants went to China to seek out new trade opportunities.[26] However, when those early European merchants arrived in China, they found a country where international trade was technically illegal. From the fourteenth to the nineteenth centuries, China managed much of its foreign trade as a system of gift exchange that historians call the *tribute system*. Foreign envoys would bring goods to the Chinese emperor as a gift, or *tribute*. In exchange, the Chinese emperor would send back gifts to reward the countries that paid them tribute. The emperor would then sell or distribute the foreign goods locally in order to finance government operations.

In other words, for hundreds of years, international trade with China was handled by gift giving. And that system of gift giving relied on trust. Envoys sent gifts to China because they trusted that China would reciprocate with gifts of equal value. In a market, a quid pro quo exchange is required by custom or by law. In a gift economy, that same quid pro quo is expected, but the parties instead rely on one another's trustworthiness.

There is little doubt that the tribute system persisted for as long as it did in part due to fear of China among the empire's trading partners in Asia. These countries may have sent tribute not just out of desire for the "gifts" that China bestowed, but also to placate the hegemon and protect against invasion. However, the fact that the tribute system continued for centuries, even as Chinese military power waxed and waned, is evidence that the system was built on the belief that gifts to China would be reciprocated in kind.[27]

Of course, absent courts and other modern institutions, what choice did they have? If a Venetian and a Chinese merchant arrange a trade of Chinese silk for Venetian wine, each merchant is relying on trust that his counterpart will follow through with the terms of the agreement. If either party reneged, there were no courts of law to enforce the agreement. Market exchange also relies on trust, and the tribute system of gift exchange between the emperor of China and their neighbors also was built on trust—just in a different form.

The Origins of Gifts

While we can see gift giving as part of the international world order as recently as a couple of centuries ago, its origins hark back to the beginnings of human society. A hunter who managed to take down a gazelle on the savannah was confronted with a problem: he suddenly had more food than he could possibly eat before it spoiled. There was no refrigeration to save the food for later, and no markets at which he could sell his meat for a storable medium of exchange like money. That same hunter had another problem. He knew that hunting required a lot of luck. He might have gotten lucky today, but there would be days in the future where his luck might not be so good. The solution was simple: give the excess meat as a gift to his less fortunate neighbors who had not had a successful hunt that day. Their sense of reciprocity would make them return the favor in the future when the situation is reversed.

The prerequisites for trust are all there. There is a gain from cooperation because we are both better off sharing the proceeds of the hunt. There is a risk because if I share with you, there is no guarantee that you will share with me. But there is room, too, for reciprocity. I share with you in the hopes that someday you will return the favor. And finally, there are opportunities to build reputation. With repeated interactions, we can learn who is trustworthy and who is not.

These "gift economies" where people give gifts to others in their village describe the organization of many premodern tribes. The practices that constitute gift economies have been thoroughly studied by anthropologists, who have documented elaborate rituals associated with gift giving. In various tribes in Papua New Guinea, for instance, people participate in the Kularing exchange. This involves setting off in canoes and traveling among a number of different islands on a journey that sometimes covered several hundred miles. They would give red shell necklaces while traveling clockwise and white shell bracelets while traveling counterclockwise.[28] In India, there is a gift-giving custom between siblings called Raksha-Bandhan, in which a sister ties a piece of string around the wrist of her brother, and the brother, in return, offers her a gift that symbolizes a promise to protect her.[29]

In modern Western societies, gifts are associated with children, holidays, and birthdays. In premarket villages, gifts were a central practice necessary for survival. That is why the anthropologists Jean Ensminger, Joseph Henrich, and their team were so surprised to learn that premarket tribes were the least likely to share when confronted with experimental economic games. We consider their work next.

Experimental Time Travel

As we peel back history to better understand the historical origins of trust, what we would ideally like to do is to run our trust game experiments on human societies going back hundreds, if not thousands, of years. While we don't yet have a time machine that allows us to do that, researchers have done the next best thing.

A team led by Ensminger and Henrich used the tools of experimental economics to examine how economic behavior has developed over time. The team identified fifteen villages around the world, chosen to represent different levels of economic development. The villages ranged from preagricultural hunter-gatherer tribes with little to no connection to outside markets (e.g., the Hadza in Tanzania, or the Tsimane' in Bolivia) to globally integrated, modern, capitalist towns in the United States. In each culture, they tried to find villages of roughly the same size so that they could set up experimental games with similar stakes. Because money was not used in all the cultures, they standardized the games to be worth approximately what a worker could earn in two weeks in each community. In the United States, this represented an amount of four hundred dollars, while in the Amazon, this represented the amount of food that a typical family could expect to hunt or gather in two weeks' time. The researchers then had villagers play the standard economic experimental games and compared the behavior across cultures. The games included the trust game that we described in chapter 1; the prisoner's dilemma, which is a game between two players where each player simultaneously chooses to either cooperate or betray the other person without knowing the other person's choice; the ultimatum game, which is a game that measures how much people value fairness; and the dictator game, where the experimenter gives some food or money to the test subject and asks that person how much they would share with an anonymous person from the same village.

The hunter-gatherers give us a glimpse into how humans might have behaved long ago and allow us to compare the behavior of our ancestors. The researchers organized the communities they studied based on degree of market integration, with

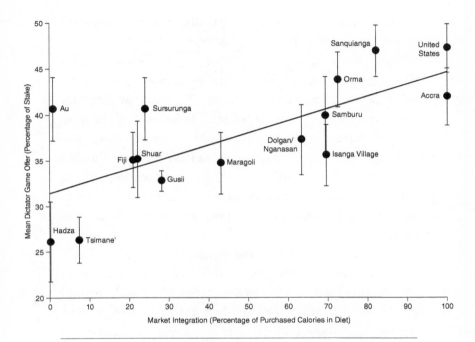

FIGURE 2.1 Mean dictator game offers for each population, plotted against mean value of market integration

Source: Ensminger, J., & Henrich, J. (Eds.). (2014). *Experimenting with social norms: Fairness and punishment in cross-cultural perspective*. Russell Sage Foundation. Figure 4.4.

hunter-gatherers and subsistence farmers on the left to globally integrated market economies in the United States and Europe on the right. Then they plotted the average altruism of each village, measured by how much each person shared with an anonymous other person in their village in the standard dictator game. A clear pattern emerged, as shown in figure 2.1.

When I ask students to predict which societies would share the most, the ancient hunter-gatherer societies or the modern capitalist ones, most come up with the same hypothesis the researchers had. They look around at modern society—filled with anonymous transactions with faceless corporations—and compare that to the village life of the hunter-gatherers, who depend every day on their neighbors for survival. Based on that, they expect that the more communal hunter-gatherers would be more likely to share. The professional anthropologists who spent years studying the gift exchange economies of these tribes expected the same. Instead, they found that the opposite was true. Villagers in the modern United States, for instance, were the most likely to share with an anonymous neighbor, and the hunter-gatherers were the least likely.

Both the students and the anthropologists missed the importance of a key feature of the standard economic experiments: anonymity. It is true that hunter-gatherers do likely depend on cooperation with their neighbors far more than modern Americans. However, when confronted with the question of how much to share with an anonymous other, a key feature of that cooperation is lost: reciprocity. Cooperation happens every day for these tribes, but it is always in the context of a longer-term relationship.

A key part of the gift exchange economy is lost when the gifts are given anonymously: the potential for reciprocity.

The evidence suggests that at least among humans, social preferences are based on reciprocity and trust. When we get a sudden windfall (either from a successful hunt or from a visiting foreign academic experimenter), we want to share it, but not with an anonymous other. Rather, people share their gains with a specific other because the sharing of windfalls becomes part of the cycle of trust and reciprocity. I share the meat from this hunt with you in the expectation that you will share the meat from future hunts with me. In other words, I share because of trust.

The researchers were surprised at what they found, but they probably shouldn't have been. Game theory would have predicted the same result. The reason is that gift exchange depends on *conditional cooperation*—defined as cooperation that relies on your partner being in good standing. Conditional cooperation, then, requires knowing your exchange partner's standing, and thus knowing who your exchange partner is.

The basics of a gift exchange economy are fairly easy to intuit based on the idea of favors owed and favors expected, but important questions remain that game theory can help answer. For example, what happens as the number of people in the tribe increases?

We can see how trading favors works between two people, but introducing the idea into a broader community creates new dilemmas. Being part of a community is good for its members because having more people means that risk is spread widely and more thinly: with only two people, it is possible that both might have bad luck at the hunt, but the law of large numbers says that bad luck should average out as the population size grows. A larger community also brings more diverse skills, and thus more opportunities for specialization in cooperation.

However, more people also means more difficulty maintaining trust. Game theorists have focused on analyzing the problems that arise as community size increases, problems that come from the "shadow of the future." Taking account of the future is important for rational decision-making involving trust, for two reasons:

1. The chance of meeting the same person in the future gives me reason to be more *trustworthy* today.
2. The benefits of meeting people in the future give me more reason to take a risk on *trusting* somebody today.

Trust, that is, relies crucially on anticipation of the future consequences of my actions—anticipation of likely consequences both disciplines the behavior of the trustee today and makes the trustor's risks worth taking. This is why patience is key to developing and maintaining trust: for many of these enforcement mechanisms to work, I have to take a risk today in the hopes of getting some future reward. That requires patience. In bilateral (one-on-one) relationships, it is easier to see that what I do today will come back around again. However, when I am just one among many in a large community, that patience is put under greater strain.

In anonymous experimental interactions, where we may never meet the other person again, the Ensminger et al. study shows that our fundamental instincts lean toward distrust. When I am engaged in an ongoing relationship with a neighbor whom I see every day, then I have a tangible reason to build up a trustworthy reputation because my reputation will likely benefit me in the future. In addition, the potential of creating a lasting relationship gives me a reason to take the risk of working to build trust because building a relationship today can yield returns in the future. All that changes as the number of people whom I regularly interact with increases.

The value of maintaining a relationship depends on the probability that I will interact with you again. Game theorists associate this probability with the *discount rate*, defined as how much you value something in the future relative to your valuation of that same thing today. For example, suppose that Wimpy from the *Popeye* comic proposes, "I will gladly give you two hamburgers on Tuesday in exchange for a hamburger today." If you accept, that implies that you have a discount rate of 50 percent for Tuesday: a hamburger in the future is worth half as much as getting that hamburger today.

The key finding in game theory is that cooperative behavior is easier to maintain when people value the future more—which is just another way of saying that they are more patient.

All of this matters to the question of community size because the less likely I am to interact with you again, the more that I will discount the value of our future relationship. If I have one neighbor, I might see that person every day. If I have two neighbors, I might see each one half as often. If I have three neighbors, I might see each one a third as often. The more neighbors I have, the less I interact with any given neighbor and the more patient I will need to be in order to maintain the relationship. The lack of interaction means that now I have less reason to invest in the relationship and less information about the people in my community.[30]

The problems generated from not knowing whom to trust in your community are mitigated by another key invention associated with community living: gossip. When I am engaged in a one-on-one, direct relationship with another, I get to observe the history of their past behavior. As communities grow, I can no longer rely solely on my own experience; instead, I come to depend on the experiences of others. By partaking in gossip, I can reap the advantages of having a larger network of relationships, while mitigating the risk by taking advantage of the trust-building done by others. Further, knowing that news about my behavior will be quickly shared helps increase trustworthiness. I have an incentive to be a good citizen if I know that news of my good behavior will get out. Or, perhaps more important, fear that news of my bad behavior will spread keeps me in line. At the extreme, the most untrustworthy members of the community become ostracized and shunned, partly because nobody trusts them and partly to serve as a warning to others to stay in line.[31]

Gossip has its own problems, of course. I need to know what information I can trust. I need to have a reason to share my information with others. The group needs mechanisms to make sure that the information shared is reliable and to mitigate incentives for deception. Anyone who has played the telephone game as a child is keenly aware of how gossip can spread misinformation. The spread of bad information is compounded when people have incentives to spread lies for their own personal gain. Many of the cultural institutions that will be discussed in this chapter, such as law and religion, arose to help deal with the problem of gossip at scale. Without those institutions, we run into limits on how big communities can grow.

Anthropologists refer to the limiting number for the size of a community as *Dunbar's number*, which for humans is around 150. Anthropologist Robin Dunbar identified this number in the 1990s by noting that among primates, there is a correlation between the size of the brain's neocortex and the size of the communities they tend to form.[32] He theorized that primates use the neocortex to keep track of their relationships. Therefore, even though humans have the largest neocortex of all primate species (see figure 2.2), which implies that we also have the capacity to live in the largest groups, we are still ultimately constrained in how big our communities can become before they fall apart.

Dunbar found evidence for his prediction by scouring the anthropological literature for the average size of human tribes, which indeed tended to be around 150. He argued that tribes would break apart due to internal conflicts once they reached sizes greater than around 150. He supported his claim by arguing that 150 has been a standard size in military units since the Roman legion, and also by looking at Facebook data: the average number of people we interact with on Facebook is around 150.[33]

Regardless of whether our social groupings can be predicted by our brain anatomy, it is certainly the case that Dunbar's number no longer constrains how we group ourselves today.

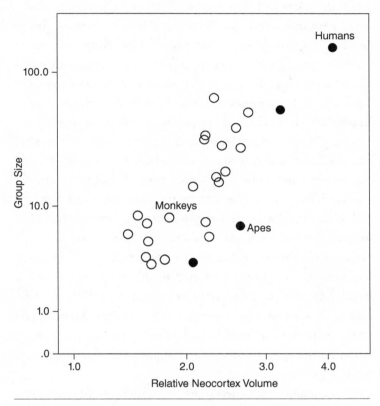

FIGURE 2.2 Mean social group size plotted against relative neocortex volume (indexed as the ratio of neocortex volume to the volume of the subcortical brain) in anthropoid primates. Filled circles: apes (including humans); unfilled circles: monkeys. The regression lines indicate grades of increasing sociocognitive complexity (indexed by the increasing density of the line).

Source: Dunbar, R. I. (2014). The social brain: Psychological underpinnings and implications for the structure of organizations. *Current Directions in Psychological Science, 23*(2), 109–14. Figure 1.

There has been a profound shift in how humans identify their group membership. Tribes became villages. Villages became towns. Towns became city-states. City-states became nations. Today, there is a growing movement toward identifying with larger classes of people, with the entire human race, or even with something larger. Coevolving with that expansion in human identity has been the development of new institutions that have allowed us to cope with strains created by associating with more people.

The gift economy originated as a system based on keeping track of favors and knowing at any moment who owed you and whom you owed. Dunbar's number suggests that our brain can manage around 150 of these accounts before our ledger gets too full. One trick that we will explore next is grouping: instead of keeping track of the favors owed me by Amy, Bob, and Carl separately, I can save mental capacity by putting them into a group and keeping track of my relationship with the group. Trust is a belief, a form of information, so we can think of the trust problem as, at least in part, a computation problem. Many of the institutions that developed to help solve the problem of trust are based on the idea of simplifying the problem of keeping track of information.

This grouping trick opened the way for trust to be established in much larger communities and generates a number of implications for how our communities are organized. It also creates strong mechanisms that induce us to define how we feel about individuals based on the groups to which they belong. This reliance on group identity has been a powerful factor in the development of human civilization and continues to exert a powerful influence on everything we do today.

We have a strong bias to prefer our own tribes in deciding whom to trust. In-group favoritism for members of your own tribe has been fundamental to the human development of trust because it makes it easier to figure out whom to trust, and because it makes the threat of expulsion a possible punishment that will encourage good behavior. A key to facilitating trust at ever-greater levels of organization (from the village to the country to the global community) is to expand our tribe to include more people. One of the first steps in the extension of trust beyond the tribe can be seen in how we organize ourselves around religious beliefs.

RELIGION

In Cambodia stands one of the great wonders of the world— Angkor Wat, a millennia-old, sprawling stone temple complex. Spanning hundreds of acres and barely emerging from the jungle, Angkor Wat is one of the largest religious structures in the world. Much of the rest of the Khmer civilization has disappeared into the jungle, but the temple remains.

When I first arrived at Angkor Wat as a tourist, I asked my tour guide what these structures were used for. Were they markets, or schools, or fortifications for military purposes? The guide replied that while the structures had many uses, their primary function was religious. That seemed odd to me. Considering the idea that civilizations prosper based on how well their institutions function, it seemed strange that this clearly wealthy civilization was able to prosper when it spent so much of its wealth on temples rather than on more practical structures that facilitated trade, or learning, or defense. However, the fact that so many of the most impressive structures from past centuries that survive to this day are religious in nature—from Gothic cathedrals to the Egyptian pyramids—suggests that civilizations that spent a large fraction of their resources on religion were common, and maybe the religious spending helped these civilizations thrive for some reason.

Perhaps religious institutions persisted because they served some functionalist purpose.[34] Just as evolutionary pressure ensures survival of the fittest in biology, the same mechanisms push the fittest societies to survive. Historically, stronger societies outproduce or conquer their neighbors and therefore are more likely to grow over time. Societies with strong religious institutions reflected those values in the architecture they built. They thrived because somehow the religious institutions fostered greater stability and social cohesion, which paved the way for the economic growth that allowed grand structures to be built. It probably should not be a surprise by now that I want to argue that one of the main reasons that religion has been such a powerful force is that it fosters trust.

In the previous section, we talked about how the Dunbar number predicts that the human brain can handle relationships with around 150 others before those relationships start to fray and groups become dysfunctional. For civilizations to grow beyond that number, we need to develop new social institutions.

Much of what is discussed in this section is inspired by the pioneering work of the economist Laurence Iannaccone, who developed game theory models to explain religious practices. Many of these theoretical models have been tested both in lab experiments and by looking at time series data. Iannaccone takes a functionalist view of religion as an institution. The usefulness of religion to its members is that it provides services that make societies that better perform that religion work. His focus was the provision of services like alms and protection, but other economists, such as Avner Greif, have emphasized the role of religious links and affiliations in disseminating trust.

Say Now Shibboleth . . .

The dilemma of extending trust to large groups that we have discussed thus far is that our brains seem to be designed to be able to handle relationships with only around 150 others. What can we do to extend that, thus allowing societies with greater numbers of people?

A story from the Bible helps to illustrate how religion can expand our circle of trust:

> And the Gileadites took the passages of Jordan before the Ephraimites: and it was so, that when those Ephraimites which were escaped said, Let me go over; that the men of Gilead said unto him, Art thou an Ephraimite? If he said, Nay;
>
> Then said they unto him, Say now Shibboleth: and he said Sibboleth: for he could not frame to pronounce it right. Then they took him, and slew him at the passages of Jordan: and there fell at that time of the Ephraimites forty and two thousand.

KING JAMES BIBLE, BOOK OF JUDGES, CHAPTER 12:5

The story illustrates one way to extend trust: instead of determining whom to trust based on our experiences with each human individual (an impossible standard), we could think about trust in terms of groups. Keeping track of the reputations and relationships among hundreds of people is beyond the computational capacity of the human brain. It becomes manageable if we can group hundreds, thousands, or even millions of people into a single group identity and keep track of the reputation of that group as a whole. While this use of group identities isn't limited to religious groups, religion has been an important part of human identity for all of recorded history. The simple idea of replacing individual reputation with group reputation leads to many implications for our model of trust.

If group identity becomes shorthand for knowing whom to trust, then trust becomes a shared resource. Greif finds examples from the late Middle Ages where a single untrustworthy action by a member of a guild, or even a city, leads other merchants from other guilds and cities to break ties with all members of the offending group.[35] All the members of the identity group benefit from the positive actions of others, but at the same time, all the members of the group suffer from the bad actions of one. The group needs to avoid having free-riders within its ranks—members who enjoy the reputation earned by the group without contributing positively to the group's reputation.

One implication of treating trust as a shared resource is that groups tend to erect high barriers to entry, thus ensuring that potential members do not take membership lightly. Examples include painful tattoos or ritual scarring, demonstration of specialized knowledge or lingo (e.g., memorization of Scripture), and other initiation rituals. Researchers on college campuses love to study the often-elaborate initiation rituals used by college fraternities and sororities. When I was inducted into a college honor society, a friend of mine was president of the society and thus was responsible for inducting new members. She tried really hard to keep a straight face while wearing a robe and going through all the required "secret" rituals. The robes, candles, chanting—it's all ridiculous, but it has a purpose. You may have heard the term *cognitive dissonance*. One of the classic studies on cognitive dissonance looks at how increasing the painfulness of a college society initiation ritual increases the loyalty of those who successfully participate.[36]

Willingness to hurdle a group's barrier to entry signals an individual's trustworthiness in two ways. First, individuals who are willing to endure the pain or difficulty of the initiation rituals demonstrate a long-term commitment to the group. Membership confers benefits: by front-loading the costs, the group can ensure members' commitment; long-term receipt of benefits may be required in order to recoup those initial, possibly painful costs. Second, these initiation practices may leave lasting and difficult-to-counterfeit marks on the initiate, so when a stranger is encountered in a foreign land, their membership is readily determined.[37]

Moreover, because the actions of each group member reflect on the reputation of the group, and group markers are often permanent (tattoos are difficult to remove and specialized knowledge or lingo difficult to forget), groups may adopt practices that make leaving the group difficult, if not impossible. Similarly, if an individual must be excommunicated, groups find ways to mark the offender in some permanent way to preserve the integrity of the members of the group.

Group membership often is associated with rules that members need to follow or else risk sanction. Some of these rules seem arbitrary, like kosher dietary rules (although many dietary rules, like a prohibition on eating pork, arose from health concerns associated with diseases like trichinosis, they have little practical use today) or the recitation of set prayers at prescribed times. But arbitrary rules serve the same two purposes as the initiation rituals: they signal to community members a continuing long-term commitment to the cause, and they serve as a signal of group membership to other members and to strangers.

Internal rules have other functions as well. The game-theoretic view of cooperation suggests many solutions for cooperative dilemmas.[38] People can adopt "pay it forward" practices, where A's kindness to B is repaid by B's kindness to C.[39] Groups can also adopt rules that punish untrustworthy behavior. In laboratory games, subjects will sacrifice their own earnings to punish those who they witness engaging in untrustworthy behavior.[40] The same kind of group enforcement behavior is observed in discrete social groups like military platoons.[41]

A practical difficulty for enforcing rules in the real world is that everybody needs to be on the same page when it comes to deciding which of many possible sets of rules to adopt. Formally, this is known as a *coordination game*. Institutions like religions and governments help to enable this process, creating centralized systems to disseminate and enforce rules among all members of the community.[42]

Members who are outside the group would not have access to information about the rules that the in-group follows. They have not demonstrated their commitment to the group, so they are not trusted. Therefore, the pattern of behavior that religious institutions tend to enforce is trust people who belong to your in-group and distrust all those who do not.

This kind of behavior is so ingrained in human nature that it is almost impossible to avoid and seems self-evident, but its existence has been verified by carefully conducted economic experiments. Researchers have run trust game experiments in labs and find that the amount of trust between two players depends on the "social distance" between them. Although the term has recently acquired a different meaning, social scientists have generally used the term "social distance" to refer to the degree of familiarity or feelings of nearness to people in a social group different from your own. The more socially similar someone is to you, the more likely you are to trust them.

In Hell We Trust . . .

The previous section approached religion from a microeconomic perspective. It used ideas from game theory to uncover the incentives and mechanisms that motivate trusting and trustworthy behavior in members of small groups. However, the macroeconomic relationships between religion and trust have also been studied.

Economists Robert Barro and Rachel McCleary studied the relationship between economic growth and religion in an influential paper they published in 2003. Looking at economic growth across a panel of more than 100 countries since 1960, they found, incredibly, that the strength of a country's belief in hell has a positive effect on economic growth. Moreover, they found that it is not religiosity per se that leads to this growth because countries with high rates of church attendance actually experience slower growth.[43]

Joseph Henrich has extended this work to look at the role that religion played in premodern civilizations. He and his colleagues reported not only that the development of religion coincides with periods of intense economic growth, but specifically, believing in a religion that has a punitive god (one that would punish you for bad behavior) rather than a naturalistic god (one that explained things like thunder and lightning) or a mischievous god (one that simply caused trouble for mortals) was the key to these civilizations' growth.[44]

Barro and McCleary argued that the effect they found is causal because they used a statistical technique called an *instrumental variable model* to identify the direction of causality. That is, it is not that fast economic growth increases belief in hell, but rather that a belief in hell causes faster economic growth. This is an important distinction because one can tell stories that go both ways. The idea that religiosity leads to growth[45] (an idea often associated with Max Weber's seminal work *Protestant Ethic and the Spirit of Capitalism*) has long been theorized, including the associations between religion and trust described in this chapter. However, we always need to be mindful of the fact that correlation is not causation. Growth may lead to higher religiosity because higher growth makes people more optimistic and grateful to a higher power. Or there may be a third factor, such as culture, that leads to both higher religiosity and higher growth.

Although religion could affect economic growth through many channels, we have evidence for the belief that trust is at least one of them. The association between religious belief and trust has been documented across countries in turn, trust has been linked to economic growth, although that is a complicated connection.[46]

Because it is always difficult to unpack the causality of macro findings, both because data are limited for events like the formation of new religions, and because you never know what caused what, it is helpful to have lab evidence to back these studies up. In one experiment, subjects (who were mainly Protestant and Catholic) came into a lab to play the standard experimental games to measure trust and public altruism, a measure of trustworthiness.[47] The researchers primed some subjects to think about religion by asking them to play some word games that happened to use religion-adjacent words (e.g., "she felt the spirit," "the dessert was divine," and "give thanks to God"). A control group saw only nonreligious words. They found that subjects who identified with the Protestant religion were more likely to be altruistic. Catholics were less altruistic, but only because when primed to think about religion, the Catholics in the group became less trusting. This could be because the subjects were sampled from a population where Catholics were in the minority. When primed to think about religion, their differences from their peers were made more salient, and we have already seen that we have an innate distrust of those who are different. The opposite was true for the Protestants, who made up the majority of the experimental subjects. In related experimental work, one experimenter visited shopkeepers in a traditional market in Marrakech, Morocco. He finds that shopkeepers were more likely to donate to a charity if they were asked while the call to prayer from the nearby mosque can be heard.[48] Experiments have also been done that reaffirm the observational findings by Barro and McCleary and by Henrich that it is the punitive aspects of religious beliefs that help create cooperation. Researchers have found that Christian subjects are less likely to engage in unethical behavior when they are primed to think about the punitive nature of God as opposed to the more forgiving one.[49]

We can shed more light on beliefs about hell by looking through the lens of game theory. Belief in hell can be understood as a way to extend the rules that maintain group cohesion to situations where nobody is looking. The philosopher Jeremy Bentham envisioned the design of a prison that needed no walls. He called it the *panopticon*. Instead of walls, it would have a central tower that could look into the room of any prisoner at any time. The prisoners couldn't tell when they were being watched, but they knew that at any time, they might be.

According to Bentham, the panopticon needed no walls because for any prisoner, the possibility that he might be under observation at any time would be enough to ensure his good behavior, and thus enough to maintain discipline. The belief in a god that might be watching your behavior constantly is a way of extending that feeling of being under observation.

In a neat demonstration of the effect of being watched, Mary Rigdon and her collaborators had subjects play a simple altruism game.[50] When deciding whether and how much they wanted to share with an anonymous other, they recorded their answer on an answer sheet that had one of two logos, as shown in Figure 2.3. When presented with a three-dot logo that looked somewhat like a watching face, people were more likely to behave altruistically.[51]

FIGURE 2.3 Watching face configuration (left); neutral
configuration (right)

Game theory has also described how belief in the supernatu-
ral power of God was used to screen out bad actors. The economic historian Peter Leeson looked at the practice of medieval
ordeals like witch burnings.[52] Trial by fire is a commonly paro-
died medieval practice (because it is entirely ludicrous) in which
an accused witch was given the opportunity to prove her inno-
cence by being scalded by boiling water or burned by a hot iron.
The premise was that if she were innocent, God would spare her
suffering, but if she were guilty, she would burn. Leeson found
that this practice was surprisingly common, and perhaps more
surprising, people would survive the trial by fire more often
than not. Leeson speculates that the priests who administered
the trial had ways to secretly control the heat of the flame. For
example, by adjusting the timing of the prayer or the placement
of the iron in the fire, the priest could make the rod less hot than
it seemed. Another plausible alternative is the use of chemicals
like naphtha, a petroleum derivative that has been known since
the Greeks, which burns at relatively low temperatures. It is a
chemical commonly used by magicians and fire eaters to perform
feats involving fire.

Leeson supposed that the priest could make an offer modeled
as a simple choice: the accused could either accept trial by fire
or admit guilt and go to jail. So long as the accused genuinely

believed in the power of the fire, then the guilty would admit their guilt and go to jail, while the innocent would accept the trial by fire. The priest would know that only the truly innocent would accept the trial, and therefore would substitute the actual fire with naphtha fire, which would spare the accused witch's life.

The flip side of the fire-and-brimstone, Old Testament–style God that talks about punishment is a more benevolent, New Testament–style God that focuses on the rewards of heaven. Insofar as the rewards of heaven go to those who were judged not naughty, but nice, it works much the same way as the threat of punishment in hell. While experiments have shown that punishments generally work better than rewards in enforcing discipline, the value of a more positive view of the future is that it helps to ensure cooperation by extending the shadow of the future.[53]

Recall that the game-theoretical approach to trust argues that how much we cooperate depends crucially on how much we value the future (and hence our reputation). In any given interaction, we have a temptation to act selfishly, but that temptation is moderated by the knowledge that bad behavior will negatively affect our reputation, and thus our future interactions. Someone who did not expect to live very long would have less reason to behave in a trustworthy manner today.

The medieval worldview was often bleak, and life expectancies were short. The idea of an eternal soul gave people hope and reason to care about and plan for the future.[54] By extending our hope for the future, religious belief increased people's trustworthiness, which also expanded our willingness to trust.

Our discussion about religion has focused on three ways that religion fosters trust:

1.   Religion fosters trust because it helps us consolidate information about the reputations of different groups of people, thus helping us keep track of who is and who isn't trustworthy.

2. Religion changes behavior, perhaps because of fear of a venge-ful god. This makes people more trustworthy.

3. Religion makes us more patient, perhaps through belief in an afterlife or by the fear of always being watched, and patience fosters both trust and trustworthy behavior.

But I wanted to end this discussion about religion with an important caution about the findings in this literature.

The development of religious institutions allowed humanity to extend the rules that govern trust from small Dunbar groups of 150 to globe-spanning religious empires eventually numbering in the billions. However, one consequence of these institutions is that they strengthened the biases that we have toward trusting members of our in-group and distrusting outsiders.

It is rational to place your trust in your in-group because you know them best. They were socialized with the same rules for promoting trustworthy behavior that you were. You belong to the same information networks (i.e., gossip networks) that help identify and isolate bad apples right away and increase the trust among those who belong. You share customs and practices that demonstrate enduring commitment to the collective whole. All in all, these practices create strong incentives to rely on stereo-types and inferences based on people's identities.

While this fosters trust for those within a group, it discourages diversity, both because it excludes ideas from the outside and because it discourages departures from the norm. It has been convincingly shown in experiments that diverse groups are more creative.[55] Scott Page has an interesting theoretical model showing how diverse groups outperform groups of high achievers when seeking solutions to new problems.[56] The best performers at a given task tend to approach the problem in mostly the same way. Therefore, it is redundant to build a team of only high performers. Page showed that diverse groups tend to come up with better solutions to problems because they do a better job of considering the broadest range of solutions to the problem.

In part, the costs of the homogeneity associated with tribalism is mitigated as institutions developed, allowing ever-larger tribes. Extending the definition of "tribe" to larger groups means larger societies. Larger societies can produce more growth through greater diversity which allows greater specialization of labor. But the growth of tribes also increased the consequences of out-group animus. Tribal conflicts between two neighboring Dunbar-sized tribes evolved into globe-spanning crusades and jihads, with devastating wars costing thousands or even millions of lives.

For all the benefits of religion identified by Weber in his best-known book, his second-best-known book, *Economy and Society*, extols the virtues of bureaucracy.[57] Weber liked bureaucracy because it instituted impartial rules that constrained the tribal nepotism of the venal leaders it replaced. While this section focused on the development of religious institutions that fostered the development of large-scale trust, the following section discusses the development of legal institutions that offered an alternative mechanism to achieve the same things.

MEDIEVAL MARKETS AND INTERNATIONAL TRADE

Motivated by an ad I saw in a magazine while on a flight to Paris, I took the light rail on a seventy-minute trip from Paris to the town of Provins, lured by the promise of jousting and falconry and mead. It was a veritable medieval times, set in a real medieval town, and it offered a chance to escape the American visitors who crowd the usual Parisian tourist destinations each summer.

While it was lovely to mingle with French tourists enjoying medieval catapult demonstrations and staged sword fights, the nicest surprise from my visit is that Provins was also the home of one of the most important economic developments in medieval economic history: the Champagne Fairs. Provins, a medieval town in the French province of Champagne, was the site of this development, which helped spur the growth of international trade and perhaps also marked the beginnings of the modern economy.

In 1990, a game theorist (Paul Milgrom), an economic historian (Douglass North), and a political scientist (Barry R. Weingast) published a game-changing paper on the history of the institutional rules that underpin the modern market economy. As noted in the introduction, modern economic theory developed through the twentieth century, largely presuming a frictionless competitive marketplace. This presumption wasn't so much a failure of imagination as it was a failure of mathematical dexterity. Just as a student new to physics often begins by assuming a frictionless surface or an ideal gas or an infinite plane, it was useful and productive to presume a functioning market economy without looking too deeply at its underpinnings. However, by the end of the century, there was a growing appreciation of the inadequacies of this approach. In particular, as economics struggled to guide the transition of communist countries to market economies while much of the developing world floundered in poverty traps, it became more and more clear that the economics profession did not fully understand much of what made modern market economies work.

One response was the development of New Institutional Economics (NIE), a new approach within economics that sought to bring to light the societal structures that markets rely upon—structures that we previously took for granted. NIE looks at big-picture, macroeconomic systems like markets and uses microeconomic tools like game theory to uncover the rules that make them work. The paper by Milgrom et al. was a seminal contribution to this approach. By illuminating the systems that allowed judges to preside over merchant disputes at the Champagne Fairs in late medieval France, these researchers helped us get a better understanding of one of the origins of the institutions that allow international trade to function.[58]

It was within that academic context that I found myself standing in awe in the reconstructed courtrooms in the town of Provins, in the French province of Champagne, watching an animatronic judge mutely render his judgments. I had the room to myself. Most normal tourists were out watching equestrian shows or other colorful revelry, only slipping into the dark, cool stone halls to escape the heat. However, I stood there in awe because the animatronic judge represented a key development in market economies: the creation of a new kind of trust.

What Is a Market?

Like the neoclassical economics of the mid-twentieth century, I think most of us don't give much thought to what it means to have a market. If you do a Google search for definitions of a market economy, the results involve terms like "prices," "supply," "demand," "buying," and "selling." However, all those terms raise further questions: What is a price? What is buying? What is selling? Never mind the even more abstract concepts of supply and demand.

Simply put, *selling* is the exchange of a good for money. *Buying* is the exchange of money for a good. The *price* is the amount of money being exchanged. These definitions seem simple enough, although they hide the fact that they all rely on having an understanding of *money*. We will return to the concept of money later, but for now, you can think of a *market transaction* as one where the price of an exchange is based only on the good and/or service being transacted, not on the identities of the people involved.

To sociologists and anthropologists, the advent of market economies represents a significant break in the organization of human societies. To an economist, the most important impact of markets is a change in how scarce goods and services produced in a society are allocated to the members of society. The market represents a shift from a system in which the product of the society is distributed on the basis of relationships to one where distribution is based on a system of anonymous rules.

The development of markets was crucial to allowing human societies to expand beyond the tribal, relationship-driven particularism of gift economies, allowing societies to grow beyond the scope of our immediate relationships and creating the opportunity for a fairer system—one in which your economic well-being is not constrained by whom you know. But the development of markets was a turbulent process, marked by friction with the gift-based economies and religious institutions that we have discussed so far.

From the experiments in hunter-gatherer communities by Ensminger and colleagues, we learned that our tribal forbears likely relied on gifts but were unaccustomed to giving gifts in anonymous situations. Rachel Kranton was one of the first game theorists to discuss the tensions that arise when a gift economy and a market economy interact—partly to better understand how we evolve from one system to the next, and partly just to get a better grip on what happens when two societies with different systems come into contact with one another.

Kranton notes that we cannot a priori say that one system is better than the other. Gift economies may be preferred if market institutions are weak and relationships are strong, while market economies may be preferred if the opposite is true. She shows that in cases where a society might be better off transitioning to a market economy, the transition is undermined if the market is thin.[59] That is, if everyone is obtaining what they need from gift relationships, no one will be buying or selling on the market. Conversely, the arrival of a market can undermine a well-functioning gift economy. Part of what sustains trustworthy behavior is the possibility of losing someone's trust due to bad behavior. If someone ostracized from their relationships can turn to the market to buy and sell the goods they need, that makes it harder to sustain a gift economy. Gift economies and market economies may both be viable under different circumstances, but Kranton's work shows that when the systems meet, each has the potential to disrupt the functioning of the other.

Further, religion and markets have long been in conflict with each other: Jesus cast out the money changers from the temple, while the prohibition on charging interest on loans (i.e., usury) is common in religions around the world. Markets challenge the power of religious authorities.

And despite the advantages of markets, it is easy to forget just how fraught market transactions can be and how ephemeral this idealized world of frictionless exchange actually is. Between the buyer and seller, each side has both the incentive and the opportunity to cheat the other. The goods can be counterfeit; the money can be counterfeit. The seller can abscond with the cash without delivering the goods. The buyer can take the goods without paying. As exchanges get more complicated (like the purchase of a house), the opportunities for fraud and misrepresentation multiply.

For much of history, reputation and the market economy worked hand in hand. Buyers and sellers transacted, but each side relied on reputation—both to determine whom to trust and to incentivize trustworthy behavior. People bought and sold in transactions with the same people over and over, and the introduction of people who specialized in a given commodity helped solve the problem of the Dunbar number. Instead of having to keep track of the reputations of everybody in the community with whom I needed to trade, I just needed to keep track of the reputations of the merchants for each commodity that I needed to buy or sell. In simple medieval communities where most markets traded in only a few different goods, the number of vendor reputations that had to be tracked was much more manageable.

Many of the systems of trust in the modern economy that we will come back to in the next chapter are simply digitized versions of the same ideas that evolved over past centuries. For example, seller scores on eBay are simply reputation in digital form, while review sites like Yelp are the modern-day gossip network. However, as the Ensminger et al. experiment showed, modern institutions did require people to reorient our thinking from particular to anonymous exchanges. The big change that arose was from trusting only people in your own tribe (however broadly construed) to trusting anonymous rules and institutions.

Let us return to the home purchase example. This is perhaps one of the most complicated transactions that a typical consumer in the modern economy makes, but we do so protected by a great many institutions. Because most of us buy or sell homes rarely, we cannot rely on reputation. Instead, we rely on inspectors and actuaries to inspect the house and uncover and make public information that had been private to the seller. We rely on credit rating agencies to check the credit of the buyer. We rely on government regulators that require houses to meet certain requirements. We rely on courts who will hear our case if we decide that a lawsuit is called for. We rely on escrow companies to hold the deed for the house while these details are being resolved. We rely on police to enforce the deed. Interestingly, many, if not most, of these institutions are private institutions that may be regulated by the government but do not rely on government enforcement, per se. In fact, we can trace the DNA of these institutions back to the twelfth and thirteenth centuries in Europe, when governments were more prone to rob you than to enforce your contracts, especially for disputes that crossed territorial borders. In such an environment, it was prudent not to have to rely on the government but to find private alternatives instead. It was to one of these institutions, the Champagne Fairs, that Milgrom, North, and Weingast turned their attention.

The Champagne Fairs

In the twelth and thirteenth centuries, the Champagne region of France was at the crossroads of Europe. Various towns in Champagne would host a monthlong annual fair where merchants from across Europe would gather to arrange for trade in goods such as textiles, leather, and spices from places like Italy, Spain, and northern Europe. Merchants met for the usual reasons: goods that were common and cheap in the south were rare and expensive in the north and vice versa, so there was profit to be made in the dangerous and laborious journey needed to complete the exchanges. In the eighteenth century, one of the first economists, David Ricardo, famously based his theories of comparative advantage on the medieval trade of English wool for Spanish port wine.

Also, for the usual reasons, transactions were risky and required trust. Money was typically not carried by merchants on their persons for fear of theft, so accounts were settled at the end of the fair. Sometimes merchants lacked the money to pay up front, so, as businesses of today do, they made deals to take delivery now but arrange payment at a future date (typically at a subsequent fair). More specifically, they would take delivery of their newly acquired goods, bring them back home and sell them, and then pay back their debt at the subsequent fair. Often, the risk involved was just the time it took to arrange delivery of the cargo. Between the time an agreement was made and the time(s) the goods and money were exchanged, there was ample room for treachery. Perhaps the seller found a new buyer who could offer better terms. Perhaps the buyer "lost" the money. Perhaps the seller tried to replace the original merchandise with goods of inferior quality.[60]

The merchants met in Champagne in part because of its convenient location at the center of many trade routes, but more important, because institutions existed there that facilitated trust. In part, these institutions were governmental. The count of Champagne had consolidated enough power to achieve a certain amount of independence from the king of France (although the region remained part of France). The count promised safe passage for merchants, and he established courts to settle legal disputes.[61]

But Milgrom and colleagues argued that the formal legal system in Champagne was insufficient, as it lacked the power to enforce contracts outside its borders. This problem, they reasoned, was solved by the emergence of a private court system. Judges were paid by the merchants directly rather than funded by any government (whether the count's or the king's). Punishment, when it was judged necessary, was meted out by blacklisting guilty parties: the blacklist was publicly posted and other merchants would not trade with merchants on the list. Blacklisted status could be lifted after a stipulated period of time or when a fine was paid. Private arbitration continues to be common to this day, especially in cases that cross international borders.

Milgrom and colleagues thus showed, in their landmark paper on the private courts of the Champagne Fairs, how private institutions could form to facilitate trust—private institutions that did not require the coercive power of the state to enforce compliance. The functioning of such an institution, as they analyzed using mathematical game theory models, requires reliable adherence to a number of key norms:

- The merchants must report honestly.
- The judges must adjudicate honestly.
- Other merchants must be willing to punish defectors.
- The punished must be willing to pay fines.
- The merchants must be willing to pay the judges for their services.

When a society arrives at a state in which enough players are following the relevant norms and rules that all other players will find it in their best interests to voluntarily comply with them, that society has reached what game theorists call *Nash Equilibrium*. The voluntary compliance feature of the Nash Equilibrium was key to their purposes. It is easy to understand why I am willing to follow rules if the police will throw me in jail if I don't. What is less obvious is why I follow rules and act honestly when no police exist. There are judges, but then the question becomes why the judges adjudicate honestly. Also, there are other merchants who will mete out punishments, but why would merchants punish if it is costly to do so, and why would they punish only those who deserve punishment? Milgrom et al. constructed a mathematical proof of the Nash Equilibrium in order to answer these questions.

And so, they concluded, the judges adjudicate honestly and reject bribes because their reputation is at stake, and they know that they won't get paid in the future if they are caught taking bribes today. The merchants report honestly because they know that judges will honestly punish bad behavior and will not succumb to bribes. The other merchants are willing to punish defectors because they will be deemed dishonest and blacklisted themselves if they do not. The merchants will pay the judge for his services for the same reason. The punished will pay his fines because that is the only way to regain his livelihood.

There are so many invisible forces driving our behavior; most of these we take for granted and don't think much about. Today, we may follow norms and rules out of convention or fear of criminal prosecution, but Milgrom, North, and Weingast showed that a system of behavior could be constructed such that everybody follows the rules out of pure, rational self-interest.

One thing to note about the shifting of the basis of trust from individual relationships to systems like the Champagne Fair is that much of the risk and vulnerability associated with these transactions is reduced. While this is great for the people involved at the time, it is bad for the development of trust. This tension is heightened as we move to more formal systems of government. While stable institutions are good for trust, institutions that are too strong may interfere with trust-building. We turn to this tension between trust and the law next.

THE RULE OF LAW

Varys's Riddle:

In a room sit three great men, a king, a priest, and a rich man with his gold. Between them stands a sellsword, a little man of common birth and no great mind. Each of the great ones bids him slay the other two. "Do it," says the king, "for I am your lawful ruler." "Do it," says the priest, "for I command you in the names of the gods." "Do it," says the rich man, "and all this gold shall be yours." So tell me—who lives and who dies?

GEORGE R. R. MARTIN, *GAME OF THRONES*

This riddle is relayed by the conniving advisor Varys, a character in Martin's fantasy series *A Song of Ice and Fire*, later adapted into *Game of Thrones*, a wildly popular television series. What is the nature of power in society? Why do people follow orders, either from a king, a priest, or a rich merchant? More generally, why do people follow rules? More concretely, why do Americans in the twenty-first century continue to abide by the Constitution, an imperfect document signed in 1789, when the world has changed so much?

Thomas Hobbes famously argued that in humankind's "state of nature," "life is nasty, brutish, and short", a constant "war of all against all."[62] While our collective mythology of tribal life derives in part from Jean-Jacques Rousseau's idyllic vision of the noble savage, Steven Pinker documents the murder rate over the long sweep of history and argues that our hunter-gatherer forebears lived in far more violent times, where murder was much more common.[63] Studies of skeletal remains in prehistoric sites find that an average of 15 percent of all people died violently. Studies of medieval Europe where we have written records show the death rate has fallen even further, from a rate of 100 violent deaths per 100,000 people per year in 1300 to close to 1 death per 100,000 people per year today.

In premodern times, conflict was often settled using violence, making cooperation tenuous and trust essential for allowing cooperation to help us rise above our own individual means. The question then is why and how we came to trust in the abstract rules that compel us to obey our political leaders, obey our religious leaders, or even obey the rules of the marketplace.

In prior sections, we have discussed how trust evolved in the context of religion and trade. In our functionalist view, religion creates the trust that allows larger-scale cooperation, which creates stronger, more prosperous societies. Religion creates trust by inculcating social norms and beliefs into its members.

These religious norms enforce standards of behavior because members believe that bad things will happen to them if they do not follow the rules and that they will be rewarded if they obey them. These norms strengthen and persist in populations because they foster stronger societies that are more likely to survive and grow.

Moreover, as communities grew and the scope of markets grew to international levels, we saw how informal legal systems developed in Europe and elsewhere. Judges kept track of the reputation of international traders, and traders trusted the judges because the judges cared about maintaining their reputations as well.

Therefore, we could say that the man with a sword in Varys's riddle might obey the priest because of the religious norms he was inculcated with, and he might obey the wealthy merchant because of the market institutions that create incentives for even the rich to keep their promises, but why might the swordsman obey the king? What gives rulers political power?

While *Game of Thrones* poses the question, game theory provides us with an answer.

Game Theory and the Rule of Law

While the previous section was preoccupied with the role of trust in facilitating trade in early economies, trust is just one of many fundamental dilemmas in communal life that game theorists seek to understand. The most fundamental of these dilemmas is the collective action problem. Governments come in many forms and play many roles, but economists are most interested in how they solve the collective action problems involved in organizing individuals to act for the collective good. These collective action problems come in two flavors: the first is inducing people to cooperate in pursuit of prosocial activities—working together to build public works like irrigation systems or to organize a militia for common defense. The second is reducing antisocial activities—preventing violence, theft, fraud, and (hopefully) the squandering of resources. But both are just versions of the classic prisoner's dilemma. The cooperative choice to make would be to do what is best for the public good, but each individual member would prefer to shirk their responsibility and pass it off to someone else.

An alternative notion of the purpose of government, which goes back to at least Hobbes, is the government as centralizer of power.[64] In the modern economy, governments make the rules, collect taxes, and provide social services. Crucial to its ability to function in this capacity, the government has to be able to make rules and expect that they will be followed. Most of the time, we don't give much thought to why we follow the rules. The traditional view is that we follow the rules because if we don't, there will be consequences. If we don't pay our taxes, there will be a fine. If we don't pay the fine, our property will be seized. If we don't give up our property, we face jail time. If we refuse jail time, we face the risk of violence.

At the heart of this notion of government, underlying all of our rules, is the idea that the government holds a monopoly on the legitimate use of violence. Government maintains law and order, outlaws the use of violence by others (murder and armed robbery, for instance, are disallowed), and enforces the rules through the mechanism of the threat.

Hobbes argued that citizens put up with this system because the order created by government is better than the nasty world that would exist without government. People follow through on transactions, contribute taxes, and eschew violence because of the implicit threat of punishment; they put up with being threatened because it is better than living in society ungoverned. This is a rigid view of government based on strict rules, and it does not acknowledge the role of trust and human relationships.[65]

While this view of society initially seems to be a reasonable representation of modern life, the view breaks down upon closer inspection. The first piece of evidence that should give us pause is that order in society is not maintained only by fear of the law. Recall the Ensminger et al. experiments on premarket tribes. That research had two key takeaways, the first being that people in premodern economies are less likely to cooperate in anonymous economic games, and the second being that people in modern economies are in fact quite likely to cooperate in anonymous economic games.

The most forceful refutation of this comes from the work of Elinor Ostrom, the first woman to win a Nobel Prize in economics, who was part of the wave of NIE that we introduced with the Milgrom et al. model earlier. This school of thought is based on the idea that if you want to understand the rules of society, you can't just look at the top—at the leaders who centralized power—you have to look at the local level. Rule-making is decentralized and comes just as much from socially evolved norms of behavior as it does from official edicts.

Generalizing the ideas raised earlier, Ostrom examines how diverse populations (not just the modern educated Western ones normally studied by academics) solve collective action problems, and she identified eight qualities of efficient systems of norms:[66]

1. Clear definitions
2. Being appropriate to local conditions
3. Broad participation
4. Effective monitoring
5. Appropriate sanctions
6. Effective conflict resolution
7. Self-determination
8. Nested authority

Although there's no reason to believe that every society will have the most efficient qualities, we might expect that due to evolutionary pressures, more efficient systems are more likely to survive. She also argues that underlying each of these eight attributes is trust and reciprocity.

The central contribution of Ostrom's view is that stability and the rule of law don't have to be top-down. We don't necessarily need government edicts and authoritarian rulers to create stability. Instead, cooperation and order and the rule of law can come from the bottom up. From leveraging individual relationships based on trust and reciprocity, societies of greater and greater size and complexity can be built.

Her view is that instead of seeing government as some power from on high that creates rules that impose order on the citizens down below, we should think of society as being built on the relationships that connect the citizens within it, and the super-structure of government is built as a reflection of those underlying relationships.

Trust and Government Stability

There is an even more fundamental question about the relationship between trust and government, which is how much we trust the system itself (and how much trust is necessary to keep the system intact).

The original Hobbesian view of government was that people tolerated the rule of a monarch, even if it was sometimes autocratic and cruel, because the monarch maintained order: being ruled by that monarch was preferable to the chaos that would occur otherwise. Calvert formalized this idea with game theory, showing that in a community of people who are constantly confronted with situations where their neighbors may cheat them (i.e., prisoner's dilemmas), it becomes optimal for them to choose (any) one of them to be ruler, with the power to adjudicate disputes—even though that ruler would likely use that power to their own advantage.[67]

However, any cursory look at history will show that this tacit agreement between the ruler and the people will break down from time to time, typically in the form of violent revolution. Several of the leading theorists in this area—Daron Acemgolu, James Robinson, and Simon Johnson—argue that the main reason why governments fail is inequality. Looking at the history of revolutions around the world, they argue that governments fail when the elites let the gulf of inequality get too wide—this sparks unrest, which leads to revolution.

Like NIE, Acemoglu, Robinson, and Johnson focus their attention not just on macroeconomic measures like inequality, but on the game-theoretic basis of the rules that govern a society, and specifically how those rules can be either *extractive* (i.e., favoring the rich) or *inclusive*. While trust is not a direct part of their theory, inclusive rules likely foster trust—and a look at the data shows that inequality and trust are intimately linked. In their book, Acemoglu and Robinson note that part of what determines a country's success is when the people "trusted the institutions and the rule of law that these generated and they did not worry about the security of their property rights." They go on to compare the difference in outcomes between Mexico and the United States, noting that "in surveys Mexicans typically say they trust other people less than the citizens of the United States say they trust others. But it is not a surprise that Mexicans lack trust when their government cannot eliminate drug cartels or provide a functioning unbiased legal system."[68]

Acemgolu, Robinson, and Johnson make two key points. First, the driving factor behind the wealth of nations is strong institutions. Wealthy countries may also be ones where the people exhibit a lot of trust, but that trust comes from having governments and rules that promote growth and stability. Second, the cause of societal upheaval is inequality. The working class tolerates a ruling elite so long as the benefits of that tolerance outweigh the costs of revolution.

One of the most important insights from Acemoglu, Robinson, and Johnson on the study of institutions is their finding that the mechanism driving economic progress is indeed robust institutions. Economists are very careful about making causal statements. While nobody disputes that countries with better economic outcomes also have better institutions, it is not obvious whether the better economic outcomes caused the institutions to develop or the better institutions caused greater economic growth. Their careful empirical work shows that countries possessed of a natural environment conducive to Europeans' setting up inclusive institutions during the era of European colonization had better economic growth even centuries later than countries where European colonization set up extractive institutions. That finding also allows them to conclude that the higher levels of trust that we see in more stable governments comes from better institutions and stronger rule of law.

Their research also shows that the rule of law breaks down due to unchecked inequality. Acemoglu and Robinson's argument is based on the idea that the working class tolerates the elite because they believe that the implicit threat of revolution will lead the elite to continue to support efforts to spread the wealth of society. We could say that there is an implicit contract between the workers and the elites. The workers trust that the elites will look out for their interests in exchange for the working class allowing the ruling class to stay in power.

One place where the implicit contracts that bind society together is made explicit is when a country writes a constitution. U.S. Supreme Court confirmation hearings tend to bring out a standard set of debates and concerns; one of these is the question of constitutional interpretation. The originalist interpretation of the U.S. Constitution argues that the law today needs to abide by the original intent of the writers of the document, who lived over two hundred years ago. This has always seemed strange to me. Why are we using a two-hundred-year-old document to adjudicate issues that come up today, surrounding the Internet or cybercrime or DNA sequencing or gay marriage? Economists are obsessed with optimizing: policy makers should be making the best possible choice—the choice that does the most to improve human welfare. It is hard to imagine that choices made two centuries ago would somehow be the optimal ones for the issues and people living today.

The theory of repeated games provides a different insight into why originalism might make sense, and why this debate is so important. It suggests that the Constitution acts as a coordinating device, and as such, it functions to reduce conflict. It almost doesn't matter what rules were chosen two hundred years ago—what matters is that there is *some* set of rules that we all agree upon.

An apocryphal psychology experiment that has made its rounds helps illustrate the idea:

A group of scientists placed five monkeys in a cage. At the cage's center was a tall ladder with a bunch of ripe bananas at its top. Every time a monkey started up the ladder, the scientists soaked the other monkeys with cold water. After a while, any time a monkey started up the ladder, the others would grab it and beat it up. Soon none of the monkeys dared to go up the ladder, regardless of the temptation. Next, the scientists removed one of the monkeys from the cage and substituted it with a new monkey. As soon as this new monkey spotted the bananas, he tried to climb the ladder. The other monkeys beat him up at once. After several beatings, the new member of the group learned not to climb the ladder—even though he never really knew why it was "forbidden." A second new monkey was substituted for one of the original five, with the same result—and the first substitute monkey participated in the beatings. The process was repeated with a third new monkey, then a fourth, and finally a fifth, each time with the same result. In the end, the cage held a group of five monkeys who had never received a cold soaking—but who would beat up any monkey who attempted to climb the ladder.[69]

The basic idea is that we all abide by rules. We abide by them because we will be punished by others for not doing so. We sometimes punish people to enforce these rules even if we don't understand why. Even if those rules don't follow any logic. But the reason why we do is because without rules to maintain order and cooperation, life is a war of all against all, where life is nasty, brutish, and short.

This originalist view of the Constitution is a bit odd: in another context, it might be unusual to obsess over preserving rules laid out by a document that is almost two and a half centuries old. However, this preservationist instinct can be understood using the models of Calvert and Acemoglu and Robinson and Hobbes. In each case, society has decided to follow a particular ruler. There are many other rulers they could have followed, and there is no reason to believe that the current ruler is the best one. But it is the threat of the chaos that would occur when countries transition between regimes that makes the working class willing to go along with the current ruler in charge.

We can think of the U.S. Constitution as taking on the role of the ruling regime. Just as there are many possible rulers, there are many possible Constitutions. Other countries change theirs regularly.[70] In the United States, trust in the Constitution plays a crucial role in maintaining order. There may be value in pursuing unconstitutional government policies, but the benefits of such pursuits must be balanced against the risk of the chaos that might occur if trust in the Constitution breaks down.

In my own research with Xinyue Zhou, Stephan Meier, and Wenwen Xie, we ran experiments confirming that people dislike inequality, but their desire to reduce inequality is moderated by their desire to preserve order.[71]

It has been well documented in many lab experiments that people would like to reduce inequality. In our experiment, students were told that there are two other participants in the experiment—one who will be paid four dollars and another who will be paid one dollar, even though neither did anything in particular to earn the money. Students were then given the opportunity to transfer money from the more fortunate student to the less fortunate. What we found was when the transfer size was small (say, one dollar), most were happy to agree to the transfer. However, when then transfer size was a bit bigger (say, two dollars), the majority rejected the transfer. What was notable is that under both types of transfers, the final difference in income between the two students would be one dollar: one would have three dollars and the other would have two dollars. The difference is that in the case with two dollars, the identity of which student was "rich" and which was "poor" would reverse.

We believe that this behavior is driven by the fact that people have two competing desires: to reduce inequality, but also to maintain order. In the animal kingdom, animals in the same group will often have some ritualized fight to create a pecking order (whether or not they are the sorts of animals that peck). However, once that pecking order is established, the animals will enforce the order and deter others from challenging it. The reason for this is that constant challenge to the established order will weaken the group as a whole against outsiders. We think that the same is true for human societies. We favor policies that reduce inequality, but only insofar as they don't radically disturb the existing order. We all implicitly know that too big a challenge to the order will lead to a period of chaos that will be bad for all.

We interpret this result as evidence that generally people prefer more equality, but they hesitate when the option to create that equality upsets the existing order. Also, we find that this isn't just an American phenomenon, but universal. For example, Plato noted that "Meddling and exchange among these three classes is the greatest harm that can happen to the city and would rightly be called the worst evil one could do to it." while Confucius wrote, "Let the ruler be a ruler, the subject a subject, the father a father, the son a son." The effect is evident in countries ranging from the United States to China to India to Australia. The effect was strongest when tested on nomadic Tibetan herders. We also found that the respect for hierarchy over stability develops in children as young as seven or eight years old. It seems like it is universally agreed upon that inequality is bad, but instability can be worse. Maintaining trust in the system sometimes takes priority. This chapter began by looking at how the history of human trust started, based on personal one-on-one relationships, and then showed how the progress of human history has been about building the institutions—like markets, religions, and governments—that allow us to trust one another at scale. At the beginning of this section, we asked this question: if the man with the sword holds all the power, why does he follow orders from kings, or merchants, or religious leaders? It's because in a world dominated by men with swords, life is nasty, brutish, and short. Therefore, we follow the rules handed down by merchants, church leaders, and kings because it creates the stability and trust that civilization is built on. In today's modern world, we have become so accustomed to these rules that like the monkeys with the ladder, we have forgotten why we follow them. Still, as we see in the next chapter, trust is still deeply interwoven into the institutions of the modern economy—institutions that both rely on trust and are designed to maintain it.

3

TRUST IN THE MODERN ECONOMY

N chapter 2, we told the story of human civilization as the story of how we learned to trust one another. Part of that story can be seen in our biology. Evolution has given animals the tools for cooperation, and we have inherited those same genetic predispositions to trust—at least when it comes to our immediate family and those around us. Over time, institutions developed to expand our circle of trust. Religion gave us reasons to behave in more trustworthy ways and methods to keep track of who is likely to be trustworthy. Markets developed rules to do the same. Adam Smith noted that even in an individualistic, free market economy, the magic comes from how the market coordinates the division of labor: as previously noted, a factory of pin makers, each specializing in one part of production, can produce vastly more pins than an equal number of traditional pin makers working alone. Those rules became formalized by governments, which expanded their scope into all parts of our daily lives. Governments, particularly democratic governments, rely on the rule of law, and the functioning of the rule of law relies on trust as well. Each institutional development allowed our circle of trust to grow, but each also made whom and how we trust more impersonal—a characteristic that I think many of us would ascribe to the modern market economy. It is to this subject that we now turn our attention.

This chapter digs into the topics that most people would identify with economics. We will first look at the role of trust in money, banking, and contracts; and then the workplace and advertising. Finally, we will consider the role of trust in the online economy by examining the role of trust in the sharing economy and in blockchain.

Even though we noted that some of the most important economists, like Kenneth Arrow and Amartya Sen, have long discussed the importance of trust, the role that trust plays in the modern economy is not often acknowledged in either economics courses or popular culture. Trust is taken for granted, even though it is essential. In this chapter, we hope to uncover the trust that is at work in our daily interactions with the market economy, and how the institutions of the market economy are designed to facilitate trust.

MONEY

U.S. law has required all U.S. currency to contain the words "In God We Trust" since 1956, although the phrase has been used regularly on U.S. coins and bills since 1864.[1] The aim of facilitating trust—not in God, perhaps, but in money itself—drives many decisions about U.S. currency design.[2] We can see an attention to trust in the anticounterfeit features literally woven into or stamped onto our paper money: these include microprinted words, invisible patterns that show up under special light, and hidden threads buried inside the paper. But more symbolically, we can see trust at work in the fact that the validity of U.S. currency has been constant over the centuries. Unlike other currencies, which are regularly retired and replaced, U.S. currency stays legal tender forever—at least, that is the promise. Trusting that promise is integral to how money works in an economy and is part of why the U.S. dollar is the most trusted currency in the world.[3]

But What Is Money?

Every discussion of the history of money includes some discussion of the stone coins used by the residents of the Micronesian island of Yap. The coins vary in size from an inch or so in diameter to twelve or thirteen feet, and they were used as currency in Yap until the early twentieth century. Part of the reason that economists always begin discussions about money by talking about these coins is that the Yap islanders, as John Maynard Keynes put it, are "a people whose ideas on currency are probably more truly philosophical than those of any country."[4]

These coins were used like any other currency. The largest were time consuming to make, so they were mostly used for large transactions. Like gold, they derived their value in part from their rarity. One might use a coin as a dowry or as a ransom, but also for more mundane transactions like the exchange of food.

The stones were constructed like a wheel for easier transport and could be rolled from hut to hut as payment for goods and services. However, the largest of the stones were still quite unwieldy. Over time, it became customary to transfer ownership by simply telling everyone in the community that ownership had changed hands, while the stone stayed where it was. The physical location of the stone did not matter—only the community's collective agreement about who the owner was mattered. In fact, it was reported that once, when a stone was being transported by boat to another island, it fell overboard and sank to the bottom of the sea.[5] However, the tradition of maintaining ownership by oral history was so strong that the physical location *still* did not matter. The coin that was lost forever under the water was still transacted in the usual way. Islanders bought and sold things with it, and for all intents and purposes, the sunken coin was still accepted as currency under the usual rules of ownership established by the Yap society.

Why do economists love this story so much? Because it tells us a lot about how all money works.

It is probably a surprise to most people that most economists (at least most microeconomists) don't think a whole lot about money. Economists sometimes draw a distinction between the "real economy" and the "monetary economy." Our real economy models are about labor and capital, demand and supply, more tangible things rather than numbers on a ledger. Money is a useful yardstick for measuring those things, but just as most physicists don't spend much time thinking about inches or kilograms, most economists don't give money much thought most of the time.

However, that's not to say that monetary economics isn't important or interesting. Sometimes things that happen within the monetary economy wind up affecting what happens in the real economy. But more fundamentally, you quickly fall down a long rabbit hole when you ask the deceptively simple question: *what is money?* Because part of the answer is that money is an illusion. Money is a solipsism. Money is an act of faith.

Think back to the section in Chapter 2 on hunter-gatherer gift-giving economies. In these economies, the exchange of goods and services is mediated by favors. In a market economy, the exchange of goods and services is mediated by money. Well—money is really just an accounting mechanism that keeps track of who owes a favor to whom. Suppose that Amy caught a gazelle last week and shared her extra meat with Bob. Now Bob owes

Amy a favor. Suppose that this week, Carl has extra berries and Amy would like some. She could transfer the favor that Bob owes her to Carl in exchange for the berries. It's already confusing to keep track of the favors owed among Amy, Bob, and Carl. Imagine the complexity of keeping track of all that in a tribe with dozens of people.

Things would be a lot simpler if Bob had been able to pay Amy for her extra meat in cash. Amy could then use the cash to buy berries from Carl. The cash keeps track of the favors. It also takes the particularism out of the system. So long as the money here is universally accepted, Amy can spend that cash anywhere. She doesn't have to worry if Carl doesn't like her or if Carl is sharing only with members of his family or with people who share his religious beliefs. It means that we can trade with anyone who accepts the currency rather than trading only with those whom we trust. The burden of trust shifts from needing to trust the other person with whom you are trading to needing to trust the money. Just as those giant stones on Yap were used to keep track of favors, the money that we use today is basically doing the same thing.

For money to work, economists believe, it should have six properties:[6]

1. Durability—We can't make it from a material that deteriorates too quickly.
2. Portability—Money should be easy to move.
3. Divisiblity—It should be possible to subdivide a basic unit of currency.
4. Uniformity—Each unit should be the same.
5. Limited supply—Money must be scarce.
6. Acceptability—Money should be widely accepted by others in the community.

Traditionally, we think of money in the form of precious metals like gold or silver coins, but many other things have been used—and not every money system has all six of these properties. The stone money of Yap failed the portability test in spectacular fashion. Between Africa and Asia during the Middle to late Middle Ages, rare shells from the cowry sea snail were used. In earlier times, it was salt (the word "salary" comes from the Latin *salarius*, "salt"). In prisons, inmates used to use cigarettes, which gave way to cans of mackerel as no-smoking rules gained favor. Both cigarettes and mackerel cans are uniform and storable. Outside of prison, they would fail the scarcity test, but within prison, the tight control of what is allowed inside makes both a scarce commodity, much like gold and silver.

The most interesting lesson from Yap, though, is not just that money can take almost any form, but that it doesn't have to take a form at all. When the huge stone coin fell to the ocean floor, never to be retrieved, it was the idea of the coin that contained its value. Islanders on Yap knew that they could own a coin even if that coin were not physically in their possession—even if it were at the bottom of the ocean. The same idea has been at work around the world for centuries, during which time many people used slips of paper to represent ownership of gold bars stored in a vault somewhere, never to be seen by its "owner." The revolutionary idea occurs when you realize that if you never see the coin, maybe you don't need the coin at all.

The History of Money

The idea that money doesn't have to represent a physical thing like a stone coin or a bar of gold, but instead could simply represent faith, as in the "full faith and credit of the U.S. Treasury," was a giant conceptual leap that took off in a big way in 1971, when the United States went off the gold standard, but it had its beginnings centuries earlier. The use of slips of transferable paper to represent the ownership of physical assets like gold and silver has a history extending back a thousand years.

Medieval merchants, wary of bandits, were rightly reluctant to carry large sums of gold and silver on the open road, so banks emerged as a place to store and transfer precious metals. The banks would issue a paper declaring ownership of an amount of gold, for instance, and merchants could carry and transfer the paper instead of the gold itself. Just like the stone coin at the bottom of the ocean, all that had to be transferred was the ownership of the gold itself. This practice began with the Knights Templar and the medieval crusaders and pilgrims who traveled between Western Europe and Jerusalem. The journey was long and dangerous. The ability to travel without being laden with gold made the trip much safer.

While we think of money as something that governments issue, up through the Middle Ages, the dominant institution securing money in Europe was the church and, later, private banks. To this day, the currency that circulates in Hong Kong is issued by private banks such as HSBC. However, in most countries, the rise of the nation-state was accompanied by a nationalization of the currency, so nations took control of the money supply.

Governments had an interest in controlling money because the ability to print money was of immense value. They could print money to help finance wars and print extra money to create infla-tion, which would make it easier to pay their debts. There were limits, of course. Up until the twentieth century, paper money printed by governments was supposed to be backed by gold or silver. Like the islanders of Yap who transacted using giant coins lost at the bottom of the ocean, or the Christian pilgrims who used paper that represented gold held in Crusader temples, paper currency was meant to represent precious metals that were held in a vault somewhere for safekeeping.

However, like banks everywhere, governments were quick to realize that when the economy was stable, most people would be happy with their paper money and wouldn't bother asking for the gold. Therefore, they were free to print more paper than there was gold in the vaults. The government just had to keep enough gold in the vaults so that anyone who did request money could get it. If a bank never expects more than 10 percent of people to come asking for their gold, then keeping a reserve of 10 percent would allow each dollar of gold to create ten dollars of paper money. Effectively, governments could give ten different people the right to claim each gold bar in the vault. So long as no more than 10 percent of these people ever came to ask for the gold, the government could create nine virtual gold bars for each actual bar of gold that it had in its possession.

So long as people trusted in the stability of the government and the ability of the government to convert paper into gold, governments would have the ability to print far more cash than the gold it actually possessed. Of course, if that trust were to falter, the currency would lose its value as people rushed to convert their paper money into gold and the economy would crash. The Chinese were perhaps the first to realize this (in the eleventh century), but the practice became ubiquitous in the centuries that followed.

Even the value of money that was made of metal rather than paper could be manipulated by governments. Those who play enough computer games are familiar with the exchange rate between gold and silver coins in fantasy games. By long convention, mostly for the sake of simplicity, one gold coin can be exchanged for ten silver coins in video games.[7]

The relative price of any two commodities should be determined by supply and demand, so a fixed exchange rate between gold and silver isn't realistic. However, it was practical to have a relatively fixed rate so that merchants could know how to set prices for when customers wanted to pay in gold and when they wanted to pay in silver. In England between the sixteenth and the nineteenth centuries, this job fell to the Master of the Mint (something like a central banker today). Perhaps the most famous person to hold this position was Isaac Newton—the same Newton who coinvented calculus and modern physics. By offering different exchange rates between gold and silver, the mint could regulate the relative amount of each in circulation, which would effectively control the rate of inflation and regulate the money supply.

One of the most famous unsuccessful candidates for president of the United States was William Jennings Bryan, whose most famous speech was about the "cross of gold." He delivered this speech at the 1896 Democratic National Convention, arguing for an increase in the use of silver within the monetary system as a way to increase inflation; this, he argued, would help farmers get out of debt.[8]

Money became nationalized because whoever controls the money in a country reaps substantial benefits. The nationalization of currency allowed governments to print money when needed, while controlling the rate of inflation by regulating the amount of gold and silver in circulation. However, governments that nationalized money were also providing a useful service. They helped combat the debasement and counterfeiting of money that occurred in a free market for currency.

Today, the term "debasement" mostly refers to someone who acts immorally, proving themselves to be untrustworthy, but the original meaning referred to the practice of reducing the gold and silver content of coins. Imagine that you wanted to buy an economics book and the cost of that book was 1 ounce of gold. Suppose that you have a single, 1-ounce gold coin that you could use to pay for the book. You could make the money go further by shaving off the edges of the coin and hoping that the bookseller doesn't notice. Then, if you shave off enough gold edges, you could melt those shavings into new coins. The value of the gold has been debased because it no longer weighs a full ounce.

We see the legacy of debasement in currency today—the U.S. quarter still has ridges on its edge because adding ridges to gold and silver coins was a way to prevent shaving. If the ridges were shaved off, the fraud would quickly be detected.

Of course, savvy merchants were aware of debasement and could weigh the coins given to them. However, other schemes could be used to defeat the scales: for instance, the gold could be mixed with other substances. The carat measurement used for gold (and other precious minerals) refers to the quantity of impurities present in the substance. Pure gold is referred to as "24-carat," but if the gold is mixed with other base metals and is only 75 percent pure, then it is 18-carat gold. In old Bugs Bunny cartoons and on Olympic podiums, you still see the biting of gold coins (or medals). This is because real gold is soft, and a bite should leave an imprint.

It is hard to tell by looking at a gold coin whether it is pure gold or if it has been debased, and methods like the bite test work only so well. Mints began imprinting coins with official seals as a guarantee of authenticity.

Trust increases the value of currency because it makes buying and selling easier. Without a guarantee of authenticity, using a coin required careful measurements, risk, and uncertainty due to the possibility of counterfeiting. Coins were mostly valued for the precious metals they contained, so in Newton's time, it was normal for a single transaction to use coins that were minted in places ranging from London to the Roman Empire. Merchants had to be aware of the various metal qualities and weights and markings, each of which would impart a different value to the coin. Paper currency was even worse. In colonial America, for instance, paper currency would be issued by multiple states and different banks. In addition to avoiding counterfeits, a merchant would have to determine how much to trust the reputation of each issuing bank. When collecting on your bar tab in colonial times, a bartender would have had to consult a book that gave the relative value of different banknotes, and the book would have to be updated as the reputations of the currency issuers shifted.[9]

Nation-states had an advantage when making currency because the value of a currency depended on the trustworthiness of the institution backing that currency. Nations operate on a larger scale than banks or individual localities and have the ability to tax to pay their debts and moreover can require that taxes be paid using the printed currency; these factors increase their trustworthiness in monetary matters.

Nations have multiple incentives for increasing the trustworthiness of their currencies. The more trustworthy a currency, the higher its value, which in turn gives the nation more purchasing power. Naming an eminent scientist like Isaac Newton as head of the mint was one strategy to improve the trustworthiness of British currency. Making counterfeiting a high-profile crime was another. The United States established the Secret Service after the Civil War to police counterfeiting, long before it got its (better-known) duty to protect the president.

Fiat Money

For most of history, paper money was a placeholder, usually standing in for gold or silver locked away in a vault somewhere.

It wasn't until 1971 that the United States, under President Richard Nixon, eliminated the gold standard, which had previously backed each U.S. dollar with a promise of physical gold. Much of the world followed, moving to a monetary system in which the major currencies of the world were backed only by the words (i.e., the fiat) of the countries that issued them.

A *fiat* is a proclamation, a declaration, an arbitrary order[10]. By fiat, the money in circulation in 1971—which, up until then, had been convertible into gold, suddenly (almost magically) became just pieces of paper.

The fact that we treat fiat money as having value isn't that crazy when you think about it. The value that we place in gold is not primarily due to its chemical properties, or even its aesthetic properties. The main reason why we place value in gold is because it's rare. All the gold that has ever been mined could fit in 3.27 swimming pools.[11] If we ever found the elusive alchemical process to convert iron to gold, then suddenly gold would cease to function as a currency. This helps to explain why a piece of paper can function just as well as a coin of gold if we can make sure that the piece of paper remains rare. This requires trusting the government not to print too much money at a time.

Imagine that you have just found a magic lamp that grants monetary wishes. At any time, you could use the lamp to wish for a million dollars, a billion dollars, a trillion dollars—however much you wanted. The government has such a lamp, and it regularly takes advantage of it. The term for the money that the government makes by printing it is called *seigniorage*, and it works out to tens of billions each year.[12]

However, just because the government can print as much money as it wants (these days, it just needs a computer terminal to change some numbers in a database; it doesn't even need paper anymore) doesn't mean that it would be beneficial to do so.

The value of paper money derives from its usefulness (the demand for money) and its scarcity (the supply of money). As the supply of money goes up, the value goes down.

The government needs to print more money every year just to keep up with the growing economy. As the economy grows, more stuff is bought and sold—this means that the demand for money is going up. Therefore, we need more money in circulation to keep up with the demand. The government benefits directly from the billions of dollars that it gets from printing money, and benefits indirectly by keeping the economy stable. Too few dollars in circulation will make buying and selling stuff more difficult and slow the economy. On the other hand, too many dollars means that the supply of money is going up faster than the demand, which drives the value of money down. We call this *inflation*.

Central banks are always trying to strike a balance between too much and too little money in the economy. Our models and measures are imperfect, so that is hard to do. Central banks do make mistakes (part of the research that first made Ben Bernanke well known as an academic was showing how overly tight monetary policy helped cause the Great Depression).[13] However, we will see that sometimes central banks produce too much money quite deliberately. The temptation is great, and we have to trust them to be responsible.

Monetary policy happens on such a tremendous scale it often feels abstract, like an act of nature. But the roots of money are quite simple, and quite human.

To make fiat money feel more tangible, the other example that economists love talking about—besides the giant stone coins on Yap—is the Capitol Hill Babysitting Co-op (as popularized by Paul Krugman). In the 1950s, a group of parents in Washington, D.C., would take turns babysitting each other's children. Like the premodern hunter-gatherers who would take turns sharing the meat from a hunt, the system was based on an informal exchange of favors that we are all familiar with. I babysit for you, and so now you "owe me one" and will babysit for me in the future. We are also all familiar with the feeling that this informal system of favors might be unfair, with some families doing more babysitting than others. Therefore, this group of D.C. families decided to formalize the system by forming a co-op.[14] They would keep track of who babysat for whom using coupons. If I babysat for you for one hour, you would pay me a one-hour coupon, which I could then use to pay someone else. To get the system started, they gave all members twenty hours of free coupons when they joined.

A problem soon arose. People were saving their coupons for a rainy day, so they weren't spending them. As a result, there weren't enough coupons circulating, so when families wanted to babysit, nobody was willing to part with their precious coupons. There was too little money in the system. To address the problem, the administrators started giving away more free coupons. This soon caused the opposite problem: there were now too many coupons in circulation, and people who wanted to buy babysitting services couldn't find anyone who needed more coupons. Keeping supply and demand in balance is the most important part of a central banker's job.

The co-op had another feature. It took work administering the program, keeping track of coupons, and matching babysitters and babysittees. Therefore, all members of the co-op had to provide fourteen hours of free babysitting services each year that went to administrators. You could imagine unscrupulous administrators upping the fee to increase the amount of babysitting services they would receive. Or you could also imagine unscrupulous administrators keeping the number of coupons in circulation low so that the coupons they held onto would be more valuable. Fortunately for the co-op, the administrators were genuinely trustworthy. This has not always been the case when it comes to national governments.

In 2019, the inflation rate in Venezuela was over 2 million percent. The amount of cash needed to make purchases required money to be stacked into blocks, and purchases were made based on their weight. This recalls the inflation rate in Weimar Germany in the 1920s, when people carried money in wheelbarrows. The government tried to print higher-denomination notes to keep up—but as more higher-denomination bills were printed, their value only plummeted faster. At one point, single notes worth one hundred trillion marks were in circulation. Picture a $20 bill, now replace that 20 with one hundred trillion to get an idea of what this looked like. This kind of hyperinflation actually happens surprisingly often, with currency denominated in the billions and trillions circulating in Zimbabwe in 2008, Yugoslavia in 1994, and China in 1949, just to name a few.

Trusting the Moneymakers

Previously in this book, we discussed how we came to trust the rule of law. Later, we will discuss how we trust the people in charge. In most modern democracies, it has been decided that we can't trust the people in power to control the supply of money. Actually, a better version of that statement is that everyone, including the people in power, is better off if elected officials do not have direct control of the money supply.

We will discuss how a democracy allocates decision-making authority between the voters, elected officials, and unelected judges or bureaucrats. Judges and bureaucrats and central bankers are for the most part largely given free rein to make decisions, with only loose accountability for their actions. The reason behind this, in the case of money, is that neither rulers nor voters should be trusted. Voters will be tempted to print more money to create inflation that lowers their debts and pays for social services and government spending. Rulers have the temptation to print more money to pander to voters and consolidate their own power. In cases where rulers or voters have too much power over the money supply, the fear of hyperinflation looms, and people put less trust in the money supply.

As a result, the Federal Reserve governors in the United States and similar officials in other countries are given a great deal of independence. In the United States, they are appointed for fourteen-year terms—beyond the span of any presidency and largely insulated from political interference. This separation of powers has deep historical roots.

True fiat money was largely a twentieth-century invention, but the gold standard was not entirely dissimilar in its functioning. Historians often credit the Chinese with the invention of paper money in the eleventh century. They issued paper that was convertible into gold and silver in theory, but that conversion was often not honored by the government in practice. The paper retained some value because it could be used to pay taxes, but because it was broadly recognized that the issuing government was untrustworthy, the currency quickly fell out of favor.[15]

However, as noted previously, rulers could benefit from having the ability to produce money when needed (especially in order to wage war), and citizens also could benefit from the more liquid money supply. However, rulers were constrained by distrust. People knew that the temptation to print too much money was too great.

Rulers faced a similar problem when it came to borrowing money. Governments issue bonds to borrow money from citizens. This practice is especially common in times of war.[16]

Issuing bonds may seem different from printing money, but in practice they are very similar. A *bond* is a loan to the government.

In fact, when we talk about the Federal Reserve "printing money" today, they often are doing so using U.S. Treasury bonds. But when it comes to money-printing, just as citizens have to trust the government to pay back its bond debts, they have to trust the government not to print too much money to do so. So when it comes to bonds, citizens have to trust the government to pay back their loans with interest without bankrupting itself.

Economists Douglass North and Barry R. Weingast also developed the mathematics behind an idea discussed by political scientist Hilton Root. This was the idea of "tying the king's hands," a practice employed during the 1600s in France and England. This was a period when the power of the king was thought to be absolute (think Louis XIV), and yet institutions existed that limited the king's power.

Institutions developed where the authority to tax and manipulate currencies devolved. In France, so-called tax farmers were given the authority to collect taxes and hold sovereign debts, and in England, Parliament maintained the threat of removing the king or queen to keep him or her in line. While one could see these developments as limits to sovereign power, these historians argued that these institutions were ultimately good for the royals in both England and France. By restricting the monarch's authority, it made him or her more likely to honor debts, which in turn made it more likely that people would lend money to the Crown, which helped both nations raise armies and wage wars.

The idea that we need institutional checks on the authority of the sovereign exists to this day. Central bankers in the United States and elsewhere are generally granted a lot of autonomy. As previously mentioned, in the United States, the Federal Reserve chair serves a fourteen-year term, longer than any president will be in office. Once appointed, Congress and the president have little authority in influencing the chair's behavior.

The Federal Reserve is required by an act of Congress to aim for maximum employment and stable prices, but within that broad mission is a great deal of room for independent decision-making. Keeping prices stable means not printing too much money. Maximizing employment requires providing enough money in the system for people to use to buy and sell things. Money is a tool for exchange. As an economy grows, you need more money. Keeping the need to increase the money supply to keep up with economic growth balanced with the need not to print too much money is the main remit of the Federal Reserve.

The reason to give the central banker independence is clear. The central bank has good reasons for increasing the money supply and has information about the demand for money that may not be readily available to the public. A government may be tempted to try to print a little extra to help pay off its debts and fund projects that some politician in power favors, perhaps to help win reelection. For that (and other) reasons, politicians should not be trusted with the ability to print money. By delegating that authority to an independent body, the government raises more money at lower interest rates (we will see in the next section that interest rates are a measure of trust: the more trust, the lower the interest rate). By giving up some independence, both politicians and citizens are better off.

When we started this section, I argued that fiat money was basically paper backed only by the promise of the government. But that isn't entirely accurate. The example from medieval China is instructive. The U.S. dollar isn't backed only by a promise, but also by the U.S. armed forces. The one thing that gave Chinese paper money value in the Middle Ages, despite the temptation to print too much, was the fact that the Chinese government required payment of taxes using paper money. Governments enforce their tax rules through the threat of force. The same is true today. Ultimately, U.S. paper money has value because the government requires residents to use it to pay their taxes.

The latest evolution of money, however, eliminates even that last step. Instead of fiat money, which is backed by trust in the government along with the threat of force, we have recently seen the emergence of digital money, backed only by trust in an algorithm. We will return to bitcoin and other cryptocurrencies at the end of this chapter.

INVESTMENTS AND BANKING

"What stocks should I buy?" That is the question I invariably get when small talk with the person next to me on a flight leads to the revelation that I am an economist. Either that or "Is the Fed going to raise interest rates?"

Here is something most microeconomists wish you knew. The majority of economists are microeconomists[17] (rather than macroeconomists) and most microeconomists rarely think about stock markets and interest rates. Still, financial markets can be interesting to microeconomists because microeconomic models like the trust game help us understand how finance works and what role it plays in an economy.

Many people see the stock market as a giant casino: a game played by the rich that generates little value for society. And to some extent, much of what happens on the trading floor of a stock exchange is not dissimilar from what happens in a casino. The exchanges are zero-sum, and every winner creates a loser. But finance as a sector makes up 20 percent of U.S. gross domestic product (GDP).[18] That is, one-fifth of the total value the economy creates each year is created by finance (broadly defined to include finance, insurance and real estate). The financial system undoubtedly suffers from inefficiency and corruption, and monopoly power might mean that some of those earnings are undeserved. Much of that 20 percent figure, however, represents a real contribution to the well-being of society. If we take a step back and look at the origins of all those stocks and bonds being traded, we can begin to see why finance might be so valuable and how the financial sector might genuinely create one-fifth of the value in the economy.

To an economist, the role of an economy is to produce stuff that people want. That stuff can be tangible, like corn or cars, or it could be intangible, like vacations or education.[19] Producing stuff requires inputs. For a long time, economists have found it useful to categorize inputs as either *labor* or *capital*. To make corn requires a farmer, but tools like tractors and land are needed too. The role of finance is to match workers like farmers with the tools they need to produce. A farmer with only a few tools can still grow food, but a farmer with many tools can produce much more. The so-called green revolution in agricultural technology, which massively increased the productivity of farmers in the 1950s and 1960s and thus is credited with helping the world avoid the starvation predicted by Thomas Malthus, basically involved matching farmers with better tools—tools like fertilizer and pesticides, but also other new technologies.[20] The job of finance is to match workers (labor) to the tools they need (capital), and for that, those in the financial sector get paid their 20 percent cut of national GDP.[21]

The benefits of matching labor with capital can be enormous. For most of human history, most farmers operated on a subsistence level, producing enough food for their own family. In the United States today, just 2 percent of the population produces enough food for the entire country, and much of the rest of the world as well. Providing farmers with adequate tools (like better pesticides or new farm technology) can greatly increase their productivity.

The problem is that this relationship between labor and capital is fraught with risks. In its most basic form, the worker holds an advantage. Absent external enforcement by a legal system, the owner of capital has to trust that each worker will diligently perform the work, fairly share the profits, and not abscond with the money. In fact, the experimental economic study of trust—and what we now call the trust game—began with what its authors originally called the *investment game*.

The need for trust in the labor-capital relationship is even more evident if we consider historical examples. In the Middle Ages, the wealth of nations was largely driven by trade. Venetian merchants amassed great wealth by transporting trade goods on long, dangerous sea voyages or on multiyear journeys along the Silk Road. The merchants who provided the financing were different from the merchant-adventurers who undertook the journey, like Marco Polo.[22] A financier who supported a young adventurer in undertaking such a journey, paying for the merchandise and the travel expenses, had to have great trust that the traveler would return with his money.

Even today, when we have courts and contracts that help to alleviate the need to trust the people with whom we transact, the same kinds of problems remain. Courts will never be able to cover every potential dispute, and not every eventuality can be covered by contracts; most interactions in the modern economy rely on trust relationships, including the relationship between investors and firms.[23]

Financial Markets and Trust

If you look up the word "trust" in the dictionary, the first definition is the one that we have been using throughout this book so far, about general trust between two parties, but the second definition is a financial one, a financial arrangement where one person holds property for another. Often, the word "trust" is used in the context of banks. Lots of financial words evoke trust. Money printed by the United States is backed "by the full faith and credit" of the U.S. government. "Credit," from the Latin *credere*, literally means "to trust." Banks are typically incorporated as *trust* companies, organized to act as *fiduciaries* (from the Latin *fidere*, also meaning "to trust") who serve as *trustees* of the money held by others (e.g., the money held in a trust fund on behalf of a minor).

Trust is also embodied in the architecture of banking. Living in New York City, you sometimes find yourself standing in a surprisingly grandiose pharmacy with extra-tall, vaulted ceilings and concrete columns, instantly recognizable as a former bank. As more and more banks moved online, they left behind grand, old buildings that were repurposed as drugstores, ice cream parlors, and pop-up stores.[24]

In most towns across the United States, older banks boast an impressive façade and a unique architectural style, as if to say, "You can trust your money with us." The money spent on a bank's accoutrements long served as a costly signal (act of trustworthiness) of the financial solvency of that institution. Banks were trying to send the message that they could afford to own a fancy building that would be enormously costly to abandon and difficult to sell if the bankers were ever inclined to leave town with everyone's money.

Just as it's easy to think that economics is about money, it's even easier to assume that financial markets and banks are all about money. We might picture a financier as a Scrooge McDuck, swimming in a giant bin full of gold coins and counting his stacks of money all day. However, economists like to think of money as a placeholder.

We sometimes think that the primary role of a bank is to keep our money safe, and it does do that. But it might be better to think that a bank's main job is putting our excess resources to good use. When we have money to save at the end of the month, however much or little that is, we did more work this month than was needed to obtain the goods and services required to satisfy our immediate wants and needs. If we put that money into a bank, most of it will be loaned to someone who has a productive use for it. The borrower may use the money to pay for college or to open up a hair salon. The bank is using our money to create value. In return, we get some of that added value back in the form of interest.

So, in any given month, whatever portion of the value that I create from teaching economics classes that I *don't* spend on my family's immediate needs goes toward financing somebody else's education, home purchase, or small business loan. When the Federal Reserve requires that U.S. banks keep a reserve of 3 percent of deposits (this number changes from time to time and can differ depending on the size of the bank), one hundred dollars of savings can support 97 dollars in loans.

All of this requires a great deal of trust. The savers must trust the banks with their savings. In turn, the banks need to figure out which borrowers to trust.

In 1982, Frank Tortoriello of Great Barrington, Massachusetts, needed money to relocate his deli. Tortoriello couldn't get a loan from the bank, so instead he printed up a bunch of ten-dollar sandwich vouchers, which he called "Deli Dollars," and they could be redeemed after the deli was relocated. He sold these vouchers for eight dollars, effectively offering his customers two dollars of interest if they gave him a loan. His bank wouldn't trust him with the money—but his customers did.

Normally, we rely on banks to decide which borrowers we should trust with our savings, but Tortoriello showed that banks aren't really necessary; they're just middlemen. His Deli Dollars scheme actually skirted federal securities regulations, since he was basically issuing bonds, but the Securities and Exchange

Commission (SEC) decided not to investigate. U.S. regulations don't normally allow businesses to raise money with so little oversight; Tortoriello's clever fundraising plan could easily be copied by a fraudster who had no intention of opening or reopening a business. U.S. regulators have requirements to protect investors, for example investors must have a minimum of $200,000 in annual income or 1 million dollars in savings before the SEC will allow them to invest in unregistered ventures.[25] This is to make sure that investors have enough income to recover from a bad investment where they lost their money. We will see how blockchain technology is letting more companies bypass banks and regulators, getting funding instead directly from their customers. But in general, the modern financial system relies on institutions like banks and regulators to verify and ensure the trustworthiness of those who invest in it.

Something else interesting happened once those Deli Dollars were released into the world. People began using them for other things, like payments to contractors—some were even donated to a church collection plate.[26] People were using these paper notes, which promised delivery of a sandwich in the future, to pay for goods and services today. They were units of currency operating, we might say, on the "sandwich standard." The reuse of these Deli Dollars by parties other than the original borrower and lender is an example of a *secondary market*. We will return to the secondary market because the breakdown of the secondary market helped trigger the Great Recession.

Interest Rates

Finance generally divides the world of investments into two categories: equity and debt. An equity investment entails ownership of an asset and means that you get a share of future profits, whatever they may be (even if there are losses). A debt investment means that all you can expect to get back at the end of the day is your initial investment—but as compensation, your investment is returned with interest.

The neat part is that the interest rate is pretty much a yardstick for measuring trust. Or, more specifically, it is the point where the trust of the lender meets the presumed trustworthiness of the borrower.

Usually, the interest rate for debt is measured as the sum of two numbers, as follows:

$$\text{Interest Rate} = \text{Base Rate} + \text{Spread}$$

The *base rate* is usually either the interest rate associated with U.S. Treasury bonds, the London Interbank Offered Rate (LIBOR), or more commonly for consumers, the prime rate. It represents the cost of capital, or the amount of money that the bank has to pay to obtain the money. The base rate can be thought of as how much interest you would be charged if the lender trusted you completely. Because a loan to the U.S. government is considered more or less perfectly safe, it is often referred to as the *risk-free rate;* the interest rate that the U.S. government pays when it borrows sets the benchmark for loans to borrowers who are not expected to default. Similarly, the *prime rate* is the lowest interest rate that a bank charges to any of its retail customers. That is, it is the rate that the bank charges its most trusted customers, the ones who the bank is most sure will pay back the borrowed money. For everyone else, there is a *spread*, which is the amount of additional interest paid by the borrower each month to make up for the increased risk the lender is taking. From the lender's point of view, the spread compensates them for the risk they are taking. From the borrower's point of view, the spread is the extra cost that they have to pay because of the lender's lack of trust.

Here, the guts of the trust interaction are fully exposed. We can look at the interest rate that someone is offered and place a precise numerical value on the bank's belief that the borrower will default on (i.e., not pay back) their loan. For example, if the bank thinks that there is a 5 percent chance that you will default on your loan in any given year, they will (more or less) charge you an extra 5 percent interest to make up for that risk. In other words, the spread that you have to pay to borrow from that bank is 5 percent.

The more trustworthy the bank thinks you are, the lower your offered interest rate will be. We can mathematically unpack the interest rate even further by looking at credit scores. Banks use your credit score to determine your creditworthiness (i.e., trustworthiness). The higher your credit score, the more trustworthy lenders believe you to be. This means that you will be offered a lower interest rate, which makes it easier for you to borrow money, to repay your debts, and to invest in assets like a home.

Of course, we never fully know how trustworthy you actually are—indeed, you yourself don't know. Someone who pays all their bills on time is likely to do so in the future. Someone who regularly misses payments is less likely to pay back their debts in the future. But most people who wind up defaulting on loans never expected to default; they were forced into it as a result of unpredicted circumstances, like losing a job or incurring large medical bills. Your credit score is one way to guess at what your default risk might be, but it is only a guess.

That guess is all the more imprecise because your credit score can be based only on your credit history: how good you have been at making payments on past debts, the types of credit you use and have access to, and how long you have had credit. Other information about you, including social characteristics like age, race, and gender, cannot be used to determine your creditworthiness in the United States.

China, on the other hand, is exploring the expansion of credit scores to "social credit scores." The rise of Big Data and the surveillance state means that more information is being collected than ever before. Information about past criminal offenses is used to assess trustworthiness. But what about jaywalking? What about being rude? What about missed alimony payments? What about high school grades? And why use credit scores only for borrowing and lending—why not use them to determine whom to hire for a job, whom to rent an apartment to, or whom to let onto an airplane? All those questions involve trust—so why not quantify that trust in a number? In the United States we generally accept that credit scores can depend on the number of credit cards you possess but cannot be based on what college you went to. We generally accept that credit scores can be used to determine which apartment you can get but are uneasy when dating sites use credit scores to determine who you can date. How do we decide what goes into these scores, and what they can be used for? The answer to these questions is at the intersection of trust and dignity. We will return to them in chapter 5.[27]

Secondary Markets and the Financial Crisis of 2008

Perhaps the most significant economic event in the past half-century, the Great Recession of 2008–2009, occurred due to a breakdown in trust—specifically, trust in the secondary markets of the financial system. Harking back to our previous example, the deli owner Frank Tortoriello issued Deli Dollars to his customers to pay for his deli expansion. That was a primary market because it was a transaction between the person who needs the capital and the "investors" in that enterprise. The secondary market was created when some of them started using their

Deli Dollars for transactions that didn't involve Tortoriello or the deli at all. When people buy and sell Walmart stock on the New York Stock Exchange, they aren't buying it from Walmart, but from other investors like themselves. Thus, stock exchanges and other exchanges are secondary markets, and many investment banks make their money buying and selling in these markets.

On September 15, 2008, one of these banks, Lehman Brothers, filed for bankruptcy. A *bankruptcy* is when you default on your credit obligations to others and say that you are no longer able to fulfill your commitments. Investors had trusted Lehman, and that trust was broken. The bankruptcy set off a wave of panic and the start of the Great Recession, an economic calamity that many feared would rival the Great Depression.

The symptom that economic commentators were most afraid of was a breakdown of the commercial paper market. *Commercial paper* refers to large loans taken out by well-established firms to meet short-term obligations. Unlike a mortgage, which is paid back over a long period of time, like fifteen or thirty years, commercial paper loans are typically due within thirty days. Consumers might encounter commercial paper as part of their money market accounts, which a bank offers alongside checking accounts as a way to earn a slightly higher return on savings, but most consumers never think about it, if they even know what it is. Commercial paper is also generally regarded as such a low-risk, boring investment that Wall Street rarely thinks about it either. Few think that companies like General Electric or Exxon won't be able to pay back their debts in one month's time, so trust in the ability of these companies to pay back these loans is normally high—which means that the spread on interest rates for commercial paper is normally close to zero.[28] Until September 2008, that is.

Early 2008 was a time when even an unemployed worker with a bad credit history could get a loan to buy a house if they were willing to pay a high-enough interest rate, but by the end of 2008, the wealthiest corporation in the world couldn't get a thirty-day loan to cover a short-term expense like payroll. The collapse of a market like commercial paper is devastating to economists. Economics is all about how society allocates scarce resources, and economists believe that markets are the best way to handle that allocation. Markets are created when people can make a trade that makes both sides better off. When that power to trade is multiplied across all the sectors of an economy, wealth is created and increased. Markets lifted the world out of medieval poverty. But when a market fails, the effects can echo throughout an entire economy.

The breakdown of this market was shocking for two reasons. The first is that the trust that allows markets to function was shown to be more than just a question of numbers. Bankers rely on mathematical equations to determine what interest rate to charge and what interest rate to accept. In principle, those equations should work for any level of risk that would allow trading to continue. But for a few days in September, the traders who used those models ceased to trust them. It wasn't just that the risk had become too high—there was a renewed fear of "unknown unknowns." (As Secretary of Defense Donald Rumsfeld famously declared, there are known unknowns and unknown unknowns. Known unknowns are things that you aren't sure of but can make an educated guess about. Unknown unknowns are things that you never thought of in the first place.) People were unwilling to trade with each other because there were too many unknown unknowns. They didn't trust their models.

The second lesson from the breakdown in this market was that we are all embedded in a web of trust. Normally, when we offer someone a loan, we are asking whether we trust that other party to pay us back. However, the financial crisis reminded us that those transactions do not happen in isolation. We examined the development of the rule of law earlier in this book and will examine how trust behaves as a contagion later on. The financial crisis highlighted the importance of both. There was uncertainty not only about how the government might react to the events on the ground, but also how the bankruptcies might spread throughout the system. When I was deciding whether to make a trade with your bank, I worried not just about whether you had enough money to pay me back, but whether the people who owed you money would be able to pay you back. Failure is contagious. In order to trust you, I have to trust the system.

The financial crisis was also when the proverbial crash on Wall Street came crashing onto Main Street as well. For a long time, finance appeared to be a game, with ups and downs that were of little interest to most people. The secondary markets for financial securities seemed to have little direct impact on the lives of most people. Once a company issues stock or incurs debt to pay its workers or build its factories, whatever happens to those pieces of paper that signify ownership of the stock or bond afterward has little effect on those factory workers. All that buying and selling between large financial institutions that make for an energetic trading floor is largely irrelevant to what economists call the *real economy*. However, the financial crisis showed why those secondary markets matter. The ability to raise new capital, to invest in new factories, or simply to allow a company to pay its workers while it awaits payment from customers relies on the existence of functioning secondary markets. Banks aren't willing to lend to companies if they aren't able to resell those debts to somebody else. Whereas banks do invest some of their own money to companies that need it, banks mostly invest on behalf of others. Your local bank takes the money that you deposit in your savings account and invests it in local businesses. A large investment bank takes money from large investors like pension funds and gives it to places that need it.

People sometimes feel as though the problems of the financial markets are irrelevant to anyone not in finance. But when the credit markets freeze up and trust in the system breaks down, businesses can't get money to pay their employees, much less open up new branches and create new jobs. It is true that people got by for thousands of years without complex financial markets, but the complexity of these markets are a big part of what sustains our standard of living today.

Economists are still debating what caused the financial crisis (was it financial deregulation, a bubble in the housing market, excessively expansion monetary policy, or excessive foreign investment?),[29] but one thing was clear: we are all connected. Bankruptcies are normal when you make investments. The whole point of investing is to help entrepreneurs take risks that they couldn't take on their own. The crisis occurred when one of those bankruptcies spread almost out of control.

CONTRACTS

Once a friend that I've learned not to mess with told me a story about how he once hired a painter to paint the apartment he was living in over the summer. He was living in a gated community and was doing renovations to the apartment. Apparently, he was unsatisfied with the painter's work and wanted him to redo it. The painter refused and tried to drive away. My friend called the security guard at the gate and told him that the painter was trying to steal his money and not to let him leave the premises. The painter was forced to return to the apartment and redo the work to my friend's satisfaction.

As it happens, having your house painted is a kind of transaction that is often used in economics textbooks to illustrate the need for trust. Not only do you have to trust the painter to do a good job, but you are also trusting them not to steal your stuff. What allows these transactions to occur is partly trust and partly the rule of law—specifically, contract law.

While our impression of the law is often shaped by the litigators we see on television and in movies, much of a lawyer's time is spent reviewing contracts.[30] A *contract* is just an agreement between two parties that is enforceable by law. That broad definition pretty much covers all forms of interaction in any sector of the economy—typically between two firms, but also between a worker and a firm.

The classic example is a seller and buyer who are arranging a sale for a future date. For example, perhaps a farmer is arranging financing for seeds and tools, to be paid back when the crops are grown, harvested, and sold. Or a home buyer might arrange a deal with a home seller before the buyer can obtain a mortgage from a bank. These are all situations that require an act of trust. They are also situations in which trust is likely secured using a contract.

The question that I want to ask here is whether legally enforceable contracts help or hinder trust and whether trust helps or hinders legal contracts. In economic language, if trust and contracts are *complements*, that means that each makes the other better. Contracts work better when parties trust each other, and strong and complete contracts enhance trust. Alternatively, if trust and contracts are what economists call *substitutes*, that means that they either crowd each other out or, even worse, interfere with each other. Places with strong contract enforcement may see no need to invest in building trust, while places with a lot of trust may see no need to invest in a contract-enforcing legal system. More concretely, when a buyer and a seller make an agreement, they could either rely on the trust they have in each other to follow through with the deal or rely on a legally enforceable contract to threaten legal ramifications (i.e., punishments) to make sure that the deal happens.

You might think that because trust and contracts are both good things, having both is ideal. However, it could also be the case that having a legally binding contract might undermine the trust that two people have in one another. Think about the marriage contract and the prenuptial agreement: sometimes spelling things out in a legal contract like a prenup could undermine the trust of the partners in their relationship.

This question of how trust and contract enforcement interact is important because both are associated with prosperity and growth. If the two work together, then strengthening one could contribute to a virtuous cycle that strengthens the other as well, contributing all the more to economic growth. But if the two are at odds, then increasing trust in society could discourage contracts, while increasing contract enforcement could harm trust, in both cases, leaving society no better off.[31]

Trust and Contracts in the Lab

The model of trust discussed earlier in this chapter defined an act of trust as fundamentally about taking a risk. A contract between two parties is an agreement about the obligations of each party and the consequences of various eventualities. Economists focus on two features of contracts that make them stronger: *completeness* and *enforceability*. A contract is more complete when it does a better job of explicitly laying out the details regarding its obligations and consequences. A contract is more enforceable when the legal system does a better job of bringing about the terms of the contract. For example, contracts that are more explicit about their terms are more enforceable than contracts that are vague. But better enforcement also comes from factors like lower court costs, fairer judges, and a generally well functioning legal system.

In general, good contracts lower the risk of working together. That reduction in risk is both good and bad for trust. It's good for trust because it lowers the risk of working with somebody new. New relationships can't form if it is too risky to work with somebody new. However, strong contracts are bad for trust if too much control takes away too much risk. Relationships can't grow if there is *no* opportunity to demonstrate trustworthiness.

A clever trust game experiment by Armin Falk and Michael Kosfeld was able to demonstrate this tension by identifying what they call the "hidden cost of control." In the classic trust game, the investor makes an investment in the trustee. That investment triples in value for the trustee, who then has the option to split the proceeds however they want between themself and the investor. On average, when this experiment is conducted in labs, subjects tend to keep around two-thirds, returning one-third of the proceeds to the investor. One could make this interaction safer if you imposed some restrictions on the actions of the trustee. Instead of allowing the trustee to divide the proceeds however they wanted, you might instead require the trustee to return at least 10 percent to the investor. You can think of this restriction as a stipulation in the contract between the investor and the trustee.

Because trustees typically return one-third, which is already more than 10 percent, you would think that imposing a 10 percent minimum wouldn't have a big effect. It takes away some of the risk, so the investor never gets zero. This should increase investment and yield higher returns for the investor. Instead, Falk and Kosfeld found the opposite. The 10 percent minimum caused trustees to return less to the investor than before the restriction was imposed. The investors would have been better off not trying to restrict the trustee's choice.[32]

This might seem puzzling at first. If the trustees were going to return one third anyway, why would they return less with the restriction in place? One-third is already higher than 10 percent, so the restriction shouldn't matter. The answer, it turns out, is that the restriction demonstrates a lack of trust. Trust relies on reciprocity, and when the investor restricts the trustee's choice, the trustee responds with less reciprocal behavior. On the other hand, when the investor does something nice to the trustee, the trustee does something nice in return. Moreover when the trustee has unfettered choice on how much to return, then what they choose to return is a demonstration of their trust-worthiness. When their choice is restricted by contractual rules, then it's less clear whether their choice was motivated by trust-worthiness or if it was imposed by the rules. That reduces the trustee's ability to use their decision as a signal. Therefore, they wind up returning less to the investor. Finally, when the investor imposes a 10 percent minimum, they are implicitly saying that they have low expectations about how much the trustee is going to return. So the trustee responds by living up (or down) to those lower expectations.

Economists have extended this idea to show that contracts could be more effective when they are incomplete.[33] When contracts leave some room for trust, they work better. We can see this in a job context where there is tension between a manager's desire to micromanage workers and their ability to delegate authority and trust their workers' judgment.[34]

So we have seen that contracts can interfere with trust within a relationship at the micro level. However, we will see that at the macro level—when comparing U.S. states or countries—trust and contracts seem to go hand in hand.

Trust and the Law: Complements Versus Substitutes

In Chapter 2, we talked about the evolution of cooperation across human history and how we moved from a society where cooperation was enforced by relationships and trust to one where cooperation is coordinated by markets and the rule of law. Of course, framing the evolution in that way makes it seem as though there is a dichotomy in how a society can be governed: either by a centralized rule of law backed by a monopoly of violence, or by a set of decentralized social norms backed by individuals' trust in each other to fulfill their obligations within the system. In fact, societies are not governed by one or the other—typically, it is some mix of both.

Historical data shows that both the rule of law and social trust contribute to the prosperity of society. The sizes of economies around the world and across time are tightly correlated with both the rule of law and social trust. Of course, all these things—economy size, rule of law, and social trust—are hard to measure, but we do the best we can using survey data, economic data, and expert assessments.[35]

I recently wrote a paper with David Huffman in which we studied how the rule of law and trust interact. In particular, we asked if rule of law and trust were complements or substitutes in promoting the prosperity of society. One key piece of evidence is that historically, trust and rule of law tend to go together as can be seen in figure 3.1.

In this study, Huffman and I explored two competing game-theoretic dynamics at work in the interactions between laws and trust. The first dynamic at work is that laws create a baseline level of stability that allows people to build trust in others. Each inter-action—each act of trust that was rewarded by a demonstration of trustworthiness—works to build more trust over time. When we learn more information about one another from repeated interactions, we are better able to discover who is trustworthy, which in

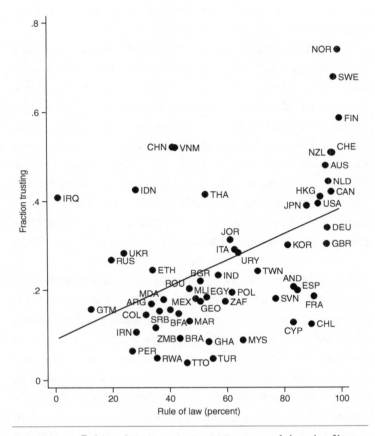

FIGURE 3.1 Relation between trust in government and the rule of law

Source: Ho, B., & Huffman, D. (2018). Trust and the law. In *Research Handbook on Behavioral Law and Economics* (Northampton, MA: Edward Elgar), 302.

turn makes it easier for us to trust. Once a baseline level of trust is established, we have the security to take more risks, which leads to more interactions. This cycle allows more and more trust to grow over time. However, this virtuous cycle can begin only if people find enough ways to trust strangers, to move beyond the small, tribal societies that are governed by personal relationships. This complementary relationship between trust and the law can be seen in the macro data, which show that a country with a strong rule of law also tends to have trusting people.[36]

The second dynamic between trust and law that is at work, however, suggests the opposite: trust and the law can be at odds with one another. While macroeconomic evidence (looking at trends across countries across time) shows trust and law operating hand in hand, microeconomic evidence (looking at individual or firm behavior, including behaviors revealed in the lab) suggests that the opposite is also possible.[37] Laws that promote order and contracts can interfere with the building of trust. Trust requires each side to take risks in investing in the other, and it requires each side to be willing to invest in the relationship. Contracts that are too controlling reduce the need for risk-taking, which limits the opportunity to build trust.

Economists and lawyers who study contracts have long observed that contracts are always incomplete. There will always be eventualities that the two parties did not include in the contract and could lead to future conflict. For example, suppose that I agree to pay you gold in exchange for your next harvest of wheat. We may do our best to specify what happens in a variety of circumstances, but there will always be some that we didn't think of. What if a wheat blight kills the crop? What if gold is devalued by a shift in monetary policy? What if bandits steal the wheat in transit? What if a war breaks out? The incompleteness of contracts in specifying what should happen in various contingencies was traditionally seen as a problem that requires parties to trust each other to overcome.

However, recent game theorists have argued that contract incompleteness is a feature, not a bug—that parties may intentionally leave some parts of contracts vague and underspecified.[38] Specifying more precise contracts may be costly, requiring more legal fees and risking potential litigation. Sometimes it is better to rely on trust and relationships to resolve disputes in good faith rather than involving lawyers.

The thing is, just as you need stability for parties to be willing to take a chance and let trust grow, you also need room to breathe, to allow parties to be vulnerable. In the Falk and Kosfeld experiment described previously, when investors imposed rules that restricted the choices of trustees you saw less trustworthy behavior, which in turn leads to less trust.

The ultimate takeaway is that rules and restrictions can make principal-agent transactions safer, but that safety interferes with the ability to build trust.

We know from historical data that trust, the rule of law, and economic prosperity go hand in hand (in hand). We also observe a positive correlation among the three. As I've said, though, correlation is not causation. An association between trust and rule of law and prosperity doesn't tell us which causes which, or whether all are caused by something else entirely. To figure that out, we usually rely on theory to give us hypotheses. The hypotheses that we have laid out in this section are:

1. Stronger contracts and the rule of law foster trust by making it safer to initiate relationships with strangers.
2. Stronger contracts and rule of law impede trust by impeding the development of relationships.

These two competing hypotheses give us different ways to interpret the positive associations among trust, the rule of law, and prosperity.

If rules foster trust, then we would believe that societies with better rules will develop more trust. If rules impede trust, then the reason why we see a positive correlation between the two is that rules foster prosperity and greater prosperity fosters trust. Or trust fosters prosperity and prosperity fosters rules.

The ideal way to resolve questions about correlation versus causality is to perform a randomized experiment: choose a number of countries and randomly give some of them strong rule of law and others weak rule of law—and then stand back and watch them for a century or two and see what happens to trust in those countries.

Unfortunately, that plan is a bit impractical. The best we can do is to simulate trust and the law in the lab and see what happens or to look for natural experiments. For the moment, we just don't know.

When we work with another person, many things can go wrong. We have expectations that might not be met. Changing circumstances may change the nature of the work involved. One way to handle those risks is to draw up a contract. Another is to work with somebody you trust. Mediating a relationship using a contract is costly because they are costly to write (lawyers are expensive) and to enforce (courts are expensive too). Moreover, introducing a contract into a relationship changes the nature of the relationship. Therefore, contracts could interfere with how we trust. Think of how introducing a prenuptial agreement changes the meaning of marriage.

On the other hand, working with somebody new is always risky. It's hard to build trust with someone you don't know. Having a contract might foster relationships by making it easier to take a chance on a stranger. In our prenup example, if you (or perhaps your family) are nervous that a potential marriage might not last, you may delay getting married until you are sure, or you may not get married at all. A prenup might allow two people to take a risk on each other and get married, creating a stronger bond that wouldn't have been possible if a lack of a prenup had prevented the marriage from ever happening.

WORK

The fundamental building blocks of an economy are labor and capital. Everything we consume, from the clothes we wear to the movies we see to where we get our education, comes from a combination of the work that somebody does (labor) and the tools that they use to augment their effectiveness (capital). Economists think of the economy as a machine that takes these fundamental building blocks and transforms them into the goods and services that all of us consume. In the previous discussion about money and investments, we talked about how economies match capital to labor (investment). In this section we focus on the nature of work.

Once I was sitting on the lawn in a park in San Francisco, waiting for a free outdoor concert and perusing an econ textbook. A woman on a nearby blanket glanced over and said, "You must be an economist. What is the biggest question economists are grappling with these days?" Not used to such big philosophical questions—I spent most of my days deriving mathematical equations—I stammered something about asking why we have jobs. The core of modern economic thought is that markets are the best way to organize economic interactions, but corporations are not organized like markets—they are centrally planned, command-and-control fiefdoms. She nodded thoughtfully and said that this was indeed a great question to be working on. Her husband was an economist who had dedicated his life's work to answering that same question.

We take jobs for granted, but if you really think about them for a minute, the existence of jobs in a market economy is sort of odd. Firms are autocratic, hierarchical regimes where orders are passed down from on high. You might even compare the organization of a large firm to socialism, where production is dictated by those on top and the bureaucracy underneath them. The ideal market, on the other hand, is a flat system of small, competing equals. In an ideal capitalist economy, market forces of supply and demand dictate what gets produced.

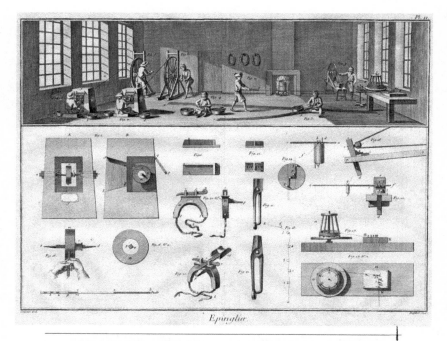

FIGURE 3.2 Elements of a pin factory. Adam Smith used pin-making to illustrate the immense productivity gains introduced by the division of labor. However, relying on so many other people to create a single pin also necessitates much greater degrees of trust.

Source: An illustration of pin-making from Diderot's *Encyclopédie*, 1762. (Wikimedia Commons)

Consider the founder of economics, Adam Smith, and his example of a pin factory (see figure 3.2). Smith begins his famous *Wealth of Nations* by pondering how a pin is made:

One man draws out the wire, another straights it, a third cuts it, a fourth points it, a fifth grinds it at the top for receiving the head: to make the head requires two or three distinct operations; to put it on is a peculiar business, to whiten the pins is another; it is even a trade by itself to put them into the paper; and the important business of making a pin is, in this manner, divided into about eighteen distinct operations.[39]

We take it for granted that these workers would all be employed at the same firm and would report to a manager, who would report to an executive, who would ultimately report to the owner or chief executive officer (CEO). All would follow orders conscientiously or risk losing their jobs. Each worker has to abide by company rules and show up on time, and workers have little autonomy to decide what to do and when to do it.

Instead, you might imagine those eighteen tasks belonging to eighteen separate, independent contractors or firms. Each makes their own rules and their own schedule. You would have a firm that purchases bent wire and sells straight wire, another firm that purchases straight wire and sells cut wire, yet another firm that purchases cut wires and sells pointed wires, and so on. You might object that it would be inconvenient to have all of these elements in different locations: it makes more sense to have them in the same place. But there's no reason why different firms couldn't share the same factory space. In some medieval factories, workers might be colocated, but each acts as an independent entity, free to set their own terms and schedules. The wire bender might work next to the wire cutter, but each works on their own.

You see this arrangement today in the organization of some hospital emergency rooms, where doctors and nurses are not employed by the hospital but instead are self-employed, each with an independent contract with the hospital itself. (This causes a nightmare for patients when some doctors in the same hospital take your insurance and others don't.) You see this as well with firms like Uber or Handy, which do not employ their drivers or cleaners or other workers directly, but instead negotiate with them as independent contractors. (This setup causes issues for the contractors, who are not protected by labor laws.)

The Theory of the Firm

The question of why we have jobs and firms was a puzzle tackled by Ronald Coase, who in the first half of the twentieth century helped to pioneer the theory of the firm, which seeks to explain why we give up our autonomy to take a job at a company rather than sell our services as independent contractors. Coase is better known for his work on *externalities*, the idea that markets work to bring about the best outcome unless some transaction cost prevents a market from working. For example, air pollution is an externality because when a factory pollutes the air, it harms millions of people. The transaction costs necessary in order for the millions of people and the factory to negotiate compensation for the harm of the pollution are impractical. That is why we need government regulation of pollutants: to internalize the externality.

Coase applied the same idea when thinking about firms. In an ideal, frictionless market, pin laborers could in theory each be their own firm, buying inputs and selling outputs for each of the eighteen steps that Smith identified as part of a pin factory's internal supply chain. However, interactions among firms can get quite complicated, requiring negotiation of contracts, dealing with missed deadlines, and quality concerns. If the wire sharpener suddenly decided to take a day off to go fishing, then the wire cutter would have no one to buy his cut wires; he'd be stuck with inventory that he can't sell or use. The pin-head flattener, who bought the wire-sharpener's sharpened wires, would have no materials to work with. In addition, each of these steps required investment in machinery, and that required investors who trusted that they would get their money back. In the end, it is easier to trust a large, immobile factory and harder to trust an individual contractor who could run off with no consequences.[40]

Theorists have spent the half-century since Coase further identifying just how these transaction costs work. Some of these costs are mundane. It takes time to find buyers and sellers. It takes time to negotiate prices. There are lawyers' fees associated with working out contracts and resolving disputes. However, other costs of having production disaggregated are more structural and related to the problem of trust.

The classic example used in this literature concerns the Fischer Body Company, which was acquired by General Motors (GM) in 1919. Fischer Body was founded in 1908 by two brothers working in the horse-drawn carriage industry, who realized that there was better money to be made making car bodies. They became the primary supplier for many GM lines, including Buick and Cadillac. GM wanted Fischer to relocate their factory next to the GM factory to cut costs. However, Fischer was reluctant. Moving their factory would improve their relationship with GM, increase efficiency, and lower costs, but it would make it harder for Fischer to sell their car bodies to other companies. Fischer rightly worried that once they became dependent on GM, the car company would want to negotiate a new contract, with terms more favorable to them. Fischer, left with few options, would have no choice but to accept the new terms. The companies were at an impasse.

Both sides would be better off if they could come to an agreement. GM would benefit from having lower costs and better integrated production, which would lead to more sales, and that would allow them to order more from Fischer and expand Fischer's production as well. But the deal couldn't go through because of lack of trust.

The solution was simple. GM made the Fischer brothers an offer they couldn't refuse. They figured out how much the Fischers valued their company at and offered to buy it from them for (somewhat) more. GM was willing and able to do this because they knew that Fischer would be worth more if they invested in their relationship with GM. The Fischers just couldn't make that investment on their own. GM wanted Fischer to specialize in GM cars, but that would also make Fischer dependent on GM. Fischer couldn't trust GM to not take advantage of that dependency. The Fischer Body example, as explained by Alchian and colleagues, became one of the foundational studies of the economic theory of the firm.[41]

But what does this have to do with workers and jobs? Firms want workers to invest in a relationship with the firm, just as GM wanted Fischer to invest in their relationship with GM. Workers may relocate to take a job at a company. They may develop specialized skills for that company. That places a substantial burden of risk on workers and makes them vulnerable to exploitation by the firm. To support workers' trust, the firm demonstrates its trustworthiness by making a long-term commitment to the worker in the form of a job. A *job* is a promise that helps convince a worker that it is safe to invest in the firm. Once that commitment has been made, long-term employment allows trust to develop more and more over time.

Hierarchy and Authority

While one defining feature of the firm is the long-term, ongoing relationship between firm and worker, another defining feature of firms is hierarchical structure. Unlike the ideal of perfectly competitive markets, where we see large numbers of undifferentiated buyers and sellers who interact more or less as equals, transactions within firms are typically very hierarchical in nature. Workers almost always know their place in the hierarchy of a firm: they know to whom they report, and they know whom they outrank, whether it is by higher position or seniority.

There have been many theories of hierarchy over the years. In one experiment my co-authors and I conducted, we showed that people prefer preserving hierarchy because hierarchy promotes stability and because conflict is costly and painful.[42] Hierarchies exist within organizations for the same reason that they exist in nature: animals create pecking orders to avoid spending all their time fighting for dominance. Once a pecking order is established within a flock of chickens, the members of the group will fight to preserve that order. Spending too much time fighting each other makes the pack more vulnerable to predators. My coauthors and I showed that this instinct to preserve hierarchies can be found in humans: we documented the instinct across cultures and showed how it develops in children as young as seven years old.

A second model of hierarchy is based on the idea that organizations favor hierarchy because they take advantage of a tournament structure for promotions. Firms almost always have a pyramid structure, in which only a select few get the chance to advance to the very top. Each level of hierarchy is smaller than the one below it. A tournament structure makes advancement the prize. This creates incentives for hard work and provides a way for firms to identify and reward talent.

A third theory of hierarchy is that the hierarchy exists for the sake of the workers. In an oft-told story by economists who work in this area, it was common in the Middle Ages to see teams of men pulling barges of goods along a river.[43] The men were whipped regularly to keep up their speed. A woman with a good heart passes by and prevails on the whipper to have mercy on the men. The whipper tells the woman, "You have this all wrong, miss. The men don't work for me; I work for them. They pay me to whip them because they don't trust their teammates and think they will slack off without proper incentive." In this conception of hierarchy, authority is centralized in organizations so that someone is accountable for ensuring that everyone works the way they're supposed to. That accountability increases everyone's productivity, which can lead to higher wages for the workers and increased profits for the organization.

There are many good reasons, then, for hierarchies to develop within a firm, but hierarchies also can cause problems. Hierarchy creates centralized authority, which is useful for motivating workers to work and for resolving conflicts. However, by taking autonomy away from workers, the organization suffers adverse consequences as well.

However, centralized authority has trade-offs.[44] By wresting autonomy from subordinates, it makes it harder for workers to make decisions on their own and take the steps that could lead to innovation. Ideally, authority to make decisions should be entrusted with those who have the best information for the choices that need to be made. But this requires that managers trust their employees to use their autonomy for the good of the firm, not to avoid work.

A modern practice emblematic of this dilemma is the trend among modern tech firms like Amazon and Sony to offer unlimited paid time off to their workers. The idea is that the firm trusts its workers enough to use that privilege responsibly. A coauthor and former student of mine, Jiayi Bao, has studied such policies.[45] She has found that such policies could increase firm profits by attracting more talented workers; moreover, by allowing workers to take care of their personal lives when they need to, the policies give them more space and energy to work hard in their jobs.

When the firm demonstrates trust in their workers, the workers reciprocate and work hard for the firm. At the same time, you can easily imagine how unlimited paid time off could enable an untrustworthy worker to take advantage of the firm, doing no work and still getting paid.

At the same time that modern workplaces are giving workers more freedom, they are also exerting more control. Many firms use software to monitor every minute of their employees' days, taking screenshots of their computer screens or tracking their location using the global positioning system (GPS) apps on their phones. Such monitoring can reveal all the time that workers spend chatting with friends on Facebook or Instagram, or the time that they spent on the beach on days they called in sick. Such monitoring could prevent lazy workers from dragging everybody else down, but they also demonstrate a lack of trust.

We previously discussed how overly controlling contracts can destroy trust. By refusing to be vulnerable and by not taking a risk on their workers, the firm harms trust: such control doesn't allow workers to demonstrate their trustworthiness, and it doesn't allow the firm to demonstrate how much they trust and value the workers. This dampens the desire of workers to demonstrate reciprocity.

We can more directly examine how this kind of trust applies in labor markets by comparing jobs that pay a salary to jobs that pay a piece rate. Workers who earn a salary get paid for their time and earn the same regardless of how much they produce. Workers who earn a piece rate (like many garment workers) are paid for each item completed (say, each article of clothing sewn) rather than for hours worked. Lazear found that when a windshield installation company switched between paying by the hour to paying per windshield installed, productivity increased 44 percent, the company attracted higher-quality workers, and profits increased.[46]

Still, in the modern economy, jobs that pay salaries or for hours worked are much more pervasive than jobs that pay piece rates. Why? The key is trust. In jobs where the output is clearly observable, like windshield repair or shirts sewn, then trust is less of an issue. However, in most jobs, an element of trust is needed.

In fact, a growing body of labor economics research suggests that the labor relationship can be thought of as being based on gift exchange, echoing the premodern societies discussed earlier. The employer offers the gift of employment and a wage, and in return, the employee offers the gift of their labor. This notion of labor flips the traditional way that we think about work, where a worker labors and gets paid by the employer for their labor. In laboratory experiments,[47] subjects were randomly assigned to play the role of either employer or employee. "Employers" offered "jobs" to other subjects who acted as employees during the experiment, and the employees were given tokens that they could use to perform "work" for the employer. Researchers found that often the best employment relationships are ones where the employer "gifts" the employee the wages first, rather than contracts where the worker does the work first and is paid a piece rate for their services. The employee "works" hardest when they are paid first. They feel obligated to live up to the trust placed in them by the employer.[48]

BRANDS

Do a web search for "the brand you trust" and you will find that tagline associated with 3M, Black & Decker, Johnson & Johnson, Genie garage door openers, Bertolli pasta, and more. The phrase has become so cliché that it hardly has any meaning at all. Creating trust in a brand is a fundamental feature of modern capitalism, and our exposure to brands begins early. Walking around Disneyland with two toddlers, I was impressed at how effectively Disney has monopolized all the brands that kids care the most about: Disney princesses and Pixar toys for sure, but also Marvel superheroes and *Star Wars*. We actually avoided most of those toys when my first son was young, but he learned all about them from his friends at school. Once he was infected with all the brand marketing, he passed on those obsessions to his little brother. One of my younger son's first words was "Iron Man." Research shows that when shown fifty brand logos, children as young as three or four could recognize and understand the product associated with 38 percent of them.[49]

But the whole purpose of branding is to build trust. When villages were small and most of our market interactions were with people whom we knew personally, then we would build trust with those local merchants and artisans directly. When the efficiencies of mass production meant that we started buying more and more from national chains and faceless international conglomerates, we needed some other way to keep track of whom to trust. Thus, the brand was born.

More recently, modern consumer culture has linked more and more of our identities with the brands we consume. Our decisions about what to buy and consume communicate more than we realize about who we are: not only are brands useful for building trust with corporations, they also allow consumers to create trust with like-minded others whom they do not yet know.

Thus, the purpose of brands is twofold: to replace the individual reputations of a collection of individuals associated with the same organization into a shared, collective reputation, and to help consumers signal their identity so that they may find others whom they can trust.

Brands as a Mnemonic for Reputation

To an economist, the purpose of brands is to solve an information problem. George Akerlof, in his Nobel Prize–winning paper "The Market for Lemons," famously showed how uncertainty about quality can make a market fall apart. Why does the value of a new car drop precipitously the second you drive it off the lot? It is because we assume that people would probably sell a newish car only if there were something wrong with it. The problem compounds because the immediate discounting means that people who may need to sell a high-quality, slightly used car would be reluctant to do so, reducing the quality of goods available on the market. This causes a vicious cycle that leads markets to unravel. Just a little bit of distrust about the quality of available goods will make people with the highest-quality products exit the market.

Brands arose to solve this uncertainty problem. Recall that humans have biological mechanisms that allow us to keep track of the trustworthiness of around 150 individuals—Dunbar's number. The modern economy has taken those mechanisms and channeled them into trust in a couple hundred brands. When driving in an unfamiliar place, hundreds of miles from home, there is comfort in finding a McDonald's or a Starbucks and knowing exactly what to expect when you walk in the door.[50]

The trick that a brand pulls off is that it takes a large group of people—for instance, McDonald's employs 1.9 million people around the world—and allows them to share in a single reputation through association with the brand. This also means that the actions of one affect our trust in all: a McDonald's employee contributes to the trustworthiness of the brand's reputation when they provide good service.

Earlier in this book, we saw that religion can enhance trust by enabling a set of people with common values and practices to share a single reputation. A corporation preserves its brand by using many of the same mechanisms that religions use to preserve the reputation of its followers.

A corporate brand works to instill the values of that brand in all the corporation's employees. My first job after college was at the investment bank Morgan Stanley. They gave us this little Rubik's Cube–like desk toy that had a different corporate value printed on each cube face: "Innovation . . . Integrity . . . Value . . . Teamwork . . ." The toy came with a letter that discussed all the money spent on the brand consultants who developed the words that the company would be based on. The toy was widely mocked by my cynical coworkers, but the idea intrigued me. How and why do firms invest so much in the corporate culture of their workers?

The reason is that in a large organization with a broad diffusion of responsibility, it is tempting and easy for one individual to free-ride on the efforts of others, not putting in any effort themselves. As in religions, members can be excommunicated (fired) for harming the reputation of the group. Therefore, corporations adopt rituals and stories to inculcate norms and expectations (rather as religions do).

We see the importance of corporate culture in lawsuits that target an entire firm due to the actions of one of its members. I used to find it odd when a corporation like Walmart would be sued for bad behavior by by one of its workers: Why blame an organization of 2.3 million for the actions of a single individual? Seen through the lens of corporate culture, though, that shared responsibility makes more sense. We trust the individuals who work at Walmart because of our trust for Walmart as a whole. That means that we also hold all of Walmart responsible for the actions of individuals.

Brands and Identity

A less appreciated role of brands is that they not only help us figure out which products and companies to trust, but also help us identify who among our peers can be trusted based on the brands that they consume. Brands help us identify our tribe. Today, that means something somewhat different from what it meant to hunter-gatherers, or what it means to religious groups, but the logic is much the same.

It may be a surprise to some, but economists still debate the purpose of advertising. Many are skeptical of the ability of advertising to truly persuade,[51] though some believe that advertising might serve to inform consumers: there are so many products on the market, and ads help tell us what is new. But for brands like Coca-Cola, which everyone already knows about, why do we need more advertising?

One theory is that the ads are there to help us feel good about our purchasing decisions. Those who have purchased iPhones feel better about their purchases and are more likely to remain loyal customers if they see a great ad for Apple products.[52]

Another theory popular among economists (though it probably sounds insane to everybody else) is that ads are simply there to "burn money." A famous ad for a jobs website during the height of the dot-com bubble showed a monkey burning hundred-dollar bills. The "advertising as money-burning" theory is that only highly profitable companies have money to waste on advertising. Super Bowl ads would be the height of this kind of costly signaling, with companies paying over a million dollars for a thirty-second spot. Remember the reason why peacocks grow extravagant tail feathers, even though the tails make them clumsier and more vulnerable to attack? It's because only the strongest peacocks could survive with such a handicap. Therefore, peahens find fancy feathers irresistibly attractive. Similarly, Doritos hopes that you will find their chips irresistible once you see that they've been so successful at selling their delicious chips that they can burn a million dollars on an amusing half-minute video.

The model of advertising that is most relevant to my own work suggests that ads help shape the identities that we associate with a given product. Apple has famously associated their "Think Different" brand identity with "The crazy ones: The misfits. The rebels. The troublemakers. The round pegs in the square holes." They want customers to believe that owning an Apple product will make you one of them. It's not what you buy when you buy Apple—it's who you are and who others perceive you to be.

The idea that our consumption shapes our self-image is an old one in economics, going back to Thorstein Veblen at the end of the nineteenth century. Veblen's theory of the leisure class described our desire for *conspicuous consumption*: choosing clothing (and later, cars and lawns) so we would look and behave like the rich, at least as far as we could given our limited means. Every person, in this view, is striving to look richer than they actually are. The idea is that in the competition for scarce resources, we want to associate with those with the most: looking rich could attract better partners—in marriage or in business.

This picture suggests that fashion trends, whether they are clothing styles or baby names, come from the elite: the rich start wearing pointy-toed shoes or naming their children Aiden, and a decade or so later everyone is doing it.[53] Today, however, we recognize that our desire to be seen is more complicated. My coauthors Jonah Berger, Yogesh Joshi and I asked in a recent paper why many trends don't in fact start from the "top" but instead emerge from poor or marginalized groups—young people of color, for instance, or gay and trans communities.[54] In part, the answer is that we no longer want to be identified with the rich and powerful, but rather with our community. Identity has shattered into a million subcultures, and we no longer want to be identified only with the elite, but also with our tribe.

Millenia of biological programming has trained us to associate with our tribes, but today we have more choice about which tribe we want to belong to. Some products we buy are still associated with money. Apparently, of the thousands of goods and services on the market, the one that best predicts whether you are financially well off is whether you have an iPhone.[55] Most smartphone users use Android, but that often comes as a shock to Americans who live in "blue bubbles" that tell other iPhone users with whom you are texting that you are also using an iPhone. This is because Apple's branding worked. We associate Apple with the free-spirited and the creative. We want to be identified with such people, and we want to associate with others who share that identity.

Of course, everything we do and own conveys information about who we are, from the names we give to our children, to the clothes we wear, to the scents of our soap and perfumes, to the handbags we carry and the cars we drive. We signal using our experiences as well. The college we went to is conveyed by school shirts and rings, and our vacations get shared on social media and via Christmas cards. The movies and television shows we watch appeal to our shared identities, and our tastes in media get revealed around the proverbial water cooler (more likely Slack or social media these days). Even if we aren't intentionally showing off when we make our purchasing decisions, all our consumption choices nonetheless shape how we are perceived by others.[56]

But what do movies or iPhones or handbags have to do with trust? The answer is that the things we like to consume are shaped by the people we are around, and people with similar preferences are likely to have other similarities. Earlier in the book, we argued that laughter fosters trust because a shared sense of humor suggests shared values and shared norms. Now, it is not just jokes that we share, but media and our fashion tastes, and these cues help us identify others on whom we can rely.[57]

THE FUTURE OF TRUST IN THE MARKET ECONOMY: THE SHARING ECONOMY AND BLOCKCHAIN

On July 23, 2013, federal authorities shut down the website known as the Silk Road, a giant online emporium found on the so-called dark web that made it as easy to trade in illegal drugs and other illegal services as it is to order socks from Amazon. In the two years that the website operated, it transacted 1.2 billion dollars in sales among 150,000 buyers and 4,000 sellers, earning the founder, Ross Ulbricht (known by the moniker "the Dread Pirate Roberts," a reference to a character in the *The Princess Bride*), almost a hundred million dollars.

Ulbricht wrote a manifesto about his vision for creating an online libertarian utopia where free markets prevailed. He envisioned a market where transactions occurred between anonymous buyers and sellers, subject only to the laws of supply and demand unfettered by government regulation and the norms of decency that govern the normal workings of the modern economy. The capitalism that most people in a modern economy encounter when they go to the supermarket for a carton of eggs or a box of cereal is very different from the libertarian utopia that Ulbricht was advocating.[58]

For much of the history of economics since Adam Smith, the idealized version of the market was one where we had large numbers of anonymous buyers and sellers transacting seamlessly in a frictionless market. However, for much of the history of the modern economy, transactions were not made anonymously, but rather (first) face to face or (later) from trusted brands. These transactions were protected by contracts and courts and regulators. The Silk Road website aimed to show that a market could function without all of that—without government intervention or social norms.

The success of Ulbricht's market showed that it could work. It wasn't an unqualified success in terms of creating a frictionless ideal market. It adopted many of the tricks that online sites like eBay had adapted from conventional markets, like escrow and reputation systems. But the fact that that it worked so well using only the tools available to a website administrator is a remarkable success.

We saw in earlier chapters that the limits of human cognition mean that we can keep track of the reputations of only a couple hundred entities at a time. In the prehistoric era, that means that our communities were limited to smallish groups. Through much of recorded history, it meant that we mostly transacted with people we knew, or others in the same religion, or under the legal aegis of a nation-state. One of the most important innovations of the twenty-first century is to show that markets may be able to operate without the legal and moral strictures that helped maintain trust and cooperation over the previous two millennia.

But the Internet has created innovations that are so powerful that they have begun to fundamentally change the role of trust in the marketplace. That innovation was so powerful that even criminals like the illegal drug dealers on the Silk Road were able to buy and sell with some degree of efficiency. Today, that trust is so powerful that it has allowed us to invite strangers to use our cars (Uber), to live in our homes (Airbnb), and to guide our restaurant and other business choices (Yelp).

Two big ideas are associated with the new sharing economy:

1. Buyers can be enabled to trust anonymous sellers online because online systems are good at spreading information (as the law merchants of medieval France did). In this case, the systems disseminate the reputations of sellers, and reputation is the basis of trust.
2. Because reputation is easier to share, the need for firms to solve trust problems is reduced. As a consequence, firms can disaggregate, and traditional, big conglomerates are being replaced with platforms.

Currently, the biggest buzz in tech is blockchain. The hype about it has been so strong that the Long Island Iced Tea company changed their name to the Long Blockchain Corp, even though their main product was still iced tea. They were simply trying to capitalize on the speculative frenzy for anything blockchain-related. The fundamental promise of blockchain is to replace trust with an algorithm.

Online Reputation Systems and Platforms in the Sharing Economy

On the Internet, nobody knows if you are a dog. Therefore, we need systems to establish our reputations while online. The first and simplest step in this direction was simply to assign each buyer and each seller a number that would measure their reputation. Experiments using eBay and other platforms have demonstrated that the reputation system allows strangers to transact, that higher ratings lead to higher prices and higher revenues, and that entities with low ratings are forced out of the market.

These online review systems spill over into the outside world, with sites like Yelp allowing independent restaurants to gain market share over chains, while customer complaints via Twitter or online apps make it more likely that consumers will get a response when they have a bad experience. The innovations in online trust continue, with services that better summarize user comments, new processes to appeal ratings, and more customized ratings that account for the differences in tastes between users.

Such online reputation systems may have an even more consequential impact in the developing world, allowing them to sidestep the development of modern-day market institutions like banks and credit cards. Payments by phone took off in Africa and China earlier than in the United States or Europe, and that allowed digital features like escrow and online reputations to become widespread before they were available in places like the United States.

While much of the online economy looks something like the offline economy—in that big companies make or buy products that they sell to consumers—one of the key features of the former is that so many of the biggest companies act as middlemen, connecting buyers and sellers but not actually making the product themselves. The quintessential platforms are online auction sites like eBay. Amazon started as a traditional company that purchased books and sold them to consumers, but today more than half of their sales come from them actually serving as a portal for other companies to sell their goods to consumers, much as eBay did.[59]

The buying and selling part is less obvious for companies like Google or Facebook, but Google's search engine is primarily a way to connect searchers with information on websites, while Facebook connects people to each other. They both make their money selling consumer attention to advertisers. More recently, there has been a proliferation of more "pure" platforms in what is often called the *sharing economy*. Companies like Uber connect consumers who need a taxi service to private drivers who want to offer rides. Airbnb does the same for people looking for a place to stay. Companies like Prosper connect people who want to lend money to people who want to borrow money, basically turning individuals into banks. Companies like Doordash or Grubhub connect restaurants with people who want to order food delivery.

Economists call these companies that connect buyers and sellers *platforms*, and they represent a new(ish) way to structure the market.[60] Some of the biggest ideas in economics are organized around different ways of structuring the market. Adam Smith's vision of the "invisible hand" of market capitalism involves millions of individual buyers and sellers interacting in a system of *perfect competition*. Karl Marx's vision of capitalism was about the aggregation of power, and it led to other thinkers like Joseph Schumpeter, who argued that the natural tendency in markets is toward monopoly, where a single company dominates a specific sector of the market.

Platforms are a hybrid of the two. The goal of the platform is to become a one-stop shop for some particular sector. Uber wants to be the one place where consumers go when they need a taxi. Their goal is to become a monopoly.[61] However, Uber is also disaggregating sellers into something that looks like Smith's vision of perfect competition: millions of interchangeable providers of an undifferentiated product.

There is an ongoing debate about the benefits of this disaggregation. Uber drivers have brought lawsuits claiming that they should count as Uber employees rather than independent contractors; similar lawsuits have been ongoing for a number of platforms, including Handy and Airbnb. Debates have also been occurring about how much a firm should be allowed to outsource.

Big companies like Apple used to hire their own janitors. Now they pay a separate company for janitorial services. Whereas the relationship used to be one based on an ongoing trust relationship, the new system is based on a market one.

The benefit of disaggregation is that it allows companies to specialize. Apple would say that their core competency is that they are better at making computer and phone hardware than anybody else. The company shouldn't be spending their time learning to offer janitorial services. Letting somebody else handle those services frees up Apple to focus on what Apple is good at. It also creates opportunities for janitorial entrepreneurs to make janitorial services better.

However, the cost of disaggregation is that it replaces a long-term, employer-employee relationship with a short-term market relationship. Large companies developed when we needed people to invest in an ongoing relationship. Reporter Neil Irwin recently contrasted the once-giant Kodak with modern firms like Apple.[62] At Kodak, janitors were paid relatively high wages and given the opportunity for education and advancement within the company. When a firm hires their own drivers or janitors, then the nature of the relationship leads to longer-term investments for both sides. The workers invest in the firm and the firm is invested in the workers. The downside is that once you become invested, it becomes harder to leave. This makes the system less flexible. A long-term worker can, over time, become irreplaceable. This makes long-term workers sort of like mini-monopolies. Platform economies turn that relationship around, restoring competition to the firm-worker relationship. The nature of these platforms is to change the nature of the relationship between workers and the work they do. By disaggregating workers, they make them interchangeable.

One key part of the trust equation that we have not discussed up to now is what happens when the relationship falls apart. In game theory, this is called the *outside option*. In business school negotiation classes, we call this the BATNA (which stands for "best alternative to a negotiated agreement"). For instance, if my boss doesn't give me a raise, I will exercise my BATNA and go to another company. Or if I can't get a good deal from this car dealer, I will take my BATNA down the street at another dealer. It is a useful business skill to be able to determine someone else's BATNA. It will help in knowing how far you can push during salary negotiations or in trying to get a good deal on your car.

But having a good BATNA has an ambiguous effect on trust. On the one hand, having good alternatives to a relationship means that parties to the relationship have to work harder to demonstrate their own value—their own trustworthiness. On the other hand, having good alternatives means that relationships are more fragile. If something bad happens that undermines trust in the relationship, it becomes easier for one or both parties to look elsewhere. (Later, in Chapter 5, we'll look at how apologies can work to restore relationships when something goes wrong, and how my own experiments with the Uber platform demonstrate how apologies work in the platform economy.)

In other words, too many alternatives can be bad for trust because they make it easier to quit a relationship in favor of another one. At the same time, having too few alternatives is bad for trust because I don't have to invest in the relationship if I know that you have nowhere else to go. Platforms have done a good job of taking advantage of both extremes. In some interactions, like the choice of drivers who use the Uber platform, platforms generate a great many alternatives, which keeps service costs down. For other interactions, like the choice of platforms by consumers, platforms try to corner the market.

Internet commerce began with a lot of idealism about frictionless markets. Competition was only a click away, and consumers would have unlimited choice. To some extent, that has happened. But there has always been a push-and-pull between the ability to easily shop around and the convenience of one-stop shopping. While early online commerce came to be dominated by a few giants like Amazon, the Internet now is increasingly populated by platforms that connect large numbers of small buyers with large numbers of small sellers.

Platforms like Uber, the Apple App Store, and Airbnb connect millions of buyers with millions of sellers. These platforms excel at promoting competition among the sellers with them. But there is relatively little competition among platforms in any given sector. If you want to find a driver to take you to the airport, Uber will connect you to dozens of drivers who are just minutes away. But if you want an alternative to Uber to find drivers for you, your options are much more limited. Maybe Lyft, but not much else. Platforms create systems to lock you into their system. That gives them monopoly power. Once a platform has that power, that reduces their need to innovate and to continue to invest in improving their services.

One technology that platforms use to create monopoly power for themselves is the reputation system discussed in the previous section. Once you have established a good reputation on one platform, and once you have built up trust in one platform, it becomes less and less likely that either buyers or sellers will switch away from you.

The tendency of platforms to centralize power is both good and bad. It is convenient for consumers to have a one-stop shop for car services or phone operating systems. All my friends and family use iPhones, so when I switched to Android, it created many annoyances. Being locked into a single system provides lots of opportunity to develop trust with that system. And big companies have the resources to invest in innovation. But at the same time, being locked into the same system creates complacency. Why invest in the relationship when your customers have nowhere to go?

The contemporary economy, therefore, presents a kind of paradox: at the same time that we are worrying about firms becoming too big, with single brand names dominating an entire sector, we are also worrying about firms becoming too small, relying on contracts and markets to provide what they once provided for themselves (like janitorial services). Getting that balance right has been an active area of study by economists since the Microsoft antitrust litigation of the 1990s, and for the first time in a long time, antitrust regulation has become a part of political discourse again, as presidential candidates and other office-seekers bring up monopoly power in their campaign speeches.

Blockchain

If the sharing economy is the first major paradigm shift in trust in the twenty-first century, maybe the next one will be blockchain. In all the hype around blockchain, what might have gotten lost is that it is a revolution in how we trust. The major application of blockchain was bitcoin, the digital currency that has become the currency of choice for illicit transactions and was the currency used on the Silk Road website. In fact, the most common use of bitcoin (accounting for half of all transactions in 2018) is for illicit activity.[63]

It's not surprising that the first application of an innovation in trust is related to money. We began this part of the book by talking about money, as money is one of the most basic building blocks of a modern market economy, and that particular building block is built on trust. People often describe bitcoin as the first digital currency, but that name isn't quite right. Most modern currencies, including the U.S. dollar, are mostly digital. Economists call the physical money (the dollar bills and coins) in the economy M_0, and this accounts for only about 20 percent of the measure that we usually use for money in circulation, M_2.[64] The rest is digital, recorded in computer databases in banks across the country and around the world. When I buy a cup of coffee for four dollars using a credit card, the money is transferred between banks by a keystroke, not by any actual paper money changing hands. The banks simply subtract four dollars from my account and add four dollars to the coffee shop's account. The United States and other industrialized countries moved away from needing to move bags of paper around years ago. Bitcoin works the same way. The difference is instead of storing those transactions in databases at a bank, Satoshi Nakamoto designed bitcoin to store the transactions on blockchain.

Instead of storing a list of transactions on a single computer server controlled by a single entity, information on blockchain is distributed on many computers (millions, in the case of bitcoin) spread around the world. It's like having a bank account, but copied millions of times. Once a transaction is completed, your bitcoin account is updated across millions of computers and can be changed only with permission from a majority of those computers. Whereas one person could hack into your bank's computer and change your checking account balance, it's unlikely that any person could hack into the millions of computers that would be necessary to mess with blockchain.

So, because the point of blockchain is to solve problems of trust, it is worth taking a second to think about which problems blockchain can actually help us solve. Today, we take for granted that the creation of money is in the purview of government. However, this has not always been the case. In the past, anyone could mine gold to use for money, although governments quickly moved to monopolize gold supplies. But in principle, the option to mine gold was available to anyone. We use the term *banknotes* for money because originally, the notes that were circulated were mostly provided by banks. The paper was exchangeable for gold and supported by the reputation of the banks that issued it. This was normal practice in early America, and private, bank-issued currency is still widely used in Hong Kong today. In general, the authority to print money became associated with the government because greedy governments wanted moneymaking authority for their own purposes, but also because governments became the easiest to trust. Any individual bank could default, but national governments tended to be more reliable and trustworthy in the long run.

In recent years, proponents of a new kind of currency claim to have solved the problem of trust using technology, in the form of a mathematical algorithm. The key feature of money—what gives it value—is rarity. The rarity of gold is maintained by the small amount of physical gold out in the world. The rarity of fiat money is maintained by governments trying to protect their reputation for austerity and good judgment when printing money, and more specifically by the independent central bankers who have been given that responsibility. However, despite the institutions that are in place to help promote the trustworthiness of governments in their moneymaking role, they are still run by people, and people are fallible.

Bitcoin and the new multitude of cryptocurrencies aim to solve that problem. Instead of currencies that are sustained by trust in other people or institutions, they are currencies whose value is protected by cryptography and which rely on trust in an algorithm. Bitcoin is based on a ledger, which you can think of as a database, or even just a spreadsheet. Just as a bank keeps a list of all its clients and how much money they have, and just as the islanders of Yap kept track of which stone disk belonged to whom, and just as premodern tribes kept track of who owed whom a favor, the bitcoin ledger keeps track of how many bitcoins each user has.

When I want to buy something using bitcoin, I authorize the ledger to decrement my account by 1 and increase the account of someone else by 1, in the same way that a bank transfers money when I write somebody a check. Of course, you wouldn't want people messing with the numbers for nefarious ends. You trust a bank to keep your account figures straight because their reputation is on the line. Banks traditionally invested in fancy, impressive-looking buildings because by spending their assets on something immobile like a building, they signaled that they were not an outfit likely to take depositors' money and vanish into the night. In modern society, governments and law enforcement and the rule of law ensure that banks will honor their contracts.

Bitcoin is different. It was started by an anonymous person or persons working under the pseudonym of Satoshi Nakamoto, supposedly an expert in cryptography and popular with the hacker community. Such provenance might not ordinarily engender trust, but Nakamoto found a way to build trust into the very technology that enables the currency (a technology that they pioneered)—namely, blockchain. Whereas banks (including central banks) store their information on some central server that could potentially be altered by whoever controls access to the server, bitcoin stores its ledger in little bits and pieces on computers spread around the world. No single person controls access to the ledger, so entering false transactions is difficult.

Bitcoin basically operates like the everyday currencies like dollars and euros that we use every day, except that instead of placing your trust in the central bank's reputation and the efficacy of local law enforcement to keep their records straight, you are placing your trust in an algorithm. It is reasonable to distrust an algorithm, as early cryptocurrencies have already been hacked several times due to mistakes in the systems of applications that work with them. Millions of dollars of bitcoin and ether (another cryptocurrency) were stolen. It is also reasonable to be skeptical of the sustainability of bitcoin, as running the algorithm requires computing power comparable to that used by a small country, although other cryptocurrencies have been designed that operate more efficiently.

I think most of us (in the developed world, anyway) do trust banks; therefore, the advantages of using bitcoin and other cryptocurrencies are unclear. Bitcoin is useful when you don't trust your bank and when you don't trust local law enforcement. This could be useful if you live in a country where the government and institutions are unstable—or if you are a criminal and therefore don't have access to traditional banks for the storage and transmission of your ill-gotten money. One of the major uses of bitcoin is the purchase of drugs and other illegal goods and services on the dark web.

Advocates of bitcoin point to one other design feature of the currency that addresses a failure in trust. Bitcoin was designed with a system that regulated the creation of more bitcoins. The threat of inflation and hyperinflation to the value of a currency has been a constant theme throughout this section. The value of gold is protected by the difficulty in mining gold, but bitcoin, like fiat money, is really just a few 1s and 0s on a computer. We trust central bankers to manage the quantity of money in circulation. Bitcoin relies on its algorithm.

Ordinarily, the supply of money has to grow to keep up with demand. As a currency is used for more and more transactions, more and more of it is needed—but if the quantity increases too fast, you get inflation, and the money loses value. Bitcoin does not have this problem because the money is all digital. As the number of transactions grows, prices can simply be set at smaller increments. For example, at the current time, the price of a hamburger is around 0.001 bitcoins. It would be hard for regular currencies to accomplish this: if a hamburger cost 0.001 cent, we would need to mint a new kind of coin—one worth one-thousandth of a dollar.

Moreover, the inventor of bitcoin designed the system to generate new bitcoins to compensate the people who are supplying the computing power to make the system work. Because each bitcoin transaction requires a substantial amount of computational effort to keep it secure, the system is set up so that people who supply the computers to perform these computations are awarded new bitcoins.

However, the creation of new bitcoins has not kept up with demand for the currency, which means that the value of the currency has at times skyrocketed (generating *deflation* and thousandth-of-a-bitcoin hamburgers). At other times the market loses faith in bitcoin and the value of bitcoin plummets (generating *inflation* and a much pricier lunch). The Federal Reserve works hard to match the supply of money to the demand to keep prices steady. There is no equivalent regulatory institution for bitcoin, and the constant adjusting of prices makes holding bitcoins risky and uncertain.

The future of bitcoin, therefore, remains to be seen with the value of bitcoin shifting wildly from year to year and month to month. However, the technology behind bitcoin has other potential applications in realms where an algorithm could become a substitute for trust. Also, the workings of bitcoin, like the giant stone coins of Yap, help expose the inner workings of our system of money, something we usually take for granted.

The current money system relies on a lot of trust. Most directly, it requires trusting the banks to keep track of your money correctly. Moreover, it requires trust in central bankers like the Federal Reserve to properly manage the total supply of money. Bitcoin sidesteps the need to trust banks by copying your information across a million computers, and it sidesteps the need to trust a central bank like the Federal Reserve by having a fixed algorithm that releases new bitcoins at a steady and predictable rate.

So bitcoin does make sense for those who distrust banks or distrust the Federal Reserve. That kind of distrust of institutions has deep roots in U.S. history, so it is understandable that there is a community of hacktivists who strongly believe that bitcoin is the currency of the future. In Neal Stephenson's 1999 novel *Cryptonomicon*, he writes about how cryptography was used to win World War II through decryption of German codes, and how a cryptographic currency (like bitcoin) and an unassailable means of sharing information (like blockchain) could save the world from despotic governments.

For those who live in tyrannical or unstable regimes, or for criminals operating outside of the law, distrust in the financial system is more than justified. However, for those of us lucky enough to live in stable, modern economies like the United States, the data suggest that we trust the banks and we trust the Federal Reserve quite a lot. Recall from our earlier discussion about investments that we can directly observe how much people in the marketplace trust a lender by looking at interest rates. The lower the interest rate, the higher the level of trust. For much of the twenty-first century, people have been willing to lend to the U.S. government at such low rates that the Federal Reserve has worried that they were too low. In other words, the Fed made the

U.S. government so trustworthy that people were willing to lend it money almost for free. The same is true for most commercial banks as well.

The same is not true for criminals, who often struggle to find financial institutions that they can trust. Criminals often use stolen art to pay for illegal transactions like drugs or weapons because they have no other way of transacting large sums of money.[65] For them, bitcoin is a huge boon.

Also, while bitcoin got a lot of its initial user base from people participating in illegal activities, it has more legitimate potential applications in countries where the central government or the banking system is unreliable. These countries largely already use U.S. dollars quite extensively, but bitcoin might be a viable alternative.

The other part of some people's distrust of the Federal Reserve comes from a belief that it doesn't increase the money supply enough to keep up with the growth of the economy. Bitcoin does little to help with that because it grows only at a fixed rate that cannot adjust (too much) to the ups and downs of economic booms and recessions.

Finally, the idea that blockchain is more trustworthy than the people at a bank because the security is ensured by an algorithm asks us to place a lot of trust in an algorithm. While these algorithms are theoretically very hard to manipulate, we are all familiar with how often software gets hacked because of vulnerabilities in the computer code. There have already been a few high-profile hacks of bitcoin and its nearest competitor, Ethereum, where cryptocurrencies worth hundreds of millions of U.S. dollars were stolen or lost.[66] While the software has been improved and could in theory be made more secure, I think a lot of us are more likely to trust our banks than to trust that this complicated piece of software won't get hacked again.

Therefore, it seems difficult to justify the high cost of storing most data that we rely on using blockchain. Whereas your bank keeps all its data on just one computer server (or maybe a few, for backup), blockchain keeps your data on millions of computers. Distributing that data uses an immense amount of energy. Part of that energy comes from each blockchain server doing pointless math to signal their trustworthiness. Recall from our model of trust that demonstrating trustworthiness requires costly sacrifice. Solving pointless math problems is a great example of this type of sacrifice, but those computations require energy, and that energy contributes to climate change. Lots of things require energy, and there is nothing inherently wrong with using energy if it is doing important work, but for the moment, bank computers can do the same job as blockchain using far fewer resources.

You may have noticed that I am a bit skeptical of bitcoin, and of blockchain more generally. I think it still has a lot of problems to work out, though it has potential. It's just that the main problem that it is trying to solve is one of trust, and as I hope you have gathered from this book so far, trust is something that humans have been developing institutions to support for thousands of years. We've gotten pretty good at trusting one another.

But I am still always optimistic about the future. And while I don't see much potential in bitcoin, there may be other applications where blockchain technologies could help. In recent years, a lot of money has been made in initial coin offerings (ICOs), where companies issue cryptocurrency to raise investment money for a new venture. Just like the Deli Dollars, these companies are issuing these virtual coins to raise money that they promise to return to investors later. However, this isn't really solving a new problem per se, because we already allow companies to issue stocks and bonds that do the same thing. An ICO simply allows firms to raise money at a lower cost. However, most of the cost savings come because these ICOs bypass SEC regulations designed to protect consumers. There may be good reason to bypass needless regulation, but many regulations are valuable. ICOs allow firms to raise money more cheaply, but at the cost of reduced protections for consumers. The SEC has already begun to crack down on the practice.

Still there are important and valuable applications for blockchain in cases where people really can't trust the government to do the right thing. For example, if citizens of a repressive regime wanted to develop a social network but were worried about government surveillance, blockchain could supply a safe haven for their data. A company could try to guarantee privacy, but even the best-intentioned company, with cutting-edge encryption, could be forced to comply with government subpoenas. Placing the data on blockchain would make the algorithms that protect the data (somewhat) more transparent.

Elections are another area where the gains from hacking are potentially large, and even in the most stable of democracies, one might have reason to distrust the people with access to the computers that determine the outcomes of elections. Some kind of decentralized blockchain could help there as well—again, so long as you can trust the algorithms themselves. Bug-free algorithms can be proved to be perfectly unhackable, but while progress has been made, perfection is difficult to attain. As computer science improves, our trust in algorithms may improve. Maybe blockchain is the next phase of the trust economy, and we will eventually put our trust more fully in algorithms. But our trust in each other is advancing as well, and it may give the algorithms a run for their money.

Recent innovations in online Internet commerce, platform economies, and blockchain have changed the relationship between technology and trust. Both platforms and blockchain offer computational shortcuts to ascertain who is trustworthy, but both require trusting new technologies. Still, they largely conform to the story that I have been painting in this book: the development of technology expanded our circle of trust from the confines of our immediate family and tribe to more and more of the global community.

However, despite this millennia-long pattern of expanding trust, there has been a recent hiccup in this trend. Even as our trust in each other has grown, our trust in experts and institutions has begun to falter. This erosion in trust of politicians, scientists, doctors, and economists has been well documented in recent decades. We will explore the reasons for this decline in the next part of the book, and will also examine the role of technological innovation in undermining trust.

4

TRUSTING INSTITUTIONS
WITH EXPERTISE

MAYBE the most crucial test for modern civilization
is whether we can adapt our biological and cultural
instincts, developed for small tribes and communities
of 150 members, to a global community of billions. For the first
time in human history, we have technologies that, if used poorly,
can have devastating consequences not just for all of humanity,
but for the entire planet. Addressing these challenges will require
all of humanity to work together cooperatively, and to do that
will require trust on a global scale.

I wrote this book in part because the story of trust in human
civilization has given me hope. We were born to trust, but we
were also born with the instincts to trust only a few. Over the
centuries, we have developed the instincts and tools and institutions to expand our circle of trust to millions—to the point
where we barely notice how weird it is that when we click
something on a computer screen, we trust an anonymous seller
on the other side of the planet to mail us some toy or knickknack.
We trust the transport system to deliver that toy in a matter of
days, and we trust our bank to handle the payments. We trust
the toy itself will be high-quality, nontoxic, and otherwise safe.
And all of that is enabled by a combination of trust in the rule of
law (to enforce contracts and regulations), trust in brands, trust

in online reputation systems, and trust in markets to regulate all those transactions.

History suggests that just as we have gotten better and better at producing food (and medicine, and all sorts of tools and technologies), we have also gotten better and better at producing trust. However, as I began work on this project, another pattern was emerging: a growing distrust of expertise. We may trust each other more, but it feels like we are trusting experts less.

The data, however, paint a more complicated story. Since the 1970s, the Pew Research Center has been polling Americans on the confidence they have in the people running various institutions. Between 1973 and 2018, the proportion of people who say they have a great deal of confidence in the media has declined from over 20 percent to 13 percent, and trust in medicine has declined from almost 60 percent to 37 percent. Trust in the federal government has declined from almost 80 percent at the beginning of the 1960s to under 20 percent in 2018, although trust in government has had many ups and downs, with trust around 30 percent during the 1970s, trust under 20 percent in the 1990s, and some periods of recovery in between.

On the other hand, trust in some institutions has increased. Trust in the military has increased from under 40 percent in the 1970s to 60 percent in 2018, while trust in the scientific community has been relatively stable moving between 40 percent to 44 percent in the same time period (see Figure 4.1).[1]

We will discuss a number of examples of eroding trust in expertise in this chapter, including the following:

- Many Americans continue to doubt the science of climate change, even as scientists have become more certain of it.
- Trust in politicians (admittedly never very high) has declined to new lows.

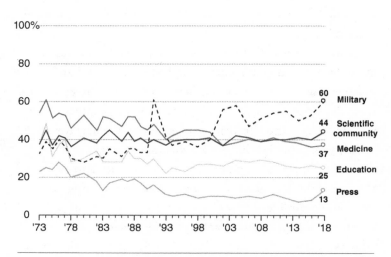

FIGURE 4.1 Percentage of adults who say they have a great deal of confidence in those running certain institutions

Note: Confidence in leaders of the military has gone up; confidence in some other institutions is declining.

Source: Pew Research Center (2019)

- Trust in medicine has declined both in the developed and developing worlds.
- Many Americans now behave as if everything we read that we disagree with is fake news.

We dive into these examples in the sections that follow. We would like to know if this is a temporary aberration (a few decades is just a blip in the sweep of history) or, if it is not, what are the consequences, and can they be averted? We would like to know if this is part of a systemic change or if trust in each institution has been declining for its own idiosyncratic reasons. Solving the biggest problems in the world will require more cooperation than ever before, and more cooperation requires greater trust.

Some common themes emerge about why trust in expertise may be in peril:

1. We now have more choices than ever before. More choice means that it is easier to look for a second opinion, and there is less incentive to invest in the relationships you have.

2. Dating to our early tribalism and the origins of religion, much trust derives from fear of the other. As the world comes together, fear of the other may become less salient, and therefore, we have lost a common enemy to foster local trust.

3. Access to more information and more education means that we may become overconfident in our own perceptions, valuing them more highly than the perceptions of experts. Some surveys find that misperceptions of science increase for those with more education and those who spend more time on the Internet. That overconfidence is linked to increased polarization. The Internet has given us greater means to find "our tribe," and so, instead of being forced to interact with those who are different, we can become more attached to those who are the same.

We will examine these themes across different institutions (specifically politics, the media, medicine, and science, particularly climate science), although I don't have any answers about what to do about it. We also should note that since 2016, the decline in trust seems to have at least momentarily reversed, with notable increases in trust for the media, but also trust across many major institutions. It is too early to tell whether this is a change in trend or just an aberration, but it is definitely an optimistic turn of events. Even if we can't fully explain these recent trends in trust, understanding how trust functions in these institutions is a necessary first step in reckoning with the problem.

POLITICIANS

These days, the headlines are full of dire warnings about the fate of democracy, with elections influenced by populist demagogues, fake news, and foreign meddling. This decline in trust in the government in the United States has been well documented in surveys (see Figure 4.2).

Of course, none of these concerns are new. One only has to watch the musical *Hamilton* to be reminded of sex scandals and fake news and demagoguery's influence in elections in the 1700s. In the farewell address that Alexander Hamilton wrote for George Washington, he warned about foreign entanglements. He was worried about French meddling in U.S. politics and warned that "foreign influence is one of the most baneful foes of republican government . . . as avenues to foreign influence in innumerable ways, such attachments are particularly alarming . . . How many opportunities do they afford to tamper with domestic factions, to practice the arts of seduction, to mislead public opinion."[2]

Reflecting the fact that trust in government is an old concern, much thought was given to trust in the drafting of the U.S. Constitution. We discussed the enduring role that the Constitution has even two-and-a-half centuries after its ratification. In this section, we focus on how the Constitution allocates power between the voters and those whom they elect. We tend to think of a republican democracy as being made up of voters and elected leaders, but of course, even those two categories are much more complicated. Most people living in the early decades

% who trust the govt in Washington always or most of the time

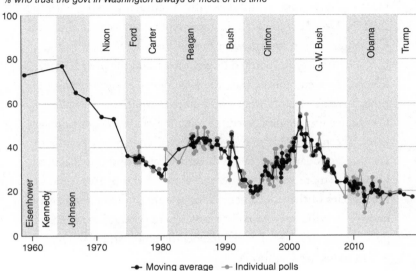

FIGURE 4.2 Public trust in government: 1958–2019

Source: Pew Research Center (2019). *Public Trust in Government: 1958–2019.*
April 11.

of the United States were not allowed to vote (at the time, voting was limited to property-owning, mostly white men above the age of twenty-one). Similarly, most government officials weren't elected. Supreme Court justices were appointed for life (as they still are today). Senators were appointed by governors. Most of the federal bureaucracy was appointed by the president (again, that remains the case today).

Trusting Politicians

One of the central questions in a democracy is the allocation of power between the electorate and those chosen to govern. People are often distrustful of concentrated power. The progressive movement at the beginning of the twentieth century led a big push to shift the United States from its more republican roots in the U.S. Constitution to a system with more direct democracy. Initially, U.S. senators were appointed by governors, and the president was selected by a committee (i.e., the Electoral College—but at the time, a state's electors were not required, explicitly or implicitly, to vote in a way that reflected the outcome of a statewide popular vote). The progressive movement effected changes in how both are chosen: today, senators are directly elected, and the Electoral College is more responsive to the votes of the people. One of the legacies of that movement is the system of direct democracy known as *initiative and referendum*, where voters directly make policy. Such exercises of direct democratic power still play a major role in states like California.

But how much direct democracy is healthy for society? In a recent National Science Foundation survey, the majority of Democrats said that the Sun revolves around the Earth or if they did know the Earth revolves around the Sun, they didn't know that it takes a year. The majority of Republicans in the same survey said they didn't believe in evolution.[3] You have to wonder to what extent voters should have a say in policy making . . .

For what it's worth, I am sympathetic with the survey takers here. The survey claiming to have found that a majority of Democrats think that the Sun revolves around the Earth probably should not be taken to mean that Democrats are shockingly ignorant about science. It may mean only that most people don't really care about giving correct answers to random phone surveys. Also, a 2015 experiment found that when you poll people on factual but partisan-tinged questions like "Was unemployment higher under Obama or under Bush?" people unsurprisingly give partisan answers.[4] However, if you instead ask them the same questions but pay them a couple of dollars if they get the question right, the bias goes away. This suggests that our partisan allegiance may not be very strong. However, I do think that it is generally true that our knowledge of most issues is quite shallow, in the sense that we believe the things we believe about the world not because we have directly observed them, but mostly because we have learned them from people we trust.

I think that it does makes sense for voters to vote based on their values. We need democracy to be responsive to voter opinion on what to prioritize: for instance, how to allocate funding between fighting poverty versus fighting climate change, or how to address questions of moral concern like civil rights. But it can be problematic when we try to legislate about questions that can be answered by science, like when one small town tried to pass a law declaring that pi equals 3.

The issue that best illustrated to me how much information it takes to make the right choice on policy can be seen in two commodities that we use every day but rarely think much about: corn and gasoline. One statistic that surprises nearly every audience I tell: nearly half of the corn grown in the United States gets converted into ethanol (basically corn vodka) and is added to gasoline. About 10 percent of the gasoline that we put into our cars comes from corn.

If you have any opinion at all about the use of corn ethanol for gasoline, it might have come from pop culture. For example, the Aaron Sorkin television drama *The West Wing* spent a whole episode on how politicians support the use of corn to make ethanol only because of the importance of Iowa in presidential elections, and ethanol policy is just pandering to Iowa corn farmers. If the topic does come up, most people I know think ethanol subsidies are dumb and would probably favor getting rid of them. I used to agree, even though the corn subsidy is one of those few things that gets broad bipartisan support among our elected representatives.

I was the lead energy economist for the White House Council of Economic Advisers. It was my job to help craft and advise the ethanol legislation that was going through Congress at the time. At that point, I probably knew more about U.S. ethanol policy than just about anybody, and my opinion on whether it was good or bad changed daily.

To really understand ethanol policy, I had to understand how and why it had replaced the chemical methyl tertiary-butyl ether (MTBE) as an oxygenate in gasoline due to litigation based on fears of carcinogens found in MTBE runoff. I learned from the U.S. trade representative that ethanol tariffs were an important bargaining chip in U.S. trade negotiations. I learned from the scientific literature that ethanol has two-thirds of the fuel economy of gasoline but higher effective octane. I also learned that ethanol increases corrosion to engines, but not in cars produced to meet modern standards, and that ethanol increases corrosion in pipelines and sometimes has to be transported by truck.

Ethanol's impact on climate change is ambiguous, and a meta-analysis of dozens of studies shows that that impact has improved with technology over time. Ethanol affects the farm economy, but it has a fairly small effect on corn prices, despite headlines blaming ethanol policy for the price of tortillas in Mexico. A biofuel provision in U.S. law helped lead to widespread deforestation in Indonesia due to increasing demand for palm oil—a deforestation that contributed to one of the largest increases in greenhouse gas emissions in recent history.[5] In sum: it took me months and years to really learn the ins and outs of ethanol policy, and throughout, I found my opinion swaying with each new fact. It seems crazy to me now that we expect voters to have opinions on whether a policy like mandating that gasoline sold to consumers contains 10 percent corn ethanol is a good idea.

I used to think that education was the key to making democracy work and that educating voters would allow them to make the decisions that hold politicians accountable. But the amount of time that it took me to amass enough information to make informed decisions about ethanol was enormous. It is wholly impractical to expect everyone to learn as much on just this single issue, much less the myriad other issues that have to be decided on any given day. That is why we have specialists. We don't expect everyone to know how to fix their own car; most people take their car to a mechanic. In a representative democracy, we elect our leaders.

And yet we are still expected to judge a candidate, as we happily do, based on their positions on issues like support for corn ethanol. At least back when that *West Wing* episode came out, it was a popular part of presidential campaigns and likely did make a difference in who won the Iowa caucuses. A *New York Times* reporter recently remarked on how surprising it was that the 2020 presidential election was the first one he covered where ethanol wasn't a major part of the primary debates.[6] Back in graduate school, I used to gather with a group of other PhD students before each Election Day to discuss the numerous ballot initiatives on issues like Native American casino taxes, property tax rates, and public transit subsidies. This group—some of the most highly educated people at one of the top research universities in the world—could barely manage to read the full descriptions of the initiatives they were deciding on, much less formulate a thoughtful, well-informed opinion about them. Understandable. We were all busy. All of us are busy. How, then, can we trust ourselves as voters with these kinds of complex decisions?

There is some hope, fortunately. While it may be futile to ask voters to decide policy, they may have a chance of doing at least a reasonable job of deciding which representatives are trustworthy. After a presidential debate, commentators often spend hours parsing body language, facial expressions, interruptions, facial tics, and language use.

High-minded pundits often complain about media obsession with such details and insist that elections should be decided based on the issues. While it is true that on some policy questions, like abortion or gun ownership, the issue is clear enough for voters to just select the candidate who shares their policy preferences, on most issues, it is more important for voters to focus not on the specific policies that candidates support, but on figuring out which candidate most closely shares their values. The policy details don't matter as much and shouldn't matter in large elections. Too much is made of whether a politician's numbers add up or whether their statements are always precisely accurate. As in the case of corn ethanol, voters will never have the time to fully digest all the nuances that go into any policy position. Even the policy debates that actually come up around abortion or gun ownership are about nuances like background checks and mental health provisions and medical exceptions. Most voters aren't going to spend the hours (or years) needed to master the details. Instead, it makes sense for them to identify the candidate who shares their values and who would make the same choice as they would, given full information. In the language of game theory and economics, voters should choose candidates who have an *alignment of preferences*. In the language of this book, they should choose the candidate whom they can *trust*.

Fortunately, as detailed in earlier chapters, millennia of biological and cultural evolution have given us instincts and systems for determining whom to trust. Unfortunately, those trust instincts can be suborned by canny marketers and political consultants for their own ends.

One interesting test of this point is the thin slicing of political candidates.[7] Subjects shown ten-second, silent videos of two competing political candidates for out-of-state (i.e., unfamiliar) gubernatorial races are able to predict with startling accuracy which one actually won. In other words, just by watching their appearance, their gestures, and their movements, they can predict which candidate the voters chose. There are two ways to interpret this result. An optimistic take is that it just takes ten seconds to decide which candidate is more trustworthy, and that the voters use this information in making their decisions. A less optimistic take is that politicians do everything they can to appear more trustworthy, and that voters are fooled by those appearances. Either way, these nonverbal cues play a significant role in who we select to make policy decisions.

Personally, I think choosing candidates based on how trustworthy they seem is a good thing. When asked to recall relevant policy facts about the world (e.g., was inflation higher under Ronald Reagan or Bill Clinton?), our recall tends to be shaped by partisan biases.[8] When Democratic subjects are told that policy X was introduced by a Democrat, they support it. When they are told that the exact same policy was introduced by a Republican, they oppose it.[9] Just as we once used religion to determine whom to trust, today we use political party affiliation. I don't think we as voters are especially good at judging policy. Let's hope that we are better at choosing representatives.

At the same time, I think we would all agree that it would be dangerous to hand over all decision-making authority to our leaders, even if they are democratically elected. The question is: when it comes to making policy decisions, when should we trust our leaders and when should we trust the voters?

The Politician and the Bureaucrat

As a teacher, it's always nice to run into former students years later and hear what they still remember from my classes. The line that I remember most from my own studies in political science is that the most important indicator of the strength of a democracy is not the set of things that people vote on, but instead the set of things that people are not *allowed* to vote on. The number of things not up for a vote in the United States is striking, when you think about it. Most notably, Supreme Court justices are appointed and serve for life, with few (if any) opportunities to be held accountable. Similarly, Federal Reserve chairs are appointed to ten-year terms (beyond the span of any presidential term) and are afforded a similar level of independence.

This broad autonomy to shape policy is evident not just for the very big, but also for the small. While laws written by Congress shape the general outline of policy and Supreme Court decisions get a lot of attention, much of the functioning of government happens out of sight—in the smaller court cases and the thousands of pages of regulations drafted by low-paid bureaucrats who are rarely held directly accountable for the effects of what they write. Some regulations are challenged and then debated in court before federal judges appointed for life, but except for a small few, most of them never get noticed by the vast majority of the electorate. And maybe all that is exactly as it should be.

One of my favorite models in game theory is a simple one written by two Nobel Prize winners, Eric Maskin and Jean Tirole. They are both known for their sophisticated mathematical modeling techniques, but the paper of theirs that I like the most uses fairly simple high school algebra to ask the important question of whom we should trust to make policy decisions: the voters, elected representatives, or unelected bureaucrats and judges? The answer, it turns out, depends on the type of policy question at issue.

Their model presents a simple game that considers a set of voters and a government official. The model then asks, for some policy choice, what would happen if the policy were decided by the voters directly, by an elected government official, or by an unelected official. A society must grapple with many kinds of policies, ranging from who must pay taxes (and how much), to what is subject to regulation, to what social programs are funded. While the policies that governments have to decide differ along a number of dimensions, Maskin and Tirole focus on just three of them:

1. How well the voters understand the issue in question (this depends on both voter familiarity and the issue's technical complexity)
2. How much the official in the game values being in power relative to how much they value serving the greater good
3. How long it takes for voters to learn whether the official made a good or bad choice

For example, on a question like abortion, voters are relatively more familiar with the technical details of abortion policies, such as what a ban on abortion might look like, and they are more likely to be able to predict what an abortion ban would look like if it were enacted. By contrast, the options regarding ethanol policy have a lot of technical complexity that is obscure to most voters, and the consequences of ethanol policy are hard to predict (its impact on climate change could be unclear for decades)[10].

In the language that we have been using in this book, policy decision-making is an act of trust that requires finding a trustworthy trustee whom we can rely upon. It is an act of trust that entails a lot of risk because the choices that policy makers make can have large impacts on our lives, but voters have a hard time evaluating the policy choices themselves. Ultimately, the purpose of government is to serve the people, so the people are taking a risk when investing specific officials with the power to make choices on their behalf. Government officials can demonstrate their trustworthiness by making good decisions for the electorate. However, at times the official will have better information and will want to make a choice that the public does not like. After all, if officials made only choices that were popular, then there would be no need to have them. We might as well just have direct democracy.

The model assumes that officials are sometimes honest but sometimes venal. Venal politicians care only about their own power—their career and their reelection. Honest politicians just want to do what's best. Even if people aren't so easily classified, it is true that at any given moment, a politician might make a choice that is more self-serving or might make a choice that is for the greater good.

A good example of this, demonstrated by Steve Levitt, is that politicians put a lot more cops on the street right before an election.[11] Levitt found that when there are more police on the street, people feel safer and are more likely to reelect the incumbent politician. Sometimes spending money for more police is in the best interest of the citizens, but other times, it is just a ploy to get reelected. The problem is that it is difficult for voters to figure out which motives are in play at any given time.

Unaccountable officials (like Supreme Court justices) in the model will just act on their own inclinations, whether venal or honest. An elected official who cares about reelection will have reason to want to demonstrate trustworthiness in their policy decisions. This has both good and bad consequences. On the one hand, it makes venal politicians at least somewhat responsive to the needs of the people, but on the other hand, it makes honest politicians want to pander. An honest elected official may know the best course of action but choose not to take it if that action would be unpopular. They would reason that they should pander in the short run and build the voters' trust so that they can be reelected and do more in the future. In cases where pandering would be bad, then assigning an unelected official would be better. However, in cases where voters are relatively well informed or when politicians are in need of more discipline, then we should have elected officials making those decisions.

As with anything in economics, whom we trust—the voter, the politician, or the bureaucrat—is a question of trade-offs. Making the right policy requires two things: the right information about the policy and the right intentions (honest, not venal). Our leaders no doubt have better information than the voters, but it is possible for leaders to have the wrong intentions. I think our elected leaders have better intentions than we give them credit for. They're more like Mr. Smith going to Washington than Senator Palpatine taking the path to the dark side. Research on trade tariffs suggests that politicians mostly make policy choices that are in the best interests of the voters, at personal cost to themselves.[12] But there is little doubt that sometimes a politician is making choices more in line with their own self-interests than the interests of their constituents. Therefore, we may want to vest some decision-making authority in the voters and risk having them make uninformed choices. Or we may want to vest some decision-making authority in unaccountable officials (judges or bureaucrats) and risk getting a venal autocrat, at least in their own small domain.

Sometimes for an official, doing the right thing isn't just about having more information than the voters, but also about having to balance the interests of the majority of the electorate and the minority. A pandering official would favor the interests of the majority even if the costs to the minority outweigh the benefits to the majority.

Maskin and Tirole summarize the consequences of their model succinctly:

(1) Accountability has two potential benefits. It allows voters to remove officials whose interests appear to be noncongruent with the electorate, but also gives noncongruent officials some incentive to act as though they were congruent (through the effect of forward-looking or partial pandering). (2) However, accountability may encourage officials to pander to the electorate and overlook minority interests. (3) Nonaccountability is most desirable when (a) the electorate is poorly informed about the optimal action, (b) acquiring decision relevant information is costly, and (c) feedback about the quality of decisions is slow. Therefore, technical decisions, in particular, may be best allocated to judges or appointed bureaucrats. (4) The most important decisions should be taken by elected rather than nonaccountable officials (although direct democracy may have the edge over representative democracy for such decisions). (5) The discretion of nonaccountable officials should be more limited than that of accountable ones. (6) Nonaccountability is preferable when the majority's preferences are very likely to inflict large negative externalities on the minority. However, representative democracy is better in this case than direct democracy, and, for moderate probabilities of negative externalities, may constitute a desirable compromise between the two extremes.[13]

Taken together, Maskin and Tirole suggest the following division of power:

- Direct democracy is best on issues when voters are well informed. We should have referenda on questions regarding values, as well as on other policy questions where the likely outcome of the policy is clear.

- The issues where mistakes are likely to have the most dire consequences should be decided by elected officials like the president or Congress.

- We should rely on nonaccountable officials when we need to protect the interests of minorities. This is often the role of the Supreme Court and other judicial officials. But we also should limit the scope of power for nonaccountable officials (precisely because they are not democratically accountable).

Democracy is hard. Policy making requires lots of specialized knowledge. It's not that the voters can't obtain that specialized knowledge; it's just that it doesn't make sense to expect them to. Adam Smith noted that the heart of capitalism is the division of labor.[14] Just as we have experts bake cakes or repair our cars for us, it makes sense to have experts do policy making for us. But power corrupts, so we need to know who can be trusted. So who should we trust to make policy: the voters, their elected representatives, or unaccountable officials? Representatives and officials have more expertise than voters but can't always be trusted to act in the best interest of voters. In fact, the systems of accountability that we design to incentivize officials can often backfire if they lead to pandering. As a consequence, who should be trusted to making decisions in a democracy depends, and will vary from issue to issue. A constitution is best designed to allocate decision-making power among all three.

MEDIA

There's a lot of hand-wringing in popular discourse these days about facts and truth and what we know. Lots of people are worried about the kinds of things that people believe about vaccines, evolution, or climate change. Much of what we believe comes from the stories that we read in the news. Fake stories about the pope's endorsement of Trump or a child sex trafficking ring at a pizzeria run by Hillary Clinton were widely spread during the 2016 election. One analysis by Buzzfeed found that the twenty most popular fake news stories about the 2016 election on Facebook got more engagement than all but one of the most popular news stories from legitimate websites.[15]

Of course, this isn't a new phenomenon. In 2007 a Rasmussen poll found that 35 percent of Democrats believed that President George W. Bush had foreknowledge of the 9/11 terrorist attacks and chose not to do anything about it. Going back further, anyone who has seen the recent musical knows that Hamilton's political career was ended by sex scandals involving fake stories leaked to the media. Also, the false things that many of us come to believe aren't just political; a recent documentary follows the community of people who believe that the Earth is flat.[16] In some of my own work, I look at how media reports of shark attacks are uncorrelated with the actual number of shark attacks.[17] People's fear of shark attacks depends on the number of shark stories that they read about in the news, but the media coverage of shark attacks depends more on what else is going on in the news cycle rather than the actual threat of sharks.

So if the stories we read in the media can't always be trusted, what can we do instead? At Vassar, one of our mantras is "go to the source," but we cannot all go to every source. A little introspection will reveal that almost everything we believe about the world around us comes from something that someone we trusted told us. Often this person is a teacher or reporter, but sometimes they're a pastor or parent. Even if we come to certain beliefs from personal experience or direct observation, we cannot expect to gain all our knowledge this way. We will see that even our own senses and introspection cannot always be trusted.

Media Bias

The source of information for much of what we know is the news media. Pioneering studies on the economics of news have looked at how newspapers and other news outlets may slant the way they present information.

My favorite example is how the British press treated coverage of two princesses. At different times, both Princess Kate Middleton and Princess Meghan Markle expressed a preference for avocados, but the same newspaper covered that story in very different ways:[18]

KATE AND WILLIAM: Prince William was given one of the green fruit—wrapped up in a bow—by a little boy who's mother is suffering during her pregnancy too . . . "He said he'd take it to [Kate] and see what happens—and said good luck for [the boy's] mummy." *Express*, September 14, 2017

MEGHAN: The pregnant Duchess of Sussex and so-called "avocado on toast whisperer" is wolfing down a fruit linked to water shortages, illegal deforestation and all round general environmental devastation. *Express*, January 23, 2019

Media bias has always been hard to study because we all think that our own point of view is unbiased truth. We tend to think news sources that share our views are unbiased, while everyone else is slanting the truth. Therefore, it is hard to escape the bias of the researchers. However, pioneering text analysis techniques by Groseclose and Milyo,[19] and later by Gentzkow and Shapiro, helped overcome this problem by using statistical models to compare the words used by newspapers to the words used by politicians. The idea was to find the politician that each newspaper sounded the most like. The political biases of members of

Congress are easily measured by looking at their voting history. Because the entire Congressional Record is digitized and downloadable, one could use machine-learning techniques to find the congressperson most similar to each newspaper and use their voting history to classify the paper's political slant. For example, Gentzkow and Shapiro find some of the most "Republican-sounding" phrases from the 2005 Congressional Record are "war on terror" and "death tax," while some of the most "Democrat-sounding" phrases are "estate tax" and "tax break." In this way, they generated a media bias score for any newspaper.

Gentzkow and Shapiro use their media bias scores to test a number of hypotheses about media bias, such as whether newspapers reflect the political biases of their corporate owners (often presumed by liberals to be more conservative) or those of their staff writers (often presumed by conservatives to be more liberal). In fact, they find little evidence for either of those well-known theories. Instead, they find that newspapers cater to the biases of their readers. The political slant of newspapers seems to align with the slant of the city in which they are based. Newspapers are in the business of selling newspapers, and consumers are more likely to buy newspapers that align with their own political predilections.

If there is only one paper in a market, it will tend to target the median. If there are several papers in a market, they will segment the market so that each targets a different portion of the population. The logic is simple: people like reading news that confirms their prior beliefs. Therefore, pandering to those beliefs sells more newspapers.

Part of the reason we tend to buy more newspapers that pander to our beliefs is due to psychological biases that cause us to distrust information that goes against what we believe. In a famous 1979 experiment at Stanford, Lord, Ross, and Lepper presented students with two studies to consider. The studies were invented but the students did not know that. One study supported the idea that the death penalty was an effective deterrent of crime, and the other provided evidence to the contrary.

STUDY A

- Kroner and Phillips (1977) compared murder rates for the year before and the year after adoption of capital punishment in fourteen states. In eleven of the fourteen states, murder rates were lower after adoption of the death penalty. This research supports the deterrent effect of the death penalty.

STUDY B

- Palmer and Crandall (1977) compared murder rates in ten pairs of neighboring states with different capital punishment laws. In eight of the ten pairs, murder rates were higher in the state with capital punishment. This research opposes the deterrent effect of the death penalty.

They then asked students which study was more convincing. They found that death penalty supporters found Study A to be more convincing, while death penalty opponents preferred Study B. Then they swapped the conclusions of the studies just changing two words in each, and showed these two new studies to a different group of students:

STUDY C

- Kroner and Phillips (1977) compared murder rates for the year before and the year after adoption of capital punishment in fourteen states. In eleven of the fourteen states, murder rates were *lower* after adoption of the death penalty. This research *opposes* the deterrent effect of the death penalty.

STUDY D

• Palmer and Crandall (1977) compared murder rates in ten pairs of neighboring states with different capital punishment laws. In eight of the ten pairs, murder rates were *higher* in the state with capital punishment. This research *supports* the deterrent effect of the death penalty.

Studies C and D were exactly the same, except that now the first study found the death penalty to be ineffective while the second study supported the death penalty. Now death penalty supporters preferred Study D, while death penalty opponents preferred Study C.

The conclusion? People trust studies that confirm their prior beliefs. Psychologists call this *confirmation bias*, but economists who study this issue note that it's potentially quite rational to place more trust in news and news sources that confirm what you already know. Economists have developed models of how a news consumer decides which source of news to trust. Consumers are trying to find the news outlet that provides accurate news. Because everyone believes their own view of the world is the correct one, people are more likely to trust news sources that confirm what they already believe. If I believe that 2 + 2 = 4, then I will be likely to distrust any newspaper reporting that 2 + 2 = 5. As a consequence, newspapers are incentivized to bias their reporting toward what their readers want to hear.

Sometimes, this bias is reflected by explicit slanting of the exact same fact, such as the following:

Mr. Smith is winning by over 4 percent in the polls!!!

versus

Mr. Smith is only up by 4 percent in the polls!!!

Or they could be selective in the news they choose to cover. Every day, more news happens than could possibly fit in a single newspaper. A newspaper's job is to decide what is "fit to print," as the *New York Times* motto says. That selection can be (and has shown to be) biased, with some news outlets deliberately omitting news that viewers or readers would not like to know about.[20]

My own work on media coverage looks at how competition affects coverage, specifically, how certain incentives work to encourage outlets to copy the news coverage of others instead of investing the resources necessary to generate breaking news.[21] The literature has always been puzzled at why newspapers expend substantial resources on investigative reporting (potentially leading to "breaking news") when they can wait for someone else to do the work and just join the herd the next day at a fraction of the cost. Joining the herd is also the safer option because reporting news contrary to expectations (as breaking news is likely to be) risks being met with readers' disbelief. However, we hypothesize that readers also place value on being first, and that those who expend the resources to investigate and break news are essentially doing so as a costly sacrifice to demonstrate trustworthiness. Just like trust can be restored by an expensive apology or created through costly initiation rituals, breaking news is a signal of a commitment to the truth, and therefore news outlets that break the news are viewed as more trustworthy.

All of this is magnified by the speed of social media, where we are deluged with stories that tend to increase our confidence in our own opinions. Our natural instinct is that more information should get us closer to the truth, and in our theoretical models, more information can only increase accuracy (or at least do no harm).[22]

But the helpfulness of increased information is subverted when the information is systematically biased. In statistical analysis, we talk about whether an estimator is *consistent*—that is, whether collecting more and more data from the same source will eventually lead to the truth. An *inconsistent* estimator will lead you to a biased view even with more and more data. Much of the information that comes to us from social media is statistically inconsistent because it is filtered in a way that is optimized to increase clicks and readership rather than in a way that maximizes our search for the truth.[23] Even before the advent of social media, marketing researchers looked at the kinds of information people share. Using data as varied as the most e-mailed stories from the *New York Times* and the spread of urban legends, they have found that the stories that we share are not the most factually accurate, and, more important, they are not a random collection of stories that average out to factual accuracy but are systematically biased to favor stories that arouse feelings of awe or anxiety.[24]

While learning about the world from the gossip of others has been around since the gift exchange economies of hunter-gatherer tribes, we have also always relied on experts like media organizations to help us sort out fact from fiction. Game theorists have asked what has happened to trust in these experts as access to a greater number and variety of news outlets has given us more choice about which pundits to trust. One consequence these models point to is increased ideological purity.[25]

Political Correctness and Ideological Purity

So far, we have argued that there are both individual and institutional reasons why people get a biased perception of the news. Even if we pay careful attention to the trustworthiness of our news sources, this attention may itself lead to even more untrustworthy behavior by the news media as they try to win our trust by slanting the news toward our biases.

The spread of fake news has instrumental consequences, which we explore later in this chapter. Misinformation about vaccines and climate change has public health consequences and skews support for public policies. However, this section is about a different consequence of misinformation and polarized news. In the United States and in much of the developed world, there is growing partisan dislike that frays the trust that we have in each other.

Research shows that overconfidence in political beliefs translates into more extreme ideological points of view. In a Pew Research center survey in which Americans were asked to rate how warmly they felt about members of the other political party on a scale from 0 to 100, the warmth they felt toward the other party declined from close to 50 in the 1970s to under 30 in 2016.[26]

The overconfidence that we feel now that we have access to more and more news has been accompanied by an increase in ideological purity in each party. In the past, it was not uncommon to find a pro-life Democrat or a Republican who was pro-environment (note that the Environmental Protection Agency was founded during President Richard Nixon's administration) or in favor of gun control. Politicians held a diverse suite of policy positions that did not necessarily conform to the party line of either party. The diversity of views led to political scientist Keith Krehbiel asking in 1993, "Where's the party?" because in his statistical analysis of congressional voting data, politicians mostly voted according to their own idiosyncratic policy positions rather than according to what the party would dictate.[27]

Now political parties have become increasingly polarized, so that to be a Democrat, you have to be pro-choice and in favor of gun control, and to be a Republican, you must be pro-life and opposed to gun control.[28] The same drivers that impel us to trust only the news that conforms to our biases also drives us to trust only those people who conform to our beliefs.

The mathematical model that prompted me to become a game theorist was a model of political correctness developed by Steven Morris. Morris's model is based on the idea that we learn from each other and that most of us have a genuine desire to be helpful to others in our social group. As a consequence, we want to be someone others trust when they need advice. However, there are some people who give us bad advice that we shouldn't trust, either because they have bad intentions or because their values are different from ours. At the same time sometimes the advice we need confirms what we want to hear, but sometimes we need advice that goes against our own inclinations. If that advice is coming from a trusted source, then that advice is helpful, but if the advice is coming from someone with different values, then it may be best to ignore it.[29] Morris's model shows that if we want to be trusted by the people whom we genuinely want to help, we should ignore the truth and just tell people what they want to hear in matters of low importance in order to build up trust—so that in matters of great importance, we can tell them the truth and give them the advice that they need to hear.

This model was developed in a time before social media; in fact, it was written at a time when the Internet was barely a thing. But it offers insight into how political correctness might evolve as key parameters in the model evolve. In an era in which our social connections are publicly exposed for all to see, and we have so many more low-stakes opportunities to demonstrate trustworthiness, the model predicts an increase in political correctness. An increase in confidence regarding our own opinions would have the same effect. Social media exposes us to more and more stories designed to confirm our existing beliefs that make us more and more confident. If we are more confident about what we believe, then we are less likely to trust someone who tells us something that contradicts our beliefs. That increases the incentive to conform. If saying what is seen as the wrong thing gets you labeled as someone not to be trusted for having bad values, then we have extra incentive to only say the "right thing."

However, while social media exacerbates the tendency to only be exposed to information that confirms your own prejudices, those that control social media platforms have the power to alter their technology to better curate the stories that we see. This is especially relevant now that social media has become a primary source of news (which it is for those aged eighteen to twenty-nine years old, according to Pew).[30] For most of their existence, platforms like Twitter and Facebook have used algorithms to maximize the time we spend on their sites, as that increases their advertising revenues. However, recent public pressure has forced these companies to consider using their algorithms for other goals, such as suppressing fake news while building mutual trust.

Facebook and other platforms are experimenting with showing people trust ratings of the news sources that produced the articles they see in their news feed, allowing the platform to determine the trustworthiness of a news source and circumventing the game that news outlets play to pander to their readers. Of course, this creates a metaproblem: it requires people to trust the algorithm that Facebook uses to assess trustworthiness.[31]

Research shows how the structure of the network affects the spread of fake versus accurate news.[32] Specifically, researchers at MIT asked whether you should see more news in your feed from close friends or distant friends. This kind of research is especially important given privacy concerns. Platforms like WhatsApp encrypt all transmissions, making it impossible for the platform to tell what kinds of messages are sent. Therefore even if WhatsApp (which now is owned by Facebook) wanted to assess the trustworthiness of the information being transmitted and filter the fake news from the real, it couldn't. However, the researchers found that just by changing the structure of the network—the web of people with whom you connect and communicate—it can diversify your media diet in a way that inhibits the spread of false or dangerous information.

For better or worse, social media has changed the curation of the news and information that we are exposed to. We have seen how this could be for the worse. Repeated exposure to the same biased information can make us overconfident about our own partisan biases and less trusting of those who disagree. Social media can become an echo chamber where ideas spread like a contagion. Models of how information spreads show that it may be rational for people to spread an idea just because they saw a couple of other people endorse it, even if their own judgment suggests that it is bad. People suppress their own opinion to go along with the herd.[33]

However, social media gives designers and regulators more control over the information we see. Whereas before, we learned about the world through gossip, now it happens through the algorithm. While algorithmic curation of gossip could have negative consequences, it also creates an opportunity to create better systems for disseminating news and improving our trust in the news we see.

TRUSTING MEDICINE

Of all the experts in our lives, perhaps the ones we need to trust the most are our doctors. It's not that big a deal if an inaccurate Yelp review leads you to dine at the wrong restaurant. As Sherlock Holmes famously said, knowing that the Earth revolves around the Sun (as opposed to the reverse) is unlikely to ever matter in your life, so it is fine to forget it or get the answer wrong. Even fake political news has surprisingly little impact on how we vote.[34] However, not trusting your doctor or getting the wrong medical advice can literally kill you.

There are, of course, good reasons for us not to trust medical experts. First, the science of medicine (like all science) is a work in progress. The headlines that we see on what is safe to eat and what isn't keeps changing. Eggs will kill you; eggs will save you. Fat is bad; fat is good. Coffee is bad; coffee is good . . . John Ioannidis and his co-authors chose a collection of common foods like wine, tomatoes, tea, eggs, coffee, etc and identified dozens of studies saying each will kill you and dozens of studies saying each will prolong your life.[35]

In this section, we consider the features of medicine and its history that make trust in doctors and in the medical profession a cause for concern. We also lay out the economic evidence for the importance of trust in the medical system because trust has been found to cause better health outcomes. Note that I used the word "cause" and not a weaker expression like "be associated with." As always, we should be mindful that correlation is not causation, and it is possible that causation runs the other way: instead of trust causing better outcomes, it is possible that healthier patients are more trusting. Economists, however, have carefully worked to tease these associations apart and argue that it is indeed changes in trust that caused changes in health outcomes and not the reverse. We noted at the beginning of this chapter that people who have a great deal of confidence in the medical profession has declined from 73 percent in 1966 to 34 percent today.[36] Researchers have identified the importance of trust in the delivery of quality healthcare but have fewer answers to the question of why trust is declining and what to do about it.

Why Trust in Medicine Matters

Why does trust matter? It is in part because we have an incredible amount of autonomy when it comes to our medical decisions. When a doctor prescribes a medication or a diet and exercise regimen, it's up to us to follow through with it. We have to obtain the medication and use it as prescribed. We have to cook healthy meals and drag ourselves to the gym. Estimates suggest that we comply with prescribed medication only 50 to 75 percent of the time. It has been estimated that if patients properly complied with medical advice, the U.S. healthcare system could save between $100 billion and $300 billion per year (or 3 to 10 percent of healthcare costs).[37]

Further, if we don't like the recommendation of one doctor, we can see another—as many as we want, in fact. Generally, getting a second opinion is good: more information typically leads to more accurate information and better decisions. But having more information can be bad if the information that we get or the way that we process information is systematically biased. In the medical context, this suggests that patients may seek out doctors who say what they, the patients, want to hear, instead of doctors who provide the best information. The ultimate example is a new kind of web platform that will match you to a doctor that will prescribe you whatever you want (at least in the context of birth control or erectile dysfunction). You choose a drug, and they find a doctor willing to prescribe it.[38]

Patients now have the Internet, WebMD, Facebook groups and chat boards, Twitter, and Instagram—each offering a range of options and opinions. Instead of picking and choosing based on statistics or data and aggregating all that information in a rational way, we tend to be drawn to the stories that make the most sense to us. We gravitate to opinions that support our hopes or allay our fears.

The ability of patients to seek out doctors who will cater to them—and the corresponding incentive for doctors to cater to patients—have been identified as contributing to the opioid epidemic.[39] Drug overdoses have more than doubled in recent decades, making accidental drug overdose the number one cause of death for those under fifty years old.[40] While addicts may eventually turn to illegal drugs, many opioid addictions began with the overprescription of painkillers.

Trust becomes even more crucial in the case of vaccinations, which are essentially treatments for diseases that people don't have yet. At least when it is one's own health at stake and the malady is immediate, patients have incentives to follow through with the best treatment even if their biases sometimes get in the way. Getting properly vaccinated is a harder case because the illness that you are trying to avert is only a potential outcome and because the benefits of vaccination often go to other people, not necessarily just the person being vaccinated. Part of the importance of vaccine programs is that when enough people in a population are vaccinated, the population develops what is known as "herd immunity." Herd immunity means that enough people in the population are immune that those who are unable to get vaccinated, like babies who are too young and people who are too sick already to get vaccines themselves, are protected because they are unlikely to encounter anyone else who carries the disease. Therefore, vaccines have the most impact when everyone (or nearly everyone) complies with the recommended vaccination schedule. In order for people to comply, they have to trust not just the safety and efficacy of the vaccine, but also the intentions of the government implementing the vaccination program.

Population-level vaccination has been one of the most successful public policies of any kind. They continue to save 2–3 million lives every year.[41] But all too often, community vaccination programs have been met with distrust. One of the very first vaccination techniques was variolation, the practice of taking pus from someone infected with smallpox and smearing it on the scratched skin of an uninfected person. Variolation was first practiced in Asia and was brought to the West by an eighteenth-century English aristocrat named Mary Wortley Montagu. Upon returning to England from Turkey, where variolation was commonly practiced, Montagu attempted to convince her fellow citizens to adopt the method. But even when she used the process on herself and her son—surely a costly signal of trustworthiness—she couldn't get others to try it.[42]

More recently, in the United States, we have seen renewed outbreaks of measles, a potentially deadly and highly communicable disease that should be entirely preventable. Some parents have stopped vaccinating their children for fear of (among other things) a nonexistent link between vaccines and autism. (Scientists are quite sure that there is no link between vaccines and autism, but one retracted study, published in the *Lancet* in 1998, has put that idea into the world in a way that has proved impossible to get out.) Part of the problem has been the success of the vaccination program. Cases of measles have been so rare in recent decades that it is difficult for parents to see the benefit of vaccination, particularly in this time of increasing general distrust.

The resurgence of measles in the United States is sadly just one of many cases of distrust in medicine worsening the impact of epidemics. South African president Thabo Mbeki famously did not believe that the human immunodeficiency virus (HIV) causes AIDS, which impeded prevention efforts in that country. During a recent Ebola outbreak in the Democratic Republic of Congo, treatment was impeded by a lack of trust in the intentions of public health officials.[43]

Sadly, some of this distrust for public health officials may be warranted. In the 1970s, India implemented a forced sterilization program that helped sow the seeds of distrust toward public health vaccination programs, distrust that persists to this day[44] More recently, the Central Intelligence Agency (CIA) was able to track down Osama bin Laden, the international terrorist and mastermind of the 9/11 attacks, in Pakistan under the pretense of running a vaccination program. Claiming to be public health workers distributing a hepatitis B vaccine, CIA agents visited households in Pakistan and drew blood samples from residents. Their true purpose was to identify relatives of bin Laden using DNA testing. Partly as a consequence, polio rates, which had been decreasing in Pakistan, started to increase in 2017.[45]

Medicine is a field that often defies simple explanations. Every person's body responds to pain, disease, medication, and treatment differently. Diagnoses are uncertain and treatments are not guaranteed to work. When there is uncertainty about the effect of somebody else's actions, those are precisely the kinds of circumstances in which trust is required.

A former colleague of mine, Bob Frank, who suffered a life-threatening heart attack despite having none of the risk factors associated with cardiac arrest, survived and went on to write a book about luck. The idea that motivated his book was that the people who are most likely to die of a heart attack are the ones who have no risk factors.[46] Healthy behaviors increase your odds of avoiding a first heart attack, but if you actually have a first heart attack, those with the fewest risk factors are the most likely to die, perhaps because healthy people have heart attacks later in life. But the idea that motivated my friend's book was that no matter what we do to take care of our health, luck still plays a huge role in deciding who lives and who dies. In the economic model of trust, the need for trust is directly proportional to risk. Trust matters so much on questions of health because the uncertainty is so great and the consequence is potentially life or death.

That uncertainty creates more room for our biases to sow distrust and more room for our minds to tell stories and invent explanations around what went wrong. Trust is a belief, and the beliefs that we form *about* our health turn out to have significant impacts *on* our health. Recent work also shows that an amazing amount of our health happens in our minds. This is true in terms of how we experience pain, how we respond to placebos, and other phenomena.[47]

Experiments in which people were asked to hold their hand in a bucket of ice water for as long as they could show that they can do so longer and with less pain when given a pill with an expensive $2.50 price tag over one with a ten-cent price tag.[48] Both pills were the same; both were made of sugar. (In fact, other research by a coauthor of mine shows that subjects can hold their hand in ice longer if they are just thinking about money.)[49] Placebos are surprisingly effective at treating symptoms of illness: not only do patients improve when given a placebo, but placebos cause actual physiological and chemical changes in the body that we can measure.[50]

One remarkable recent Harvard study showed that placebos can work even if the patient *knows* it's just a sugar pill, so long as the doctor and patient form a strong rapport. In the study, the placebo worked to treat even debilitating diseases like irritable bowel syndrome—all while the patient knew that the pill was a placebo.[51] The researchers argued that a strong patient-doctor relationship is what drives the placebo effect. Trusting your doctor can make you better, even if the doctor does nothing at all except talk to you and give you a sugar pill.

Restoring Lost Trust

Because trust is so important to our health, it is especially important to restore trust when trust is broken. While general distrust of medicine has tracked with distrust of other fields, there are reasons for distrust that are specific to medicine and need to be addressed.

Investigations have shown that different medical professionals will prescribe different treatments for different people with the same symptoms. One particularly egregious example was a dentist under investigation for fraud who was performing root canals on 90 percent of his patients with crowns. A typical dentist does this for 3 to 7 percent of patients.[52] But while that example is extreme, large-scale analysis of medical practitioners finds similar variability across the country, where the same patient may receive very different medical recommendations depending on which doctor they happen to see.[53]

In one of the most personally invested experiments I have seen, a group of researchers sent the same test patient to see 180 different dentists. Given that the patient was the same and generally had healthy teeth, you would expect the same treatment would be recommended. Instead the authors found that 28 percent of the dentists recommended treatments the patient did not need, with more overtreatment when the dentist was underbooked or when the patient presented as lower income[54]. (My former colleague, Henry Schneider, did a similar study with auto mechanics and found similar levels of unreliability.[55])

Sometimes the betrayals of trust have been so severe, their harm persists even decades later. A recurring topic on the question of trust in medicine is the Tuskegee Study of Untreated Syphilis in the Negro Male. It was a study conducted by the U.S. government between 1932 and 1972 in which 399 Black male patients who had contracted syphilis before joining the study were left untreated for decades, even though the medical profession knew by 1947 that penicillin could cure the disease. Of course, medical experiments are necessary for medical science to progress, but the study violated the principle of informed consent and withheld treatment after a cure was known. One recent study from 2016 finds that there was a substantial increase in distrust of medicine by Blacks after 1972, the same year that the details of the experiment were revealed. This distrust led to a 1.4-year decline in life expectancy for older Black men due to patients not following medical advice or not seeking enough preventative care.[56]

One consequence of how our trust evolved from the Dunbar number tribes to religions and nation-states is that our institutions sometimes generate the trust of your in-group at the expense of the out-group. We are more likely to trust those who are similar to us because similarity implies shared values, and we use the threat of ejection from the in-group to enforce group norms. Recent experiments have shown that Black patients have worse health outcomes when treated by a white doctor than by a Black doctor. The cause in this case wasn't that the white doctors provided worse care (although there is evidence of this as well),[57] but that the Black patients were less likely to comply with medical advice from a doctor whom they were less likely to trust. However, the solution to this problem shouldn't be to assign

Black patients to Black doctors we need to do a better job build-ing trust regardless of race.[58]

Given the decline in trust and the importance of trust, what can we do about it? My own research looks into the role of apol-ogy in restoring trust, at least on a small scale. Two of my papers examine the effects of trust on medical malpractice litigation. There is a vicious cycle in medicine when it comes to mistakes and bad outcomes. In patient surveys, the most common reason that patients give for suing their doctor is anger, and that anger might have been assuaged by an apology from the doctor—an apology that they never received. However, doctors are often afraid to apologize for fear that implicitly or explicitly admitting fault will increase the likelihood that they will be sued. That reluctance increases patient anger, which in turn heightens the threat of lawsuits.

To combat this problem, thirty-six states (at the time of the study in 2009) had passed laws prohibiting apologies from being used as evidence in court for cases of medical malpractice. The idea was so successful that in 2005, two junior senators named Hillary Clinton and Barack Obama tried getting federal apology legislation passed—but unfortunately, at that time they lacked the clout to make it happen.[59]

While encouraging apologies seems like a good idea, they can backfire. An act signals trustworthiness in proportion to how costly it was. Part of the cost that a doctor faces when they apologize is the implied threat of a lawsuit. These apology laws reduce the cost that the doctor faces, devaluing the apology. Even if these laws make apologies to patients more common, we might wonder whether they do anything to improve the doctor-patient relationship.

My research has found that these apologies do improve the relationship. By analyzing the database of medical malpractice litigation maintained by the federal government, my coauthor, Elaine Liu, and I found that apologies speed up settlements by 19 to 20 percent and reduce the dollar value of lawsuits by tens of thousands of dollars (the precise amount depends on the severity of the injury).

More generally, many have argued recently that the key to trust in the field of medicine is transparency. For example, the Sunshine Act provision of the Affordable Care Act, passed during the Obama administration, has required increased disclosure by doctors of payments received from pharmaceutical companies. Distrust breeds where information is lacking. Other research on apologies shows that the main reason that apologies matter in medicine is that they open a channel of communication between doctor and patient. Patients often feel left in the dark, and an apology is the beginning of a conversation that helps both sides understand one another. When people are denied information, they often assume the worst.

While apologies seem to work to restore individual violations of trust, what can we do to restore trust to the institution of medicine as a whole? Because distrust breeds in uncertainty, maybe more information can help mend things.

One of my favorite books of all time is by a fellow economist, Emily Oster, whose book about pregnancy, *Expecting Better*, advocates for a different kind of relationship between patient and healthcare provider. She focuses on the case of pregnant women, although I think that her book contains lessons for healthcare more broadly. (Her follow-up book, *Cribsheet*, does the same for the project of raising small children.) As a pregnant mother-to-be herself, she found that many of the dictums associated with pregnancy are handed down as rules rather than as informed choices: No coffee. No alcohol. No fish. No deli meats. Her book provides the data that those recommendations are based on and lets the patient decide for herself. This approach has been met with resistance, but it is a kind of transparency and openness that may have merit. More and more doctors do seem to favor this more open, patient-centric approach. However, the downside of returning so much decision-making authority to the patient is that we see doctors for a reason: they know a lot more than we do about health and medicine. The solution can't be to transfer all decision-making power to the patient. Instead, the solution needs to be to find a way for patients to facilitate communication and strengthen the patient-doctor relationship so that the best medical decisions can be made jointly.

SCIENCE

Examples of bad science abound. Some of these are pushed by activists who selectively choose research to support a particular agenda. Examples include belief in the health benefits of organic foods (they aren't healthier than nonorganically grown foods), concern about the dangers of genetically modified foods (they aren't dangerous), the denial of climate change (it's real), and the belief that vaccines cause autism (they don't).[60]

There have been genuine mistakes by the scientific community, including the claim that low-fat diets are healthy (calories seem to matter more, and carbohydrates may be more worrisome than fats) and the claim that diets high in cholesterol increase cholesterol levels in the blood (they don't).[61]

We hold many misconceptions too about scientific facts, so maybe it is good to question our trust in what we know. Sometimes we believe things simply because they fit our preexisting narratives (e.g., that corporations are evil): for instance, that silicone breast implants are more dangerous than saline (they aren't).[62] Sometimes we believe bad science that our mothers told us, like how we should drink eight glasses of water a day (that's not necessary).[63]

We distrust science for so many reasons. This is in large part because science is hard. There is so much about the world that we can never know for ourselves.

I suspect that if you are reading this book, you do genuinely care about science, and yet I bet that if you did a serious inventory of what you believe, you'd find that a lot of things you believe to be true are not. (Did any of the examples I listed above surprise you? You don't have to just trust me though, feel free to follow up with the citations in the notes if they did. You can and should question everything you read especially when it comes to scientific studies.)

It is easy to believe untrue scientific or scientific-sounding claims because distrust of science typically has few consequences for our daily lives. Moreover, much of how the world works is simply unknown. Science even suggests that some questions are in fact not answerable.

Trust in Science

While trust in science has not declined in recent decades in the same way that trust in medicine or the media has, only 44 percent of Americans surveyed had a "great deal of confidence" in the scientific community. Some distrust might be justified by science itself discovering that science is less reliable than we thought. Those who follow science news probably will have come across articles about the so-called replication crisis, which has emerged in recent years. We are starting to better appreciate that many if not most scientific studies (even those published in the most prestigious journals using the most rigorous methods) cannot be replicated. A number of prominent research groups have taken highly cited research from a given field in a given year—fields like psychology or economics or medicine—and arranged to have a new set of researchers replicate the original results. Large numbers of these replications have failed: two-thirds in psychology, one-third in experimental economics, and more than three-quarters (of pre-clinical cancer studies) in medicine.[64]

Moreover, this project was limited to highly cited studies published in the most reputable journals. As an academic, I get e-mail spam nearly every day from some new journal that sounds real because its "editors" have taken the names of real journals and scrambled up the words. For example, two of the most prestigious journals in economics are the *Quarterly Journal of Economics* and the *American Economic Review*. These predatory journals will have names like the *Quarterly Economic Journal* or the *American Review of Economics*. These journals will literally publish anything for a fee. A number of studies have sent intentionally bad papers to dozens of journals—some of these bad papers were literally just gibberish—and nearly all of them were accepted for publication. To an unsuspecting public looking for research that says what they want to hear, these journals can provide respectable-sounding evidence to back up any claim.

The failure to replicate much scientific research doesn't mean something is wrong with science, per se—this is just the way that scientific progress works. While science narratives often tell a simple story of progress, actual scientific research proceeds in stops and starts, dead ends and reassessments, trial and error, two steps forward and one step back. That's the way it has always worked. Of course, we could do better, and there are some important and interesting reforms being proposed to improve replication rates and reliability.[65] But there must be a balance between the understandable desire to wait for certainty and the need to move forward with what we know. Many terminally ill patients would love access to a potentially life-saving experimental drug, even if it might not work.

This problem is often exacerbated by science journalism. Headlines need to be attention-grabbing, and they leave little room for uncertainty and nuance. While the researchers themselves might have included all of their own doubts and uncertainties about their results in the academic journal article, that part of the message gets lost when it is transmitted to the public.

Even without the replication crisis, part of the problem is that understanding science is hard, and it may not always be worth our time to do so. Lots of basic science questions continue to bewilder me, like how exactly a child's movements on a swing cause the swing and child to move back and forth, and I will admit that I was a grown adult before I knew how a sailboat sails into the wind. As a result, we are drawn to oversimplified stories about how the world works that follow easy patterns, have fun surprises, or cater to our preexisting biases.[66]

There are many reasons why so many scientific results, even those published in top journals, have proven to be so tenuous. First, journals have a bias toward publishing things that are surprising but also plausible. Second, there is the "desk drawer effect"—due to publication biases, many valid studies that do not find a relation between two things (say, coffee and cancer) don't get published; they get left in the desk drawer. Therefore, there might be five published studies saying that coffee causes cancer, but fifty desk-drawered (i.e., never-published) ones saying that it doesn't. Third, correlation is not causation. Teasing out the differences between correlation and causation has been the driving force in economic research over the past two decades. Statistics can only ever tell us that two things are correlated. Maybe drinking coffee is associated with higher rates of cancer, but there are always four possibilities that we need to consider when we find a correlation:

- Maybe coffee caused the cancer.
- Maybe being prone to getting cancer makes us crave coffee.
- Maybe some third factor, like the city we live in, makes us both drink coffee and get cancer.
- Maybe the correlation is spurious.

Fourth, the nature of statistics means that sometimes we get spurious correlations or false positives. Using a p-value of 0.05, which has been the convention in scientific research, means that for every twenty statistical tests you run, one of them (more or less) will be a false positive.[67] Because any one study will often involve dozens of statistical tests, any given paper will likely have some false positives. And because journals tend to publish only positive results, it becomes more likely that the studies that make it into journals are the false ones.

Finally, and related to the false positive problem, is the problem that research is expensive, and too many studies are done on only (say) twenty-two monkeys in a lab. When the number of observations you have is small, it becomes harder to get reliable conclusions. For especially "noisy" environments, the number of observations you need can be quite large. For one of my studies, we had over 1.5 million subjects, and even then we were only barely able to identify patterns in the data.

I think it is important to note that all the factors that lead to false results being published are systemic, not related to bad motives of any of the participants involved. It has become commonplace to question the motives of scientists who receive financial support for their research but nearly every scientist

I have ever met all seem to be operating in good faith at least as far as I can tell.

The fact that we often do question the intentions of scientists is another systemic problem that impedes scientific inquiry. For example, Morris's influential paper on political correctness,[68] discussed in the section entitled "Media Bias" earlier in this chapter, applies here as well. The Morris model illustrates one argument against political correctness. Because some ideas are associated with noxious people, when good people discover some truths that noxious people like, they have incentive to hide that discovery because they want to preserve their reputation as a good person in order to have influence in the future for issues that matter more to them. This means that society will produce less knowledge than in a world where we didn't use the content of scientific knowledge to determine whom to trust. This is not just political correctness in the conventional sense; it also applies to the practice of selectively publishing science that follows what is acceptable in the community. Scientists who make a discovery suggesting that climate change may not be so bad or that vaping isn't so dangerous may be reluctant to publish their work for fear of being labeled a climate denier or a tobacco industry shill.

These reputational concerns that Morris identifies tends to create more conformity. We know from the replication crisis that much of the science that is produced is wrong (at least at first). Therefore, it is useful to expand the voices that we hear from within science in order to give more weight to diverse sources that did not come from the usual channels (see the discussion of Scott Page's work in chapter 2) and to be more accepting of dissenting views.

There are other reasons why scientists may be censoring what they choose to publish. In a first best ideal world, like the one in Morris' model, we would be better off if all scientists published all of their findings. However, in economics, we often ask what we should do in a second-best world, one that has inefficiencies that we can't easily correct. What if information could be misused? We should try to correct our institutions to make sure that information is not misused, but until then, maybe we should censor the kind of information that we produce. Also, sometimes it makes sense to trust the wisdom of the crowd. If I find a result that goes against what everyone else thinks, maybe that's just because I'm wrong. In an ideal world, scientists would publish all the information we discover and let the community decide which studies to trust, but in a world where people cherry-pick the scientific studies on which they choose to rely, maybe it is better to be cautious about what gets published.

Fundamental Unknowability

Three of the most beautiful theorems in math were all discovered in the first half of the twentieth century. They point to how the universe will always fundamentally be a mystery. While they may arguably be too abstract to be of any practical significance, I think that they serve as a useful reminder of the limits to what we know and the fundamental uncertainty in our world. That uncertainty is where we find the need for trust.

Kurt Gödel was a mathematician who grappled with the question of the completeness of mathematics. He wanted to know if our system of mathematics was sound. We all have learned math, but is what we learned correct? We feel that it is, but can we prove it? Gödel set out to show that it was. Instead, he proved that any system of arithmetic was fundamentally *incomplete*—that in any system of arithmetic that you can devise, there will be true statements that cannot be proved. Furthermore, no system of arithmetic could ever prove its own internal consistency. If even basic arithmetic is incomplete, then that leaves little hope for finding a complete system of mathematics, much less all knowledge.[69]

In a similar vein, Alan Turing, known as the father of computer science, showed that there will always be computational questions that no computer could ever solve. And in economics, Kenneth Arrow showed that in any voting system that a democracy could devise, there will be some fundamental flaw.

Again, one could argue that in practical terms, these theorems don't really matter. That arithmetic works for all our needs. That computers work. That even democracy works, more or less.

The flaws in modern democracies are often not related to the mechanical problem of how to count votes that Arrow grappled with. Modern democracies rest on adherence to norms and on trust, so that the actual vote counting itself is of only secondary import.

Still, I do think that these theorems are beautiful for their reminder that the universe is and will forever be a mystery. There will be truths that will never be known. And this is a good reminder for us to be humble in our certainties.

A good reminder to be careful about the knowledge in which we trust.

CLIMATE CHANGE

Every year since 1995, the United Nations has convened a meeting where the leaders of the world gather to discuss climate change. These meetings are known as the Conference of the Parties (COP), and I was lucky enough to attend COP15 in Copenhagen as a civil society observer and part of the delegation from Cornell University. I was overwhelmed by the chaos and amazed that anything gets done.

In addition to 120 heads of state and thousands of negotiators, there were tens of thousands of reporters, researchers, activists, academics, bureaucrats, and other government officials. There were so many people that it sometimes took five or more hours to get to the front of the security lines at the entrance to the convention center. I sat in on a small session given by Nobel Peace Prize winner Leyman Gbowee, wandered by California governor Arnold Schwarzenegger in the warren of U.S. office space, discussed my research at an academic seminar, attended a rally led by Bishop Desmond Tutu, chatted with Google engineers trying to save the world using Google Maps, and sat at a conference table next to activists dressed as aliens getting a briefing by the lead U.S. negotiators.

What struck me the most were the negotiations themselves. The goal of the conference was to draft a resolution, a document that ideally all the countries of the world could sign. Ad hoc print shops around the convention center would print out vast copies of the book-length resolutions as negotiators argued over their content. On the final night, a thousand negotiators met in the main convention room, trying to work out the final details. I stayed as long as I could before leaving in the wee hours to get to the airport to catch my flight. The negotiators were still at it.

The part that surprised me the most was how different this all looked from the mathematical game theory models of political negotiations that I studied as a student. The default assumption in economics and game theory is that all we care about is the outcome of the game, as measured by its costs and its benefits. In the case of the environment, the economic model of costs and benefits presumes that it is a negotiation about who pays the costs (in the form of tax distortions and cuts in fossil fuels and changes in land use and agriculture) so that we can all enjoy the benefits of a cleaner environment.

I would have thought that the negotiations primarily would have been about who should bear the costs of cutting greenhouse gas emissions so that we all may benefit. I would have expected some discussion about how those countries who benefit the most should pay the most. And for sure, this was a big part of the negotiations. China led a coalition of less-developed countries to argue that the rich countries have benefited the most from a history of greenhouse gas emissions, and therefore they should bear more of the costs. One argument under negotiation held that rich countries should pay into a fund that would go to developing countries to help pay for the latter to engage in more environmentally friendly practices.

However, that felt like a relatively small part of the negotiations. A bigger part of the debates and the edits was about procedure and about who had the right to be recognized. At times, it felt like negotiators cared more about the legitimacy of the process than the outcome of the process.

On a similar note, I was also struck by how important the smaller, face-to-face meetings were. Even though the big talks happened in large rooms with a thousand people, I got the feeling that the most important conversations were happening among just a few countries and a handful of people. One-on-one relationships seemed to play an outsize role in this discussion about a policy that will affect billions of people—both those currently alive and those yet to be born.

The Ultimate Game of Trust

The scope of the climate problem is immense. Rising sea levels means that more cities will have to look like Amsterdam and New Orleans, which hold off the oceans using billion-dollar seawalls. Storms like Superstorm Sandy and Hurricane Katrina will become more frequent and more damaging. Greater variance in weather means more flooding and more drought. Lower crop yields means higher food prices. Increased scarcity could lead to more refugees and more international conflicts, more tropical diseases, more ecosystem losses, more species extinctions. William Nordhaus recently received the Nobel Memorial Prize in Economic Sciences for estimating the costs of climate change that we can quantify, finding that damages could exceed 3 percent of world gross domestic product (GDP) by 2100, which would equal trillions of dollars.[70]

Climate change is the ultimate example of the tragedy of the commons that we have been discussing throughout this book. Not only are the stakes higher, as the fate of the planet is on the line, but the scope of trust required is on an even greater scale. Each person is making decisions that affect not just their communities but everyone in the world. In fact, it's worse than that: we are all making choices that affect the lives of those yet to be born. Even crazier, we are making choices that affect the lives of people who may or may not ever be born. There is both a spatial component and a temporal component to the tragedy of the commons.

We began this book talking about how trust developed in small, premodern tribes, in communities whose size was limited by the number of people whom each member could personally trust (around 150, Dunbar's number). Now we are talking about a problem that involves not only trusting all of the billions of people in the world today, but also trusting the countless billions yet to be born.

Chapter 2 of this book offers some optimism about how this might happen. We saw from Elinor Ostrom's research, on how small villages deal with local environmental challenges, that humans can develop rules and norms and institutions to protect shared natural resources. We saw from the development of religions how systems of beliefs can be built to take the personal trust that we have for those in our local community and extend that same trust to a much larger religious one. We saw how markets require trust and how merchants came to trust third-party judges and legal rules to help enforce contracts. Then in chapters 3 and 4 we discussed how this trust in abstract rules developed into a general trust for the rule of law, and we saw how this abstract trust developed into the complicated, multifaceted global institutions of our modern economy, from money and banking to science and medicine.

Having trust transcend species and generations to deal with the problem of climate change seems less daunting, given the long historical trend of ever-increasing circles of trust. In-group cohesion has long been enhanced by having an out-group threat, and climate change could serve as that external threat.

Of course, there is a vast gulf between the small groups of 150 that humans were evolved to trust and a problem of global and intertemporal scope like climate change. Game theory and behavioral economics can help explain the difficulties that need to be overcome:

1. The long shadow of the future
2. Social distance
3. Inattention to slow changes

Game theory notes that trust can be maintained in repeated games, but such trust is enforced by the "long shadow of the future."[71] That is, I may be able to trust you now because I expect you to return the favor in the future. This requires patience, as

I may have to suppress temptations today in the hopes that my good behavior will induce others to behave similarly in the future. This is hard enough on the small scale, where we find evidence of impatience everywhere. In experiments, we are willing to forgo a hundred-dollar payout in a week's time for just fifty dollars today. We have difficulty resisting the temptation of dessert or making our way to the gym. We don't save enough for retirement. When it comes to climate change, the timescale makes the problem of patience even harder. We won't even see the bulk of the benefits of our actions today in our own lifetimes.

A second problem of climate change is social distance. Experimental studies found that our altruism depends on social distance—we are more altruistic toward those who are close to us and less altruistic toward those who are more distant.[72] This makes sense in evolutionary terms because it improves the chances of survival of those who share more of our genes. But our genes were not evolved for a time when the scope of human civilization has expanded to billions. Therefore, I don't think it would be surprising to anybody that our degree of altruism is highest for near-relations and lowest for strangers. In lab experiments, subjects are given a small windfall (say, twenty dollars) and asked to divide it between themselves and another person. We are most likely to share with our immediate family and become less likely to share when the other person is a friend, and we are still less likely to share when the other person is another random student. The likelihood drops again when the person is from a different town, and again when they are from another country. The effect is true not just for people with different geographies, but also across demographics. We tend to be most likely to share with people we think are similar to us. This is a problem given that the victims of climate change will be concentrated near the equator, and those most at risk are people in developing countries, far from the rich nations with the resources to deal with the problem.

A third reason that climate change is difficult to fathom is that we have evolved to be attentive to change. This is true in a variety of contexts. We care more about having more money than our neighbors than about our absolute level of wealth.[73] Our happiness depends more on receiving income increases than on our absolute level of income.[74] People get scared about a sudden crime wave even if the absolute level of crime has fallen. They fear for their children when they hear about a child abduction even though our children today are safer than ever. The climate is something that changes slowly, and when it does change, we adapt quickly.

One clever study of social media finds that we remark upon unusual weather patterns by posting about them on Twitter, but after a year or two, we no longer find those unusual weather patterns tweet-worthy.[75] In my own research looking at how people adjust their thermostats, I find that people respond to warmer weather outside by setting a warmer temperature for inside their homes. People respond to change by getting used to it and then forgetting about it. The climate is changing, but at a slow enough pace that, at least in our daily lives, we adjust to it and then forget about it. The best way to boil a frog is to put the frog in while the water is cool and slowly raise the heat.

These days, environmentalists and activists are well aware of these problems: that climate requires patience, that climate involves people who are far apart, and that climate changes too slowly to notice. There has been a concerted effort to rebrand climate change to counteract these problems. Headlines point to the impacts of climate change on people in our communities today and play up the more dramatic effects of the phenomenon, like hurricanes, even though the slower changes are likely to be more costly. Environmentalists have attempted to rebrand climate change, but marketing and image management can go only so far, especially because attempts to emphasize and exaggerate the effects that we see today can sow distrust when people notice the exaggerations.

Norms and attitudes do shift, often thanks to the work of activists who change our perceptions.[76] But these days, trustworthy behavior is more often maintained by the rule of law. Part of the reason why most of us don't steal from each other is voluntary adherence to norms of behavior, but possibly the more proximate reason is concern about getting thrown in jail. We have international institutions like the United Nations to enforce law on issues of international scope, so why not try that?

Trust and the Paris Climate Accords

Every international treaty is ultimately an act of trust. We saw how governments enforce agreements and contracts by maintaining a monopoly on violence. Governments use the authority that comes from having control of law enforcement to mete out punishment for noncompliance. This works so long as the government has the support of the people, but it can also work without that support if the government can use its control of the military and law enforcement to suppress dissent. There is no one who can enforce international agreements, so it is necessary to rely on more old-fashioned methods—the methods employed by the hunter-gatherers we discussed at the beginning of this book.

If we can think of the 193 countries in the United Nations as 193 distinct individuals, then that is not too far from the Dunbar number. Then we can rely on the same kinds of mechanisms that small villages used to maintain cooperation to ensure that countries honor their agreements.

When countries agree on a treaty, which is essentially a contract, there is no authority that can enforce the contract. There is no overarching power that can force each party to comply with its terms. However, there are international judges who, though they have no direct authority, can earn the trust of agents just like the judges were trusted in medieval Champagne. The judge can order sanctions for noncompliance, and those sanctions would have to be imposed and enforced by the 193 other member-nations. Many of those 193 may not want to punish offenders; perhaps they had a close trading relationship with the offending country and it would become costly for them to support punishment. Such a system works so long as everyone is committed to the idea of maintaining an international rule of law, even if it costs member-nations in the short run.

This is a fairly weak system because many countries regularly fail to comply with international agreements. There have been many great examples of international agreement; economists are especially pleased with the role that the World Trade Organization (WTO) plays in keeping tariffs low and maintaining free trade, but countries regularly violate the free trade rules and then flout the punishments. The United States has faced sanctions for WTO violations in every presidential administration since the system was put in place.

Part of the instability in this system comes from uncertainty about the rules and about the nature of violations. We discussed the potential for blockchain technology to automate contracts, using a computer algorithm to avoid disputes. This works only if the terms of the contracts can be specified in computer code. The problem of adjudicating contracts comes in the fuzziness that is inherent in how contracts are specified. As we have seen, sometimes it is better for contracts to have some uncertainty because it allows the development of trust between the two parties.

Although these uncertainties have the potential to prompt trust-building, they also provide opportunity for untrustworthy behavior to manifest itself. According to WTO rules, a country may violate free trade rules if it does so to protect its national security. This exception has been used to raise tariffs to protect rice farmers in Japan and steelworkers in the United States, even though critics have argued that national security is invoked disingenuously, simply to protect domestic interests.

Every law and rule entails uncertainty. Even when we have courts to adjudicate, absent some central authority, those courts work only on the basis of trust. At least in the case of free trade, the system overseen by the WTO remains in place and tariffs remain fairly low. Of course, the world has been working on free trade agreements since the signing of the General Agreement on Tariffs and Trade (GATT), the precursor to the WTO, after World War II.

International climate treaties have a similar history, which goes back to the 1990s. The first major climate accords signed at the international level was the Kyoto Protocol, signed in 1997. Even though the agreements were drafted with great hope and fanfare, the protocol wasn't the success that its drafters had hoped it would be. The agreement was eventually ratified by 160 countries but placed emissions limits on only a quarter of them. Major polluters like China and India were exempted, and the United States, which played a major role in the creation of the protocol, never ratified it. The U.S. Senate rejected the protocol by a 95–0 vote.[77] Countries like Canada, Japan, New Zealand, Russia, and Australia pulled out or failed to meet their obligations. Of the countries that did meet the pollution reductions, many did so only because postcommunist economic collapse massively reduced industrial production in those countries, causing emissions to decline.[78]

This brings us to 2015 and the climate talks in Paris. Once again, as in Kyoto and in Copenhagen, the world's leaders gathered to come to an agreement about the future of the planet.

The novel idea of the Paris Climate Agreement was that it was based entirely on trust. All treaties are based on trust, but the trust here is even more explicit because the agreement is mostly implicit. The agreement has no binding emissions restrictions imposed on its signatories. Instead the agreement had three components:[79]

1. An acknowledgment that the shared goal is to limit global temperature increases to 2 degrees Celsius (ideally 1.5 degrees Celsius) by limiting greenhouse gas emissions.
2. A promise that each country would make "ambitious" cuts to their own emissions.
3. An agreement to measure and to participate in a "global stock-take," where countries gather to talk about progress and report on agreed-upon measurements. The only binding part of the treaty was that countries had to be measured by technical expert reviewers.

This almost lackadaisical approach was much derided as toothless because it didn't actually require anyone to do anything.

The agreement reminded me of another much-derided policy: No Child Left Behind (NCLB). This was the education policy enacted in 2002 as a bipartisan deal between President George W. Bush and Democratic legislators in Congress, led by Senator Ted Kennedy. The policy was an education reform that required states to show that their students were demonstrating proficiency on state tests, that schools were showing improvement, and that racial disparities in test scores were being addressed. The key point of controversy regarding NCLB was that each state could choose to test whatever it wanted. Much like the Paris agreement, which allows countries to choose whatever emissions standards they want, NCLB let states choose to define academic proficiency however they wanted.

Many skeptical commentators argued that states would just design really easy tests to avoid having to do the work to fix their schools.[80] Economists tend to assume the worst in people, and many derided NCLB because it merely asked states to test their students without placing any requirements on what needed to be tested or what was required to pass. Such testing would be a waste of time.

What the pundits didn't understand was that the law didn't need to specify *what* children learned, it just needed to change how state policy makers and parents thought about learning. By requiring schools to publicly report test data, the law was designed to change how we view education—to let voters and parents know that they have the power to hold schools accountable. This can start only if we try to measure learning and progress. Of course, lawmakers could game the system, so to speak, by making tests really easy to pass, but then that behavior would be public, and lawmakers who care about public trust and their own reputations would want to make the test quality as good as possible. Moreover, the federal government couldn't credibly specify what the children from each state should learn because the United States is too diverse a place to agree on a uniform standard that would apply to children in all fifty states. But NCLB could create a system that would rely on the trustworthiness of state policy makers to design the best system for their own constituents. The secret to the system was making school outcomes visible.

The Paris Climate Accords rely on the same trick. International climate agreements have been contentious since they began in the 1990s, with different countries having different priorities. Poor countries have thought that the rich countries should do more because the rich countries have the resources *and* the longer history of pollution. Rich countries have thought that developing countries should do more because emissions in rich countries have peaked as rich economies transition away from heavily polluting industries like manufacturing; most of the future growth in emissions will come from the developing world. Cold countries, moreover, are less concerned about climate change because warmer temperatures may actually make life better in places like Canada and Russia. Low-lying countries and countries near the equator will suffer the brunt of the damages and tend to have the fewest resources to deal with them.

Negotiating a deal that appeases all of these conflicting interests, not to mention the often conflicting interests within each country, created an impasse that, year after year, failed to be resolved. The Paris Accord found a way through that impasse by changing the terms of negotiations.

Instead of creating rules or concrete emissions targets that each country had to meet, the Paris Accord simply asked countries to measure their own emissions. It created standards for how emissions would be measured in each country and required countries to allow others to audit their emissions. Again, critics quickly called this agreement toothless and pointless, but those critics missed a key component that, while not written directly into the agreement, is critical to its success: trust. By making emissions visible, the system will create accountability—accountability between each country's policy makers and their constituents, and accountability between countries and the other countries of the world. Even though the agreement imposes no binding requirements on behavior, it relies on guilt and a desire to preserve reputation.

This mechanism uses social and political pressure to ensure that countries create policies that improve their numbers.

Still, this strategy is a gamble. It remains to be seen whether social pressure is strong enough to move a global energy system. And maybe they gave up too soon. The WTO example does show that somewhat-binding international agreements can be made. I still applaud the audacity of resting an international plan to fix climate change so completely on trust.

• • •

We have seen throughout this book how trust developed in pre-modern tribes among small numbers of people to solve social problems like the management of the shared natural resources. Over the centuries, those informal rules and social mechanisms were replaced first by religious strictures and later by more formal legal ones. But perhaps there are lessons to be learned from how our ancestors learned to work together. While formal rules were great and led to tremendous social progress and vast complex societies, maybe there is value in returning to the old, to the fundamental human relationships that led to the birth of human civilizations. And maybe those simple rules can help us solve some of the biggest challenges of our time.

5

TRUSTING ONE ANOTHER

N the first four chapters of this book, we have looked at the economics of trust from a variety of angles. We saw how mechanisms like signaling, implicit social contracts, and reputations work together to help us cooperate in the face of uncertainty and potential bad behavior. We then tracked how those mechanisms of trust evolved from the gift-giving norms of hunter-gatherer tribes to the modern institutions that govern the economy today. We saw how a variety of institutions have helped to expand our circles of trust beyond 150 people—to whole religions, nation-states, and global markets. We have been moving from trust in only those we know personally to trust in those who share our values, with perhaps the ultimate goal of learning to trust humanity at large.

There are obstacles in our path, however. In chapter 4, we saw how it looks when trust in institutions declines. In the present, the availability of more and more information has given us more permission to trust our own instincts and our own factions instead of experts.

Here, we turn to how the lessons about the theory and history of trust might apply to our personal lives. And how these lessons learned could help suggest a way toward an even more connected future.

We begin by looking at where new trust begins, by looking at our baseline level of trust when encountering a stranger. We then turn to how the rules of trust can apply to trusting ourselves. Building trust requires a lot of effort; it is an investment in the future. To be willing to make that investment, we need to learn to trust ourselves. We then cover the human institution designed explicitly to restore broken trust—the apology. Pioneering the economics of apology has been the focus of my contributions to the economic literature. And we end with a discussion about why extending our circle of trust is so important, as well as the role of human dignity within the study of economics.

TRUSTING STRANGERS

Time magazine's Lev Grossman once described Alan Moore, the writer of *Watchmen*, this way: Ask ten movie buffs who the greatest director is, and you will likely get ten different names. Ask ten comic book buffs who the greatest comic book writer is, and nine of them will tell you Alan Moore.[1] Moore's most important work, indisputably, was *Watchmen*, which, when it was published in 1986 in the same year as Frank Miller's *Dark Knight Returns*, launched a revolution in comic books. These two works are jointly responsible for the fact that the superhero genre is taken seriously today.

In any event, the twist in *Watchmen* was that one of the superheroes was going to save the world not by punching bad guys, but by destroying New York City and killing millions of its inhabitants—and then using Hollywood special effects crews to make it look like the attack was carried out by alien invaders. The idea was that the creation of an alien Other was the only thing that could get the nations and peoples of the world to stop fighting and learn to work together.

The larger scope of this book has been to look at the evolution of trust from the very particular to the national and global. But as we saw especially in the discussion about religion, one of the most powerful mechanisms for creating trust is the creation of an Other. Our instinct is to trust people like us and to exclude those who are different.

However, over time, membership in the category "people like us" has expanded, pushed in part by the expansion of the rule of law, as well as the global scope of market capitalism. Immanuel Kant once suggested that the expansion of liberal democracy will lead to an enduring "democratic peace" because two democracies will not go to war with each other. A related concept is the "McDonald's peace," according to which two countries that both have McDonald's restaurants will not go to war with each other because they share too many of the same capitalist norms and are connected by global trade relationships.[2] The political scientist Francis Fukuyama once declared that we are at the "end of history" because we are in a liberal democratic world order that is so tightly integrated that it will never be torn apart by conflicts and world wars.

But others are less optimistic. Political scientist Samuel Huntington argues that our fundamental values differ too much; he predicts an inevitable clash of civilizations. Huntington argues that big groupings of cultural values (e.g., Western, Islamic, Sinic, Hindu, and African societies) are so fundamentally different that they will inevitably tend toward conflict. The recent global rise of nationalist leaders shows that contrary to Huntington, we may be more alike than different—but contrary to Fukuyama, we are alike in our desire to look inward and favor our own tribe rather than the universal one.

Expanding the circle of trust requires taking a chance on a stranger. We begin by looking at the baseline level of trust that we have when encountering someone we don't know.

Trust and Distrust

We began this book by talking about how the tools of game theory are best suited for helping us understand how trust evolves within a relationship. This approach differs from (for instance) sociological studies of trust, which tend to examine how survey respondents answer questions like:[3] generally, would you say that most people can be trusted, or that you can't be too careful in dealing with people?

Economists are more interested in how people respond to the set of incentives found in the trust game, where a trustor takes a risk on the trustee's trustworthiness. In general, the incentives in the trust game operate at the level of that particular relationship between two people, but often when we run experiments with the trust game, we ensure anonymity between the two people involved. It was that anonymity in the Jean Ensminger and Joseph Heinrich experiments on hunter-gatherer tribes discussed in chapter 2 that showed that while such isolated tribes relied heavily on trust and bilateral cooperation in their day-to-day lives, that kind of trusting behavior did not extend to anonymous experimental settings.

An interesting question related to the generalized trust question given here is how much we invest in that initial phase of the trust game when paired with an anonymous stranger. The Ensminger and Heinrich study suggests that anonymous trust has increased as we have shifted to modern market economies. But other research is illuminating as well. Researchers show that "social distance" is key to the trust game. We are more likely to trust an anonymous other person that we deem similar to us (in age, income, or geographic location) than one whom we perceive to be more distant.

While these findings were taken from the world of experimental economics labs, we can apply these findings to the events driving today's headlines. This tension between trusting our tribe and trusting humanity generally is reflected in our politics, both locally and geopolitically. The U.S. presidential election of 2016 exposed a deep division in American politics that was surprising to many people. The same year, the Brexit referendum, in which Great Britain voted to leave the European Union (EU), demonstrated similar cleavages. A few years later, in 2019, the European Parliament election saw a dramatic rise of anti-EU parties elected into office. Many saw these trends as a step backward: a movement away from a cosmopolitan globalism in favor of a resurgence of reactionary nationalism. People had a hard time understanding the divisions and attributed malign motives to the other side.

The psychologist Jonathan Haidt created my favorite model to make sense of these tensions. Haidt's moral foundation theory tries to understand the building blocks of human morality using surveys of how people respond to ethical dilemmas. For example, he asked people how much they would have to be paid to do each of the following:[4]

- Stick a pin into your palm.
- Stick a pin into the palm of a child you don't know. (Harm)
- Accept a wide-screen television set from a friend who received it at no charge because of a computer error.
- Accept a wide-screen television set from a friend who received it from a thief who had stolen it from a wealthy family. (Fairness)
- Say something bad about your nation (which you don't believe) on a talk-radio show in your nation.
- Say something bad about your nation (which you don't believe) on a talk-radio show in a foreign nation. (Community)
- Slap a friend in the face, with his permission, as part of a comedy skit.

- Slap your minister in the face, with his permission, as part of a comedy skit. (Authority)
- Attend a performance-art piece in which the actors act like idiots for thirty minutes, including flubbing simple problems and falling down on stage.
- Attend a performance-art piece in which the actors act like animals for thirty minutes, including crawling around naked and urinating on stage. (Purity)

Haidt uses statistical techniques to analyze people's answers to these questions and finds that moral intuitions can be divided into five moral foundations. These five categories (maybe six) can be subdivided between community values and universal values. The community values, or *binding* foundations, are Loyalty, Authority, and Sanctity, while the more universal values, or *individualizing* foundations, consist of Caring and Fairness.

There are tensions among the various moral foundations, such as how much we choose to weigh one versus the other in moral dilemmas where they come into conflict. In particular, Haidt finds that in the United States, liberals tend to prioritize the universal foundations, while conservatives tend to balance all five.[5] We all agree that loyalty to one's community and adherence to authority are important things to value; the question becomes how we trade off loyalty to our own community with caring about others. For example, on the issue of what to do about international refugees, how does a country balance the very real needs of their own people with the very real needs of others?

Trust economics also offers a useful lens for understanding these divisions. One by-product of the mechanisms that we use to maintain trust has been to create sharp lines between those we trust and those we don't. This has been partly due to the information cost of keeping track of who is trustworthy and who is not, and partly due to our need to rely on shared values and shared punishments for untrustworthy behavior.

Trustworthy behavior is often maintained by threatening those who misbehave with the possibility of exclusion: excommunication, ostracization, shunning, or some other form of social exclusion. We use shortcuts like religion and culture to decide whom to trust. Such shortcuts are useful only if they provide a way to differentiate between those we can trust and those we cannot. The need for differentiation (i.e., an out-group against which to define the in-group) precludes trusting everybody. A world in which we trust everybody would be difficult to achieve without, as Moore depicted, an out-group from beyond the stars.

Trust is built around the moral foundations of community. Attributes like loyalty and respect for authority are associated with trustworthiness. The difficulty comes when the needs of the community are at odds with universal values, especially because a big part of how we trust comes from a shared distrust of the Other.

Drivers of Distrust

The previous section outlined the big trends of expanding trust and the fundamental tension between extending trust to strangers and maintaining a distrust of those outside our community. Here, we discuss three recent trends from chapter 4 that have exacerbated that tension:

1. An increase in the diversity of and inequality within our communities that exacerbates our tribal nature, because so many of our institutions about trust are based on distrusting the other.

2. An increase in choice in who we are able to connect with online, makes our online interactions more homogeneous than they would be without social media.
3. An increase in access to information makes us more overconfident in our own beliefs.

The first has come from a few sources. An increase in global migration means that many countries have experienced an influx of immigrants. In the United States, for instance, states like California no longer have a clear majority of any race/ethnicity (non-Hispanic whites make up less than 50 percent). In the United States as a whole, the same has been true when you look at schoolchildren since 2014.[6] At the same time, a combination of increasing globalization and technological automation has led to a widespread increase in inequality within most of the countries of the world. In the rich countries, this inequality is between those who have the skills and capital to thrive in a globalized and technologically sophisticated world economy and those who do not. In the developing world, we see the same pattern: those who are able to capitalize on globalization and fast-paced technological change have amassed enormous wealth, while those who are not have become richer, but at a slower rate.

Interestingly, if you look at the world as a whole, inequality has gone down. This is because the developing world (especially the fifth of the world population that lives in China, but also India and the African nations) has made great strides in catching up to the developed world, where economic growth has greatly slowed in recent decades. However, we tend not to compare ourselves to people living on the other side of the planet. Instead we compare ourselves to those in the same country, and over the span of the last few decades, inequality within countries has increased both in less developed countries like China and in rich countries like the United States.

This increase in immigration and in inequality means that we are more likely in our day-to-day lives to be exposed to people who are different from us. In my own research with Jonah Berger and Chip Heath, we used the experiments that Jonah ran to create a mathematical model on how many of the actions that we take are chosen to differentiate ourselves from others. In one experiment, undergraduate students who read an article about how graduate students on campus ate a lot of junk food were more likely to make the healthy choice when offered a number of snacks. In another experiment, students were sold yellow Livestrong bracelets. When students at an adjacent dormitory with a so-called nerdy reputation were also sold the same bracelet, the initial group of students all stopped wearing theirs. While we usually think about this differentiation in terms of how we dress, the same idea can be applied to how we speak, what we read, what we choose to believe, and whom we trust. The model that we produced was then used to examine behavior in a simulated social network and to explain the role and position of influencers, the dynamics of how fashion trends spread, and the importance of inconspicuous consumption in driving trends.

The term *conspicuous consumption* refers to the idea, pioneered by the early-twentieth-century economist Thorstein Veblen, that we often buy things not for our own pleasure, but to change how others perceive us. Think about flashy cars, high-tech watches, or expensive handbags. These days, increasing incomes and low-priced knockoffs have made it relatively easy for everybody to buy watches and handbags that look a lot like the ones that only rich people used to wear, so we instead use language or culture to demonstrate distinctions. People use exotic vacations, political causes, or specialized jargon to signal membership in their

tribe. This sometimes necessitates making such displays inconspicuous (hence *inconspicuous consumption*) because we don't
always want to draw attention to our differences, even though
we sometimes do.

One of Jonah's favorite examples of this is the six-hundred-
dollar pair of blue jeans, which looks a lot like the twenty-dollar
jeans that you can get at Walmart but can be identified by others
who are in the know. It's not the price of the jeans that matters—it
is the specialized cultural knowledge that you must have in order
to tell the difference. The model predicts that as people become
exposed to other people with different identities that people do
not want to be associated with, there is an increased tendency to
buy products and make choices that signal one's own identity.[7]
Those choices heighten our awareness of group identities, and our
instinct, developed over thousands of years of institutional evolution, is to use identity as a way to decide whom to trust.[8]

Related to this effect is that general distrust is associated
with economic disadvantage. We see this both at the country
level—lower-income countries tend to exhibit less trust than
higher-income countries—but also within countries, where
lower-income individuals tend to trust less than those with higher
incomes. Researchers generally attribute this to the fact that
those who are disadvantaged tend to encounter more hardships
and a system that seems to be stacked against them.[9] It is not
surprising that a person who has faced systemic discrimination or
indifference would not be very trusting of others.

Unsurprisingly, countries with lower levels of trust also tend to
have lower levels of cooperative (trustworthy) behavior.[10] Part of
the reason for this is uncooperative behavior is contagious. Why
should I be cooperative, a person might ask, when no one else is?
In my own research with Xinyue Zhou, encountering untrustworthy behavior is more potent in changing behaviors than

encountering trustworthy behavior.[11] We had students play trust games with each other via computer terminals in anonymous laboratory settings. When a relatively more cooperative trustworthy group was paired with a relatively more selfish, untrustworthy group, the groups tend to converge toward more selfish behavior. Groups of players played trust games with each other for multiple ten-round sessions. While just one session of interaction with a selfish group caused the selfish behavior to spread, it took three sessions with cooperative groups for the cooperative behavior to be adopted.

However, while our physical communities have been growing more diverse, the advent of the Internet and social media technologies means that our virtual communities have become more homogeneous. In chapter 3, we discussed the recent technological innovations that have changed how trust operates in the economy, most notably blockchain and the platforms that enable the sharing economy. One of the biggest companies in the world, which we haven't talked about much thus far, is Facebook: this single company has drastically altered how we connect and interact; undoubtedly, it has affected whom and how we trust.

Not long ago, most of our social interactions were with people who lived nearby in our communities, and most of our news came from the same shared local newspapers or a few shared national television networks. Today, our news is filtered and curated to show us only the news that appeals most to us. Economic research shows that news outlets cater their news to the biases of their readers because that is the kind of news that sells best. Facebook and other social networks not only mediate the friends we talk to, but also filter our news to cater to what we want to hear.[12]

The advent of Internet communication technologies, starting with e-mail but now including Facebook, Snapchat, Instagram, Twitter, Tumblr, LinkedIn, Slack, YouTube, TikTok, and others, have been amazing at letting us connect. By expanding the spread of something as simple as gossip, one of the first institutions that developed to spread trust, such institutions could potentially expand our circle of trust to the global village. However, even as these networks have allowed us to connect to people around the world, they have also let us home in on ever-more-precise versions of "our tribe" and further limit our social interactions with those who are different.

One of the earliest studies of Facebook was a test that the anthropologist Robin Dunbar ran on his own number, 150. He found that at the time, the average number of Facebook friends whom people regularly interacted with was around 150, suggesting that how we process relationships on Facebook mirrors how we historically processed relationships in hunter-gatherer tribes.[13] However, the difference is that we now have a lot more choice in who those 150 people are—who gets to stay in our network and who gets kicked out, or unfriended.

Robert Putnam has argued that even though increased racial diversity reduces our generalized trust of strangers, we could restore trust by creating new identities based on ideologies other than race. However, what seems to have happened in the United States (with similar trends elsewhere) is that we have become more strongly identified with our political ideologies: each political party has sorted into more homogeneous groups and people have built stronger attachments to their side. Along with stronger attachment to one's own party has come greater distrust for those who don't share one's own political views.

One concern is that the social media echo chamber has shifted our allegiances but made the country more divided than ever. Recent research by a former classmate of mine and his co-author shows that a major driver of this increased partisanship and ideological distrust is overconfidence in the rightness (and righteousness) of one's own opinions.[14] Perhaps having more access to partisan news and more political discussions only with friends who think alike has made us overconfident in our own views. Still, research that social media actually changes views has produced ambiguous results, and good evidence suggests that our political opinions are shaped more by our own economic prospects than the things we read online.[15] However, it is hard to imagine that the shift in how we consume information and interact with the people around us isn't changing us somehow.

One recent study out of Stanford University found that paying people to quit Facebook made them happier and less politically polarized.[16] Subjects were randomly divided between control and treatment groups. Those in the treatment group were paid to deactivate their Facebook account for one month. The researchers found that reducing Facebook usage caused people to spend more time socializing with their friends, reduced their knowledge about current events, increased their happiness, and reduced their usage of Facebook even after the experiment ended.

Researchers today are grappling with the impact of these networks and how they can be designed to minimize the spread of the misinformation that has led to such intense partisanship that it has been linked to killings in some parts of the world. For what it's worth, the best research finds little evidence that social media has had much impact on how we vote. This is consistent with other work that shows that the media that we consume actually does little to change our political behavior. Rather than causing the polarization that we see in society, social media simply reflects it.[17] However, how social media is changing society is something we need to be mindful of.

Trustworthy behavior is contagious. Part of what makes me want to act in a trustworthy way is that I want to live in a society where people are trustworthy. The advent of social media makes us ask what happens to trust when human beings who evolved to handle face-to-face interactions suddenly shift to a fast-moving, mutable, online world.

TRUSTING YOURSELF

One of my favorite TED talks is given by a behavioral economist, Keith Chen. Chen begins with the observation that the language you speak affects how you see the world. The example that he chooses is one I often puzzled over as a kid. The Chinese language has about a dozen different ways to say "aunt" and "uncle." Whereas modern English uses one word ("aunt") to describe any older female that you are related to but not directly descended from, in Chinese there are separate words designating that person as your mother's sister or your father's sister, or your mother's brother's wife or your father's brother's wife, or your mother's aunt or your father's aunt, and whether they are older or younger than your mother or father, and whether they are the eldest or youngest . . . the list goes on. The words are all different—they don't even sound alike—and every time you say hi to an "aunt," it requires a reconstruction of your family tree. Whether or not words change how you think is still being debated (this is known as the *Sapir-Whorf hypothesis*), but there is no doubt that words direct our attention to different things.

Chen's contribution to this question was to look at another feature of language: verb conjugation. In English, the word "go" becomes "went" or "goes" or "going" or "gone." Native English speakers who study languages like French or German are often befuddled at how many different forms a single verb can take. Those who speak Chinese struggle especially because even though Chinese has a dozen words for "aunt," verbs generally don't change for different tenses. The Chinese speak of the past and the future using the same verbs they use to speak about the present.

Chen's hypothesis was that the consequence of speaking about the future differently from how we speak about the present is that the future feels more distant, like it involves somebody other than ourselves, even when we're speaking about ourselves. The consequence is that our present self is going to be less nice to our future self. That sounds a bit strange, but this is how behavioral economists and others have been thinking about our approach to the future for some time.

For instance, one problem that has worried many talking heads is that many Americans save too little for retirement. If you think about it, saving for retirement is asking a lot of us. Saving today means locking money away today that could go toward the wants and needs we have today, and giving that money to some future self who may be somebody different from who we are now. Although we may not notice it, psychologist Dan Gilbert has noted that what we want out of life changes a lot over just ten years, and saving money for the future is basically trusting our future self to spend that money in a way that we approve of.[18] By the same token, our future self is trusting our present self to save money for their well-being.

Our bias toward procrastination is just one of many biases that behavioral economists and psychologists have identified in recent years; when under the sway of these biases, we make mistakes that we would avoid if we engaged in a bit more introspection. We make poor choices not just about saving for the future, but also in understanding what will make us happy, updating our beliefs based on new information, and interpreting the actions of other people, just to name a few.[19]

One of the surprising applications of many of the ideas that we have discussed in this book is that they apply not just to trust between two individuals, but also to understanding our cognitive biases—that is, to helping us understand when we should and should not trust ourselves. Beyond just understanding the trust within ourselves, however, building trust is by our definition an investment in the future. We are taking a risk now and making costly sacrifices for the sake of building a relationship that will yield future rewards. Understanding ourselves and how we might overcome the tendency to underinvest in the future is crucial for increasing trust in society.

Trusting the Future and Trusting the Past

Perhaps the mathematical model that has made the biggest difference in my personal life, has been the model of procrastination by Ted O'Donoghue and Matthew Rabin.[20] Not that it got me to stop procrastinating, but it helped make me aware of when and why I was doing it. That in turn has helped me do a better job of not feeling bad about procrastinating, and perhaps even procrastinating more effectively. Their model is based on experimental evidence that says that we tend to value things we get in the present twice as much as things we get in the future. If offered a choice between getting a hamburger today and getting two hamburgers next week, I might choose a hamburger today. In a similar way, painful things that happen today feel twice as painful as painful things that we expect to happen in the future. For example, I might agree to wash the dishes today in exchange for two nights of you washing dishes next week.

This means, of course, that I might regret the choices I made in the past. When next week comes and I am especially hungry, I might wish that I had waited to get my two hamburgers; I might wish I had just done the dishwashing last week so that I didn't have to do it twice now.

This devaluing of the future has even more invidious consequences when it comes to long-term patterns of behavior. For example, suppose that you wanted to quit smoking. The cost of quitting smoking today is substantial, but many people probably feel that lung cancer (a possible consequence of continuing to smoke) is more than twice as costly. That's why 68 percent of smokers say that they want to quit.[21] So why don't they? Our model of procrastination can help explain. While the cost of lung cancer is extremely high, the cost of quitting next week is about the same as the cost of quitting today. But the cost of quitting today feels twice as painful. Therefore, most people would rather quit next week than quit today. Quitting next week won't appreciably increase your chance of getting lung cancer, so why not enjoy one more week of smoking? Of course, when next week comes, what was once the future is now the present, and postponing just one more week looks appealing. As a result, the future never comes; sadly, we make all our choices in the present.

The same logic has many other applications, like saving for retirement or dieting. Enjoying a piece of cake today and starting my diet next week sound appealing. Similarly, starting my retirement savings next week instead of today also feels like a reasonable plan. The problem is that "next week" never comes. We sometimes naively assume that our future self will follow through with the plans that we make today, but our future self, it turns out, cannot be trusted.

One solution, proposed by Richard Thaler (who won the Nobel for his work in developing the field of behavioral economics) and popularized by Thaler and Cass Sunstein in their book *Nudge*, is to impose restrictions on our future behavior that are similar to the rules we use to reduce risk. For example, Thaler proposed allowing people to sign up for a retirement savings plan that would start next month instead of now. It might be hard to sign up to save today but relatively easy to agree to start saving next month. Similarly, he suggested a system to allow people to quit smoking next month instead of now. He suggested requiring everybody to have a permit to purchase cigarettes. The permit would be free and available to anyone of legal smoking age. Anyone at any time can choose to let their permit lapse—starting next month. Once the permit lapses, the person would have to wait a month to renew the permit. In this way, a smoker can force their future self to quit.

An alternative to imposing rules on future behavior is to make ourselves more trustworthy stewards of our future. Coming back to Keith Chen's observations about languages with a future tense as opposed to those without, procrastination problems come about because we value our future self's well-being less than we value our well-being in the present. If we are able to eliminate our bias in favor of immediate gratification, then the problem goes away. Whereas Thaler advocated exerting greater control over our future selves, Chen's work suggests that if people can learn to start seeing all their selves, current and future, as one, they will become better stewards of *their* future.

Chen looked at data about hundreds of thousands of people around the world and collected data about the languages they speak.[22] He found that people who speak languages without verb conjugation (like Chinese) were more patient than people who speak languages with verb conjugation (like English). This was the case even after controlling for culture and country of residence. His findings apply to things like retirement savings and education: those who speak languages without conjugation save more for retirement and invest more in their own future. The idea is that when we speak about the future in the same way that we speak about the present, we treat our future selves better.

The mathematics of procrastination used by O'Donoghue and Rabin, looks like the mathematics of altruism (developed by Gary Becker and others) to a surprising extent. In both cases, we are presumed to care about some other person at some percentage of the amount we care about ourselves.[23] One of the motivations of this book has been to show how trust has developed from our only caring about our immediate family and those in our tribe to also caring about others in our larger communities: caring about our nations, our religions, or humanity as a whole. Chen's results suggest that we can apply the same idea to our own future, learning to care about our future selves and future humanity in the same way that we care about ourselves and our societies today.

A Society of Mind

Although O'Donoghue and Rabin showed that we can explain a lot just by thinking about this one dimension of how our current self might have different preferences than our future or past self, the idea can be extended to what the 1970s computer scientist Marvin Minsky called a "society of mind."[24] Minsky's idea was that human cognition can be thought of as the emergent outcome of many different agents interacting within our mind. That idea challenges the traditional neoclassical economics notion that people are rational. While "rationality" is a loaded word, to an economist, it just means that people have goals and take actions to reach those goals. Minsky suggested instead that our minds can be thought of as a society of agents, each with contradictory goals.

We now know that people don't have innate goals; instead, goals (or *preferences*, as economists call them) are often constructed on the fly. Clever experiments show that our preferences

demonstrate arbitrary coherence (or coherent arbitrariness)[25]—
we appear on the surface to be taking actions toward coherent
goals, but the researchers found that they could manipulate what
their experimental subjects wanted through meaningless inter-
ventions like asking for their social security number.

One way to interpret this finding is that our actions are driven
by impulses that we don't fully understand ourselves, although
they do work together in the long run to achieve our goals, and
they can be manipulated in the short run by experimenter inter-
ventions. Many game theorists have taken this idea to create a
model of the games that people play against themselves (i.e.,
games played by one part of your mind against another). My
favorite is by Roland Bénabou and Jean Tirole, who present a
model in which we are uncertain about our own virtuousness. At
any given moment, the part of us making decisions isn't sure how
we will respond when put to a moral test. We want to believe that
we are good but fear that we aren't. This simple idea (and their
mathematical model of it) explain a wide range of findings in the
psychology literature.[26]

For example, we have talked at length about how groups ostracize those who have proved untrustworthy as a way to maintain
trust within the group. However, there is also evidence that people ostracize those who are *too* nice or *too* trustworthy. The moral
uncertainty model argues that this is because we don't want to
be reminded of our own moral turpitude. Being surrounded by
moral paragons makes it harder to fool ourselves. This is also
why certain topics are off-limits for discussion, like the selling of organs or votes or sex. We don't want to be reminded of
how morally weak we are, so we create a taboo that prohibits the
discussion.

The point of the model, which can really explain quite a lot
of human behavior, is that just as we have uncertainty about the

trustworthiness of others, we are unsure about our own trustworthiness. That uncertainty causes us to take actions to protect our self-image, and some of those actions affect our relationships with others. We shun the untrustworthy but also the overly virtuous. Further, we take pains to demonstrate to others our identity when our sense of self is threatened.

APOLOGIES AND BLAME

My roommate in graduate school had a problem. He had a friend he liked to play tennis with Sunday mornings, but she always showed up late. She would always apologize profusely, and yet the following week, she would always show up late again with another apology. Finally, my roommate got fed up and asked me why we even bother with apologies—they are just empty words, aren't they?[27] I got into the study of trust trying to answer the simple questions posed by my roommate: Why do we accept apologies? If words are cheap, then why do apologies have any meaning? The reason to care about these questions is that apologies restore broken trust, and as we have seen throughout this book, trust is the cornerstone of the economy.

Of course, trust matters not just in economic transactions, but also in our everyday interactions, and the same rules of trust that govern our financial transactions can give some insight into our personal relationships. For example, marriage is a contract (legally, of course, but also implicitly). Even without the extensive legal framework we have that governs marriage (and divorce), we have societal rules and expectations that we bring to every relationship.

In this section we turn our attention to apologies as an institution that allows people to make a costly sacrifice, because costly sacrifices are how we rebuild trust.

Why Do We Apologize?

The easy answer to all this is that apologies work and can save us a lot of money.

I first tackled this question by running a lab experiment at Stanford. I programmed a computer interface to allow students to play a repeated trust game with each other. One student was assigned the role of investor and another was assigned the role of entrepreneur. The investor was given ten credits each turn, which they could invest in a safe option or invest with the entrepreneur. The entrepreneur could selfishly keep the money or could share the returns with the investor. However, after each turn, there was some uncertainty about whether the entrepreneur would succeed. Even if an entrepreneur tried to do the right thing and share the returns with the investor, her efforts might fail. However, the investor learned only whether the project succeeded, not what the entrepreneur chose to do. Therefore, if an investor got nothing back for his investment, that could be due either to the entrepreneur's untrustworthiness or to bad luck. Between turns, I would give the entrepreneur the opportunity to apologize for bad outcomes, and I observed what happened to trust over time.

In short, I found that apologies worked. Investors trusted people more after they apologized. This worked because more trustworthy people (as measured by how much they tended to share over the course of the game) were more likely to apologize. The theory predicts that we should see more apologies when there is greater risk (when the need for trust is higher), and indeed in this experiment, we saw more apologies earlier in relationships, when participants knew less about the person they were interacting with.

Of course, this was just a lab setting. It would be good to see if apologies worked in a setting with real stakes. I focused on answering this question with another economist, Elaine Liu.

A policy setting where apologies come up a lot is the case of medical malpractice. We found that state laws passed in the United States to encourage apologies sped up the time it took to settle malpractice suits and reduced the amount of money that they settled for.[28] Moreover, by looking at the types of malpractice suits that were reduced the most, we could get a better understanding of when apologies work and when they don't (and why).

For example, apology laws had the biggest reductions on lawsuits involving minor injuries. They also were most effective in cases within the subspecialties of obstetrics and anesthesia. In terms of patient categories, apologies proved to be most effective for cases involving infants. And in terms of the types of mistakes that saw the biggest reductions, it was cases involving improper management by physicians and failures to diagnose.

This research helped inspire my next experiment, which sought to better understand what kinds of apologies work and why people often fail to apologize.

Why Do We Often not Apologize?

The medical malpractice example gives a hint as to what makes it so hard to apologize: it is often costly. In the case of medical malpractice, the cost is the potential for a lawsuit. Recall the question I started with: if apologies are cheap, why do they have any meaning? The answer is that cheap talk does not have much meaning. It is only when the apology is expensive that it signals that the apologizer is safe to trust again.

My work identifies five types of apologies; each represents different kinds of costs that can come with the words "I am sorry":

- "I'm sorry your grandmother is sick"—This is an apology that simply recognizes the pain somebody is feeling. It doesn't take responsibility for that pain; it simply recognizes it. This is often called the *partial apology*, and often gets people in trouble when people employ this apology for something they should have taken responsibility for, as in: "I'm sorry if you were offended."

- "I'm sorry. It wasn't my fault"—This is an apology that makes an *excuse* for a failure. It is also an easy, low-cost apology that works when the excuse is genuine, but it often gets people in trouble.
- "I'm sorry. Here are some flowers"—This is an apology that comes with some *tangible cost*. Flowers can be shockingly expensive. Kobe Bryant was famous for spending millions of dollars for an apology ring after cheating on his wife.
- "I'm sorry. I will never do it again"—This is a *promise* to do better in the future. The cost here is that you may forgive me, but you will hold me to a higher standard. That means if I screw up again, I would have been better off if I'd never apologized in the first place.
- "I'm sorry. I'm an idiot"—This is an apology that somehow *abases* the apologizer. It makes them look bad or incompetent in the hope of restoring trust.

Part of what makes apologies effective is that they can backfire. This also makes apologizing hard. That's good, because the harder the apology is to make, the more effective it is. But it also increases the consequences if you screw up.

I mathematically showed that these costs and consequences are necessary to give apologies meaning. I then joined with some collaborators (Basil Halperin, Ian Muir, and John List) to work with Uber to test the different kinds of apologies.

Uber provides ride services as an alternative to taxis or public transportation. It had a problem, though, in that one very late arrival at your destination (later than 95 percent of similar rides taken by other riders) would be enough to reduce future spending with Uber by 5 to 10 percent, as people switched to alternative services. Working with Uber, we worked to see how and when an apology could help.

We wanted to avoid annoying Uber's customers, so we skipped the easy apologies: the partial apology and the excuses apology. Instead we tested the other three types of apology by e-mailing customers after a late arrival. We tried:

1. A tangible apology: offering a five-dollar coupon for future rides
2. A promise-based apology: promising to do better in the future
3. An abasement-based apology: admitting fallibility for the bad experience

We e-mailed 1.5 million customers who'd had a bad ride and then tracked their spending over the next eighty-four days. What we found was that this type of apology was generally effective. The five-dollar-coupon apology generated more than five dollars in future spending. But we also found that apologies could backfire. With repeated use, apologizing was worse than not apologizing at all. This was particularly true for those who received a promise-based apology. We didn't find evidence that the abasement-based apology was especially helpful or harmful, but perhaps it just didn't work in this context. The idea for that treatment came from one of my favorite experiments in the apology literature.

Larissa Tiedens ran an experiment at the end of the Clinton administration, shortly after the impeachment hearings over the Monica Lewinsky affair.[29] She took a video of Bill Clinton's deposition testimony and edited it to make two videos, one where Clinton sounded apologetic and one where Clinton sounded unapologetic and angry. She showed each video to a different group of students. Those who saw the apologetic Clinton indeed liked him more and thought he was a better person. However, those who saw the angry Clinton liked him less but thought he was a more competent president. Importantly, those who saw the angry Clinton were more likely to want to vote for him again. Apologies worked, but at the cost of his electability and perceived competence.

Trust and Reconciliation and the Impossibility of Easy Apologies

While my interest in apologies, like the topics in the rest of this book, has primarily been about bilateral relationships between two individuals or organizations, apologies have also been an important part of how governments related to their people and how people relate to one another. We see this in calls for governments to apologize or for people to apologize for great crimes committed by entire societies—ranging from slavery to unjust war to genocide. A recent study found that a program of truth and reconciliation after the recent conflict in Sierra Leone increased trust in communities.[30]

While there are definitely examples of effective programs for reconciliation, like the one in Sierra Leone, most mass apologies rarely leave the affected parties satisfied. That's because for apologies to work, they have to be hard to make. This is true for both the biggest apologies and the smaller, everyday apologies.

Having studied apologies for nearly two decades, I'm often asked for advice on how to give a good apology. I'm never quite sure how to respond.

An apology is an act of trustworthiness. As discussed earlier, the effectiveness of an act of trustworthiness is proportional to its cost. Any advice that makes an apology more effective at restoring a relationship also makes the apology easier to give, and that lowers the cost and makes the apology less effective.

The key lesson from my research is that there are no shortcuts to a good apology.[31] Forgiveness takes time. Germany has spent decades apologizing for the Holocaust. National Public Radio's (NPR) *Lost in Translation* followed the efforts of the Japanese government as it tried to apologize to American prisoners of war (POWs) who were placed into forced labor camps during World War II.[32] The POWs always felt like they never got a proper apology. The Japanese government apologized to them publicly many times. But because each public apology felt instrumental, as if the apologizer were putting in the apology only for their own personal gain, it never felt costly enough to the POWs. Another show on NPR, *This American Life*, documented what they described as something that "almost never happens—a public apology that lands."[33] They describe the apology by Dan Harmon (creator of the TV shows *Rick and Morty* and *Community* among others) to one of his former employees for sexual harassment. He recorded a seven-and-a-half-minute apology for his podcast, and it really is quite a good apology; I encourage you seek out the transcript in the notes and read it. But what the reporters on that show did was reveal that even though the apology was "successful," the woman who was sexually harassed did publicly forgive Harmon afterwards. It wasn't something magical that was said in those seven and a half minutes that led to forgiveness. That seven-minute recording was only part of a series of apologies that went on for years, in person, on stage, on twitter, and over email. Effective apologies take time. The final apology admitted guilt and left Harmon open for lawsuits. Costly sacrifices were made. That is the secret of a good apology.

The sociologist Nicholas Tavuchis talks about the *paradox of apologies*. We want people to apologize, but our immediate response to an apology is often to punish or ostracize. An apologizer needs to be ostracized for a period of time—they must pay a price—before being welcomed back into the circle of trust.[34]

The theory of trust does have some practical advice on how to apologize. One is to know what we are apologizing for. Apologies are about building trust, and trust is about the expectation that future interactions will lead to positive outcomes. Therefore, it is easier to apologize for unintentional outcomes than for intentional ones. In many experiments, apologies for unintentional outcomes go over well, while apologies for intentional actions are seen as insincere and often backfire.[35] It's also useful to know that because effective apologies always entail a cost—often a social sanction that is worse when the apology is seen as insincere—it is important to be mindful of *when* to apologize. Usually apologies are more effective when trust is needed most. Trust is about how people deal with uncertainty, and therefore in my own experiments, apologies are most useful early in relationships or when there is more uncertainty about whom you are dealing with.

IDENTITY, DIGNITY, AND PRIVACY

In previous chapters about the role of trust in financial markets, we noted that interest rates are the purest measure that economists have to quantify trust. The interest rate that you must pay on a loan like a home mortgage is the number that represents the market's belief in your ability to pay back that loan. Lenders compete to offer you the best rate, but they must charge an interest rate high enough to cover their costs. The main cost that lenders worry about is the risk of default. In other words, they fear that you might act in an untrustworthy manner and not pay them back. Your interest rate is determined by your credit score—a way of measuring your trustworthiness.

In the United States, your credit score is based on only five factors: payment history, credit utilization, length of credit history, new credit, and credit mix. Most of us probably take this system for granted if we think about it at all. However, poke at the idea a little bit and two obvious questions emerge:

1. Why use only those five factors?
2. Why do we only use credit scores for determining interest rates?

The answers to these questions are illuminating in showing the role that dignity and privacy play in determining how we trust.

China forced us to think about these two questions when it began introducing its social credit score system, which was designed to "establish greater trust between people and businesses."[36] Instead of looking only at your credit history, Chinese instituions base your social credit score on all sorts of behavior, ranging from jaywalking to delinquent payback of fines to hours spent playing video games.

Also, while your normal credit score mostly is only used to access credit, your social credit score is used to decide if you are allowed onto trains or airplanes, if your children are allowed into certain schools, whether you can rent an apartment, how fast you can download from the Internet, whether you get certain jobs, and whom you are matched with on dating sites.[37] The scores are made available to the public via apps, so those around you—perhaps someone sitting next to you in a coffee shop—can then treat you differently based on your social credit.

While reports of the Chinese social credit score system (which, as in the United States, is derived from a mix of public and private credit scores) caused shock and consternation in the United States and other Western democracies, they are reportedly quite popular in China, where the rapid jump into capitalism has not allowed time for other trust-enabling institutions to develop. Chinese consumers rightly worry about whether they can trust the products made available to them: for example, counterfeiting is common, and on the streets of China, you can find everything from fake Apple stores selling fake iPhones to fake infant formula that has led to real infant deaths. The social credit score system is seen as a needed correction of the trust deficiencies.

In Western democracies, where consumers are generally more trusting of the products for sale and of each other, the benefits of such an extensive credit score system seem small, while the costs in terms of privacy seem enormous. However, even if the West is unlikely to adopt such a system any time soon, the way in which corporations like Google and Facebook are collecting and using personal data means that the issues remain very relevant.

The larger idea of dignity—that all people deserve equal treatment—is also the ultimate goal for our ever-expanding circle of trust.

What Can We Base Trust On?

In 2000, Amazon tried an experiment in which it would vary the price it charged consumers based on the information it knew about them. This kind of price discrimination is common in many industries—most notably airlines, where pricing follows arcane and wildly fluctuating formulas such that passengers pay very different prices for qualitatively identical seats. However, there is a difference between *dynamic pricing*, which changes prices quickly based on the time of day, and *personalized pricing*, which charges prices based on the identity of the buyer. The latter felt like a line had been crossed, and Amazon quickly backed off after customer outrage. (Higher education, in which colleges and universities charge different prices based on personalized financial aid packages, is one of the few sectors that seem to get away with personalized pricing with minimal outrage.)

The idea that people would be treated differently by companies based on their past actions or identities is something that most in the West will not accept. We can see this in the laws that have been passed in the West to protect privacy and limit discrimination on the basis of identity. It is informative to look at the ways that government regulates the factors we are allowed to consider when determining whom to trust.

In the United States, the 1974 Equal Opportunity Credit Act makes it illegal to base credit decisions on race, color, religion, national origin, sex, marital status, or age. This is essentially a regulation on what information we are allowed to use to figure out who we think can be trusted with our money. For example, studies show that women are often more trustworthy borrowers than men. Muhammad Yunus won the Nobel Peace Prize for establishing the Grameen Bank, which aimed to help developing countries by lending only to women, in part because women are more trustworthy. Artificially intelligent voice assistants like Siri and Alexa are usually presented as female (in terms of name and voice timbre) to increase perceived trustworthiness.[38] The greater trustworthiness of women should cause lenders to offer lower interest rates to women because they are lower-risk borrowers. However, lenders can base their decisions only on things like wages and past credit history—not gender. This actually has perverse consequences: because women tend to have lower wages than men, they are on average charged higher interest rates than men, even though we know that they are typically more trustworthy.[39]

I think we can all understand why we would want companies not to treat us differently because of our age, race, gender, or other key components of our identity. But we may also want some limits on how our past actions can affect how others treat us. We are comfortable with a lender using our history of late credit card payments to decide whether to lend to us, but less comfortable when the lender has access to and uses data on our tendency to jaywalk, our dating app profile, or our history of online purchases.

In other words, we believe that we have a right to privacy. One crucial element missing from the privacy debate is that the right to privacy isn't about keeping things secret; our right to privacy is mostly about how certain information is used and by whom. For example, our dating profiles aren't secret: dating profiles are quite public. And we typically don't hide our purchases, online or otherwise, when people come to visit our homes. Information about our dating interests and home decor preferences is available to some others in certain contexts. The right to privacy concerns how the information is used, and by whom.

Privacy is a relatively recent concern, and as such, the norms governing how private information is shared and used are still being contested (morally and legally). The European Union recently passed the General Data Protection Regulation (GDPR), which limits how websites use and collect our information and establishes a "right to be forgotten," which requires search engines like Google to "forget" some things that people don't want the world to remember. For example, someone who has had compromising photographs of themself posted online against their will by an ex-partner (so-called revenge porn) has the right to get those photographs removed from search engines and other websites. Likewise, someone who commits a crime but who has served their time can get a court to order that all information about their crime be removed from sites like Google so that they no longer show up on search engines.

The right to be forgotten is based on the idea that things we have done in the past should not cause us to be shunned or distrusted. This is, of course, an idea that is not without controversy. There is more broad agreement that revenge porn—naked images posted of someone without their permission to get back at them—should be scrubbed from the Internet. There is less agreement that past sex offenders should have that same right. Just as what should be allowed in a credit score is in debate, so are the limits of privacy.

In any case, privacy is fundamentally at odds with building trust, which is typically based on transparency. Recall that trust is a belief about the people you are interacting with; having more information about the people around you makes your beliefs more accurate. But providing more access to that information means less privacy. This tension between privacy and trust comes because of fundamental human dignity, which is based on the idea that different people cannot be treated differently on the basis of their identities. We enshrine a right to privacy to protect that fundamental dignity. But that right to privacy gets in the way of how we decide whom we can trust.

Dignity

But a human being regarded as a person, that is, as the subject of a morally practical reason, is exalted above any price . . . he possesses a dignity (absolute inner worth) by which he exacts respect for himself from all other rational beings in the world. He can measure himself with every other being of this kind and value himself on a footing of equality with them.

KANT, *THE METAPHYSICS OF MORALS*

Kant believed that all humans have a right to be treated in a way that does not depend at all on who they are, or what they did, even if what they did was criminal or immoral.[40] Dignity, as envisioned by Kant anyway, is an idea fairly new to economics. As expressed here, he conceives of dignity as a right to be respected that does not depend on merit, but only on being human. The fact that it does not depend on merit means that it should not depend on my identity (in terms of age or race or gender), but also that it should not depend on my past behavior. Of course, the tricky part is figuring out what this amounts to in practical terms: equality of dignity cannot mean that no person may ever be treated differently than any other, regardless of the differences in their behavior. The other question is what it means to respect somebody. The motivating example of this chapter is how credit scores determine access to credit and bank loans. The Chinese system extends the use of credit scores to things like access to schools and train tickets. Is equal treatment required in all domains, or just some? Recent debates surrounding privacy can help illustrate these conflicts better.

Most of this book has shared the economists' preoccupation with efficiency. Trust-supporting institutions have primarily been about helping people learn the most accurate information possible about the trustworthiness of the people they live and work with, and about encouraging people to behave in a trustworthy manner. In general, economists believe that more information is good because more information helps us make better decisions.

Popular outrage over the Chinese social credit system and the Big Data world, where tech companies like Google and Facebook know all our personal information, shows that there are limits to how much information we want others to know, even if placing limits on information will hinder decision-making and the efficiency of the economy overall. Part of the fear is that the information collected about us will be inaccurate or incomplete. The information that companies have is necessarily incomplete, and part of our objection must certainly be that we don't want our creditworthiness to be determined by faulty data. A lifetime of good behavior could be cancelled out by one error in judgment—the kind of error that, if we are honest, we know we are all capable of making. In the era of YouTube and social media, such errors can follow us for the rest of our lives.

People are worried about the lack of accountability in how this private information is collected. If the information dossier on someone paints a misleading portrait, we don't yet have good systems on how to correct that portrait. That notion, that online data may be inaccurate, is one that is easy to understand within the context of economics. Economists believe that more information is better because it leads to better decision-making, but misleading information leads to worse decision-making. Therefore, bad information should most definitely be regulated and suppressed.

However, I don't think accuracy is the only reason why we care about privacy. Many petitions invoking the right to be forgotten relate to the question of whom we decide to shun. As we saw in discussing trust and religion, part of the history of trust has been about how we balance these opposing forces of trusting and shunning. We use shunning as a way to punish untrustworthy behavior and as a way to separate those in the in-group (whom we trust) from those in the out-group (whom we do not). As we have seen, we have strong biological and cultural roots driving our instinct to shun. These laws are built around the idea that we may need help suppressing the instinct to shun for the sake of preserving the fundamental right to human dignity.

The right to privacy is also entwined with another idea favored by Kant—that we are all entitled to personal autonomy. Shunning is a tool of social control. It is used by religions to enforce their rules and the trustworthiness of their members. It was used by the merchants of medieval Champagne to make sure that members abided by their trade agreements. But as technology has exposed more and more of our private lives to the judgment of the public sphere, the threat of being shunned for our past actions has added further constraints on how we act, further inhibiting our ability to act autonomously.

Economics and Dignity

I have tried to structure this book around key findings from the economics literature, but this section on dignity and privacy is a bit more speculative. There actually are literatures within economics about dignity and about privacy but they are both small and limited. The literature about privacy has mostly concerned itself with what we are willing to pay for it, treating our demand for privacy like other things we consume.[41] It says less about why we fundamentally care about privacy. (Here's a hint: I think it's because of dignity.)

The literature about dignity has followed two strands. One is led by Nobel Prize winner and philosopher Amartya Sen, who argues that dignity is a societal goal, trying to persuade economists to broaden their conception of a healthy society from one with a high or growing gross domestic product (GDP) to one that succeeds on additional measures. Economists, I think, are happy to focus on a view of well-being that's broader than GDP, so long as we can capture that goal in terms of utility for the people in the society. But Sen goes further, suggesting that it is human capability that we need to maximize, where capability is derived from some underlying goal of freedom and autonomy (an idea that philosopher Martha Nussbaum extended, arguing that the goal of the human capability approach derives fundamentally from dignity).

The other strand of economic literature about dignity is more recent and more urgent. Anne Case and Nobel Prize winner Angus Deaton have echoed Sen's contention that GDP may be insufficient. Their work, however, has focused on more tangible additional measures. Notably, Case and Deaton found that in 2015–2017, life expectancy in the United States fell for the first time in decades, most notably among working-class Americans aged forty-five to fifty-four years old. Digging into the data, they attributed the decreased life span to extraordinary increases in suicides and drug overdoses. While the causes of both suicides and overdoses are complicated and multifactorial, Case and Deaton link the two, calling them "deaths of despair." While the cause of the despair is unknown, many observers have attributed the despair to loss of dignity.⁴²

The way that I think about how dignity, autonomy, and privacy interrelate is through the economics of identity. There is a surprisingly rich and lengthy body of economic literature about how we care about how we are perceived. It is often forgotten that the founder of modern economics, Adam Smith, wrote another book before writing the book he is most famous for, *The Wealth of Nations*. In 1759, Smith wrote in his *Theory of Moral Sentiments* (1759):

> For to what purpose is all the toil and bustle of this world? what is the end of avarice and ambition, of the pursuit of wealth, of power, and preheminence? Is it to supply the necessities of nature? The wages of the meanest labourer can supply them. We see that they afford him food and clothing, the comfort of a house, and of a family. If we examined his oeconomy with rigour, we should find that he spends a great part of them upon conveniencies, which may be regarded as superfluities . . .
>
> From whence, then, arises that emulation which runs through all the different ranks of men, and what are the advantages which we propose by that great purpose of human life which we call

bettering our condition? To be observed, to be attended to, to be taken notice of with sympathy, complacency, and approbation, are all the advantages which we can propose to derive from it. It is the vanity, not the ease, or the pleasure, which interests us.

Smith noted that the reason why we care about making money isn't that we want to acquire more stuff. Even in the eighteenth century, the poorest workers had enough money to buy the basic necessities of life. Instead, Smith argued, once we have enough money to pay for the basics, like clothes and shelter, we pay for nicer clothing and nicer shelter because of how these will change how we are treated. We care about nice clothes and nicer things in general fundamentally because we care about how we are treated by other people.

A century later, Thorsten Veblen wrote in *Theory of the Leisure Class* about the idea of *conspicuous consumption*—the idea that we have well-kept, lush, green lawns and drive nice cars primarily to look rich. This idea has developed into a rich body of literature, finding, for example, that conspicuous consumption was a major reason for the success of the Toyota Prius,[43] and how high performers at companies are often underpaid and low performers in companies are overpaid to compensate them for having a lower status.[44]

The idea that we buy the things that we buy out of "vanity" in order to be treated with "sympathy . . . and approbation" is an old and uncontroversial one, but in my work with coauthors, we have sought to extend that idea, considering how it applies to all the things we choose to do, not just what we choose to buy. Our model of human behavior extends the utility model that economists use to model decision-making. We categorize the motivations that people have for taking an action (like buying a Prius or taking out a loan) between the *intrinsic* (or *instrumental*) *utility* they get from that action, and the *extrinsic* (or *expressive*) *utility* they get. Intrinsic utility consists of the direct benefits of taking an action—the enjoyment of the car, for example, and its ability to transport its owner to work. Extrinsic utility is how that decision affects how you are treated by others.[45]

This formulation allows us to decompose the motivations for someone's choices into intrinsic and extrinsic sources. Some people are more likely to be motivated by intrinsic sources, while others are more likely to be motivated by extrinsic sources. In popular culture, we tend to prize authenticity; we deem someone to be "authentic" when they appear to make choices for intrinsic motivations alone. Someone whose music tastes are shaped by how that music affects their image, and thus how they are treated by others, is perceived as "inauthentic."

In recent decades, philosophers have identified personal autonomy as an important goal for society. They define personal autonomy as "the capacity to decide for oneself and pursue a course of action in one's life, often regardless of any particular moral content."[46] In both the popular sense of prizing authenticity and the philosophical sense of prizing autonomy, we see that privacy can be helpful in freeing us from extrinsic constraints. If nobody is watching what we do, we are more able to live and act in accordance with our true, intrinsic selves.

However, a commitment to autonomy and privacy places constraints on the tools that society has to create trust. In particular, a commitment to respecting human dignity places two constraints on the mechanisms that have developed to create trust and trustworthiness:

1. The way in which we assess trustworthiness (i.e., how we decide whom to trust) should not depend on the identity of the people we interact with.
2. The way in which we assess trustworthiness should not depend on irrelevant past behavior.

We saw how this approach applies to credit markets. We have laws that prevent age, race, and gender from being used to determine access to credit. We also have laws that prevent most past behavior from influencing credit decisions. Your credit score depends on factors like payment history and credit utilization, but factors like your job and where you live do not. We saw this when we talked about medicine: we should not match patients and doctors based on race, even if it would improve trust.

Karl Marx worried about commodification—that more and more of the human experience was being subsumed into the market sphere. For example, land that was once shared by all, as nature, becomes commodified when it is partitioned and priced as "real estate." Economists generally applaud commodification. The parceling of common land in England has been credited with triggering the Industrial Revolution and bringing the world into the modern age. Economists argue that many of the problems in contemporary society, like pollution and overfishing and underfunding of arts and innovation, come about precisely when those factors are not commoditized, when they are not brought into the market system of property rights and prices.

A major shift ushered in by the digital economy is that our personal information and our privacy are being commoditized. What was once secret—our shopping habits, what we do in our free time, whom we have visited—have now become public and tradable. Companies like Amazon track what we spend, our phone companies track and share where we go, our televisions track what we watch, and our social media track our friendships. Basic economics suggests that all these developments are for the better. Information that was not commoditized before, not creating value, has been brought into the market and is now paying for services that we never had before. Secrets, known as *asymmetric information* in economics, are being unveiled, providing people better information not just on whom to advertise to, but on whom to trust.

These are all positive features for promoting economic efficiency. However, they are troubling for many due to their impact on dignity and autonomy. The public and policy makers alike have become rightly worried that new technologies are impinging on our privacy, and thus our autonomy and dignity, in new and frightening ways. There have been dramatic calls to action even while people continue to happily use services like Amazon and Facebook that share their data with others. Some think that this is just because the public doesn't understand what is at risk. My contention is that people care about privacy, but only insofar as it impinges on their autonomy. For the moment, for most people, the risks of sharing data online are outweighed by the benefits. A better understanding of how and when and why we care about privacy will make for smarter regulations and better ways for consumers to protect themselves and their privacy.

6

CONCLUSION

WE began this book with the small, looking at the biological mechanisms that cause children to trust their parents and the institutions that maintained order in small prehistoric tribes. We ended by looking at how those same mechanisms are still at work now on a global scale as we try to address problems affecting the entire planet and all its human and nonhuman inhabitants.

It is easy to look at the problems that the world is facing—the global reach of environmental impacts, the increasingly partisan and acrimonious nature of our political discourse—and be pessimistic. The problems seem to be growing ever bigger while our capabilities to solve them seem to be shrinking. But taking a wider perspective gives me hope, for two reasons.

The first is that we have always had our discourse dominated by pessimists in the face of change. Matt Ridley's book *The Rational Optimist* notes that since the time of Socrates, pessimists have always been seen as serious and important, while optimists have been derided as foolish, Panglossian Pollyannas, even though time after time the optimists have been proven right.[1]

In ancient Greece, Socrates worried that the widespread adoption of a new technology, literacy and books, would lead to the downfall of civilization; he argued that writing things down will break the fabric of civilization because we will seek wisdom from books rather than from talking to each other. Socrates worried that we would get lost in books and lose the connections that tie us together. Today we celebrate reading and literacy as complements to the knowledge that we gain from each other. In fact, if anything, we worry that with the advent of social media, we learn too much from each other and not enough from books.

Thomas Malthus in the eighteenth century (in a sentiment we still hear today[2]), thought that populations were growing out of control and that civilization would collapse from widespread famine and starvation. Yet technology has always managed to keep pace with population growth, and if anything, many countries are now worried about having too few people, not too many. Today, commentators are again worried about the end of civilization as we know it. New technologies like social media are destabilizing our trust in institutions. Increased population has created environmental problems at a scale that many worry has outpaced the capabilities of our institutions to handle.

Yet on every measure of human well-being that we can measure and track, things have been on a steady path upward since the dawn of civilization. Mortality has been trending downward; happiness has been trending upward. Racial and gender disparities have declined. So has discrimination based on sexual orientation. The percentage of people in poverty globally has declined, as have deaths from diseases. Globally, inequality has declined. Girls' education levels are increasing, infant mortality is down, and access to healthcare is up.[3]

When he was guest editor at *Time* magazine, Bill Gates noted that it's not that the world is getting worse—the data show it has not. Instead things are getting better. It is only our tolerance of bad things that has been going down. Both of these should be seen as good trends, even if we feel that things are getting worse.[4]

Trust has had a more complicated path, at least in recent years; the larger trend of human history that this book has documented shows how the institutions that we have created, from religion to markets to the rule of law, have continually increased the circle of people whom we trust and expanded the capabilities of humans as a species.

While trust in expertise like media and government has had its downs (and ups) in recent decades, the arc of history suggests a positive trend as institutions develop to help us process the flow of information regarding our relationships and to create the right incentives for trustworthy behavior, all while creating ways to mitigate the risks associated with trusting one another and ways to demonstrate one's trustworthiness.

We live in a time where technology and interconnectedness have made our problems global in scale. Geologists have begun to call our current age the *anthropocene*, the era where the trajectory of the planet is primarily shaped by human choices. However, over the centuries, the evolution of human society has also demonstrated an ability to adapt, with social structures changing in order to deal with ever-increasing social dilemmas, ever-larger tragedies of the commons. This growth has not come without problems. Often the very mechanisms designed to create trust are what make us distrustful of difference. However, in each era, our ability to extend the definition of our in-group, to redefine the idea of "someone like me," has only expanded. Great challenges lay ahead, but our social evolutionary roots have given us the tools we need to succeed.

I truly do trust in our ability to overcome these challenges ahead. I hope you do too.

DETAILED CONTENTS

NOTES

1. ECONOMICS OF TRUST

1. Sen, Amartya (1977). Rational Fools: A Critique of the Behavioral Foundations of Economic Theory. *Philosophy & Public Affairs*, 6(4), 317–344.

2. In a similar way, physics tells us that how gravity affects the motions of two bodies in space (e.g., a planet and a star) can be calculated by a high school student and explained to a child. But physics also tells us that predicting the motions of three bodies in space (known as the "three-body problem") is mathematically intractable. That is, the question of how three bodies in space move in relation to each other can be solved only approximately, never fully.

3. Page, S. E. (2007). *The Difference: How the Power of Diversity Creates Better Groups, Firms, Schools, and Societies.* Princeton, NJ: Princeton University Press.

4. Arrow, K. J. (1969). The organization of economic activity: issues pertinent to the choice of market versus nonmarket allocation. *The analysis and evaluation of public expenditure: the PPB system, 1,* 59–73.

5. Arrow, K. J. (1974). *The Limits of Organization.* New York: Norton.

6. Robbins, B. G. (2016). What is trust? A multidisciplinary review, critique, and synthesis. *Sociology compass, 10*(10), 972–986.

7. McLeod, C., in Zalta, E. N. (2015). Trust. In *The Stanford Encyclopedia of Philosophy*

8. Fourcade, M., E. Ollion, and Y. Algan (2015). The Superiority of Economists. *Journal of Economic Perspectives*, 29(1): 89–114.

9. Lazear, E. (2000). Economic Imperialism. *Quarterly Journal of Economics*, 115(1), 99–146.

10. Card, D, Pischke, J. (2010). The Credibility Revolution in Empirical Economics: How Better Research Design is Taking the Con out of Econometrics. *Journal of Economic Perspectives*, 24(2), 3–30.

11. Deaton, A. (2010). Instruments, Randomization, and Learning About Development. *Journal of Economic Literature*, 48, 424–455.

12. Kuhn, T. S. (1962). *The Structure of Scientific Revolutions*. Chicago: University of Chicago Press..

13. Hill, T., Lewicki, P., Czyzewska, M., & Schuller, G. (1990). The Role of Learned Inferential Encoding Rules in the Perception of Faces: Effects of Nonconscious Self-Perpetuation of a Bias. *Journal of Experimental Social Psychology*, 26(4), 350–371.

14. Raz, J. (2017). Intention and value. *Philosophical Explorations*, 20(sup2), 109–126.

15. Tavuchis, N. (1991). *Mea Culpa: A Sociology of Apology and Reconciliation*. Stanford, CA: Stanford University Press.

16. Ho, B. (2012). Apologies as signals: with evidence from a trust game. *Management Science*, 58(1), 141–158.

17. Card, D., and S. DellaVigna (2013). Nine Facts about Top Journals in Economics. *Journal of Economic Literature*, 51(1), 144–161.

18. Angrist, J. D., and J-S. Pischke (2010). "The Credibility Revolution in Empirical Economics: How Better Research Design Is Taking the Con out of Econometrics." *Journal of Economic Perspectives*, 24(2): 3–30.

19. However, exploring the possibility that B could indeed be true leads you down an interesting rabbit hole of time and of free will that I will leave to readers to ponder on their own.

20. Zhou, X., Liu, Y., & Ho, B. (2015). The cultural transmission of cooperative norms. *Frontiers in psychology*, 6, 1554; Ho, Apologies as signals.

21. Halperin, B., Ho, B., List, J. A., & Muir, I. (2019). *Toward an understanding of the economics of apologies: evidence from a large-scale natural field experiment* (No. w25676). National Bureau of Economic Research.

22. Slonim, R., and A. E. Roth (1998). Learning in High Stakes Ultimatum Games: An Experiment in the Slovak Republic. *Econometrica*, 66(3), 569–596.

23. Dohmen, T., Falk, A., Huffman, D., & Sunde, U. (2008). Representative Trust and Reciprocity: Prevalence and Determinants. *Economic Inquiry*, *46*(1), 84–90.

2. THE HISTORY OF TRUST

1. Dawkins, R. (1989). *The Selfish Gene*. Oxford and New York: Oxford University Press.
2. Foster, K., T. Wenseleers, and F. Ratnieks (2006). Kin Selection Is the Key to Altruism. *Trends in Ecology & Evolution, 21*: 57–60. 10.1016/j .tree.2005.11.020.
3. Smith, J., and G. Price (1973). The Logic of Animal Conflict. *Nature*, *246*, 15–18. doi:10.1038/246015a0.
4. *Stanford Encyclopedia of Philosophy*. s.v. Biological Altruism. https:// plato.stanford.edu/entries/altruism-biological/.
5. Engel, C. (2011). Dictator games: A meta study. Experimental economics, 14(4), 583–610.
6. Fehr, E., & Fischbacher, U. (2002). Why social preferences matter–the impact of non-selfish motives on competition, cooperation and incentives. *The economic journal, 112*(478), C1–C33.
7. Blair, J., D. R. Mitchell, and K. Blair (2005). *The Psychopath: Emotion and the Brain*. Malden, MA: Blackwell Publishing.
8. Orr, S. P., and J. T. Lanzetta (1980). Facial Expressions of Emotion as Conditioned Stimuli for Human Autonomic Responses. *Journal of Personality and Social Psychology, 38*(2): 278–282.
9. J. P. W. Scharlemann, C. C. Eckel, A. Kacelnik, and R. K. Wilson (2001). The Value of a Smile: Game Theory with a Human Face. *Journal of Economic Psychology, 22*(5): 617–640. https://doi.org/10.1016/S0167 -4870(01)00059-9.
10. Interestingly, the same experiment shows that men are more likely to trust smiling women than smiling men, but women are less likely to trust smiling women than smiling men. The authors posit that the trust we place in smiling faces is related to mating opportunities, pointing again to the evolutionary connection between smiles and trust.
11. Provine, R. R. (1993). Laughter Punctuates Speech: Linguistic, Social and Gender Contexts of Laughter. *Ethology, 95*: 291–298. doi:10.1111/j.1439-0310.1993.tb00478.x.

12. Weems, S. (2014). *Ha! The Science of When We Laugh and Why*. New York: Basic Books.

13. Williams, J. H. G. (2019). "Why Children Find 'Poo' so Hilarious—and How Adults Should Tackle It." *The Conversation*, March 26. http://theconversation.com/why-children-find-poo-so-hilarious-and-how-adults-should-tackle-it-72258.

14. Adams, M. (2016). *In Praise of Profanity*. New York: Oxford University Press.

15. Magon, N., and S. Kalra (2011). The Orgasmic History of Oxytocin: Love, Lust, and Labor. *Indian Journal of Endocrinology and Metabolism, 15* (Suppl3): S156–S161.

16. Feldman, R., I. Gordon, and O. Zagoory-Sharon (2011). Maternal and Paternal Plasma, Salivary, and Urinary Oxytocin and Parent-Infant Synchrony: Considering Stress and Affiliation Components of Human Bonding. *Developmental Science, 14:* 752–761. doi:10.1111/j.1467-7687.2010.01021.x.

17. Kosfeld, M., M. Heinrichs, P. Zak, U. Fischbacher, and E. Fehr (2005). Oxytocin Increases Trust in Humans. *Nature 435*, 673–676. doi:10.1038/nature03701.

18. Nave, Camerer, and McCulloguh reviewed the literature and noted that Zak's methods may not accurately measure oxytocin, and larger-scale studies do not find associations between genetic markers of oxytocin and trust. Still there are a fair number of papers by Zak and others that do establish a link between oxytocin and trust. Nave, G., Camerer, C., & McCullough, M. (2015). Does oxytocin increase trust in humans? A critical review of research. Perspectives on Psychological Science, 10(6), 772–789.

19. Fareri, D. S., Chang, L. J., & Delgado, M. R. (2012). Effects of direct social experience on trust decisions and neural reward circuitry. Frontiers in neuroscience, 6, 148.

20. Cesarini, D., C. T. Dawes, J. H. Fowler, M. Johannesson, P. Lichtenstein, and B. Wallace (2008). Heritability of Cooperative Behavior in the Trust Game. *Proceedings of the National Academy of Sciences, 105*(10), 3721–3726.

21. Williams, L. E., and J. A. Bargh (2008). "Experiencing Physical Warmth Promotes Interpersonal Warmth." *Science, 322*(5901): 606–607. doi:10.1126/science.1162548.

22. Chapman, G. (2009). *The Five Love Languages: How to Express Heartfelt Commitment to Your Mate.* Chicago, IL: Moody.

23. Waldfogel, J. (2009). *Scroogenomics: Why You Shouldn't Buy Presents for the Holidays.* Princeton, NJ: Princeton University Press. www.jstor.org /stable/j.ctt7ssvs.

24. Camerer, C. (1988). Gifts as Economic Signals and Social Symbols. *American Journal of Sociology 94*: S180–S214.

25. However, a fair critique of markets is that while they do a good job at efficiently allocating resources, they may not do as good a job at ensuring a fair allocation. Government has a useful role to play in ensuring fairness.

26. Although some have questioned whether Marco Polo actually made it to China. Wood, F. (1996). Did Marco Polo Go to China? *Asian Affairs, 27*(3), 296–304.

27. Fairbank, J. K., & Teng, S. Y. (1941). On the Ch'ing tributary system. *Harvard journal of Asiatic studies, 6*(2), 135–246.

28. Bronislaw, M. (1922). *Argonauts of the Western Pacific: An Account of Native Enterprise and Adventure in the Archipelagoes of Melanesian New Guinea.* London and New York: George Routledge & Sons and E. P. Dutton.

29. Marriott, McKim (1955), "Little Communities in an Indigenous Civilization", in McKim Marriott (ed.), *Village India: Studies in the Little Community,* University of Chicago Press, pp. 198–202

30. Those with some prior knowledge of economics may note that this definition of "discount rate" conflates time preferences and risk preferences . . . The relationship between risk and time is an interesting one which has not been fully resolved within behavioral economics.

31. Kandori, M. (1992). Social Norms and Community Enforcement. *Review of Economic Studies, 59*(1): 63–80.

32. Hill, R. A., and R. I. Dunbar (2003). Social Network Size in Humans. *Human Nature, 14*(1), 53–72.

33. Dunbar, R. I. (2016). Do Online Social Media Cut Through the Constraints That Limit the Size of Offline Social Networks? *Royal Society Open Science, 3*(1): 150292. https://doi.org/10.1098/rsos.150292.

34. Pope, W. (1975). Durkheim as a Functionalist. *Sociological Quarterly, 16*(3): 361–379.

35. Greif, A. (2004). Impersonal Exchange Without Partial Law: The Community Responsibility System. *Chicago Journal of International Law, 5*(1): 107–136.

36. Aronson, E., and J. Mills (1959). The Effect of Severity of Initiation on Liking for a Group. *Journal of Abnormal and Social Psychology,* 59(2): 177–181.

37. Berger, J. A., C. Heath, and B. Ho (2005). Divergence in Cultural Practices: Tastes as Signals of Identity. *Scholarly Commons,* Penn Libraries, University of Pennsylvania. Retrieved from https://repository .upenn.edu/marketing_papers/306.

38. National Research Council, Committee on the Human Dimensions of Global Change, E. Ostrom, T. Dietz, N. Dolšak, P. C. Stern, S. Stovich, and E. U. Weber (Eds.), Division of Behavioral and Social Sciences and Education (2002). *The Drama of the Commons.* Washington, DC: National Academy Press.

39. Kandori, Michihiro, G. J. Mailath, and R. Rob. (1993). Learning, Mutation, and Long Run Equilibria in Games. *Econometrica, 61*(1): 29–56. www.jstor.org/stable/2951777.

40. Fehr, E., and S. Gächter. (1999). *Cooperation and Punishment in Public Goods Experiments.* Institute for Empirical Research in Economics Working Paper No. 10. CESifo Working Paper Series No. 183, June. https://ssrn.com/abstract=203194.

41. Goette, L., Huffman, D., & Meier, S. (2006). The impact of group membership on cooperation and norm enforcement: Evidence using random assignment to real social groups. *American Economic Review,* 96(2), 212–216.

42. Calvert, R. (1992). Leadership and its basis in problems of social coordination. *International Political Science Review, 13*(1), 7–24.

43. Barro, R. J., and R. M. McCleary (2003). Religion and Economic Growth Across Countries. *American Sociological Review, 68*(5): 760–781. www.jstor.org/stable/1519761; the researchers did their best to control for other factors, like reverse casualty, although they themselves emphasized that many other factors existed that they were unable to control for.

44. Lang, M., B. G. Purzycki, C. L. Apicella, Q. D. Atkinson, A. Bolyanatz, E. Cohen, . . . , and J. Henrich (2019). Moralizing Gods, Impartiality and Religious Parochialism Across 15 Societies. *Proceedings of the Royal Society B: Biological Sciences, 286*(1898). https://royalsocietypublishing .org/doi/10.1098/rspb.2019.0202.

45. Weber, M. *The Protestant Ethic and the Spirit of Capitalism.* New York: Scribner, 1958.

46. Putnam Robert (1993). *Making Democracy Work: Civic Traditions in Modern Italy.* Princeton, NJ: Princeton University Press; La Porta Rafael, Lopezde-Silanes Florencio, Shleifer Andrei, Vishny Robert W (1997). Trust in Large Organizations. *American Economic Review,* 87:333–338.

47. Benjamin, D. J., J. J. Choi, and G. Fisher (2010). *Religious Identity and Economic Behavior.* NBER Working Paper No. w15925, April. https://ssrn.com/abstract=1594559.

48. Duhaime, E. P. (2015). Is the call to prayer a call to cooperate? A field experiment on the impact of religious salience on prosocial behavior. *Judgment and Decision Making, 10*(6), 593.

49. DeBono, A., Shariff, A. F., Poole, S., & Muraven, M. (2017). Forgive us our trespasses: Priming a forgiving (but not a punishing) god increases unethical behavior. *Psychology of Religion and Spirituality, 9*(S1), S1.

50. Rigdon, M., K. Ishii, M. Watabe, and S. Kitayama (2009). Minimal Social Cues in the Dictator Game. *Journal of Economic Psychology, 30*(3): 358–367. https://doi.org/10.1016/j.joep.2009.02.002.

51. Fair warning—the number of observations in the experiment was quite small, and the statistical significance was marginal, although that problem is not unique to this paper.

52. Lesson, P. T. (2018). Witch Trials. *Economic Journal, 128*(613): 2066–2105. https://doi.org/10.1111/ecoj.12498.

53. Tversky, A., and D. Kahneman (1989). Rational Choice and the Framing of Decisions. In *Multiple Criteria Decision Making and Risk Analysis Using Microcomputers,* 81–126. Berlin and Heidelberg: Springer.

54. Dales, R. C. (1989). *Medieval Discussions of the Eternity of the World.* Vol. 18, Brill's Series in Intellectual History. https://brill.com/view/title/5655.

55. Cox, T. H., and S. Blake (1991). Managing Cultural Diversity: Implications for Organizational Competitiveness. *Academy of Management Perspectives, 5*(3): 45–56.

56. Page, S. E. (2010). *Diversity and Complexity.* Vol. 2. Princeton, NJ: Princeton University Press.

57. Weber, M. (1978). *Economy and Society: An Outline of Interpretive Sociology* (Vol. 1). Berkeley: University of California Press.

58. Milgrom, P. R., North, D. C., & Weingast, B. R. (1990). The Role of Institutions in the Revival of Trade: The Law Merchant, Private Judges, and the Champagne Fairs. *Economics & Politics, 2*(1), 1–23.

59. Kranton, R. E. (1996). Reciprocal Exchange: A Self-Sustaining System. *American Economic Review, 86*(4): 830–851.

60. Ogilvie, S. (2011). *Institutions and European Trade: Merchant Guilds, 1000–1800.* Cambridge: Cambridge University Press.

61. This is Ogilvie's explanation.

62. Hobbes, T. (1968). *Leviathan.* Baltimore, MD: Penguin.

63. Pinker, S., and OverDrive Inc. (2011). *The Better Angels of Our Nature: Why Violence Has Declined.* New York: Penguin.

64. Hobbes, *Leviathan.*

65. Of course, we could spend an entire semester talking about many other theories of the role of government in society, from the Marxist view that government perpetuates existing class structures; to a more modern sociological view that institutions like government are designed to self-perpetuate; to other game-theoretic views like Randall Calvert's, in which the sovereign coordinates collective action and collects rents for performing that service. For this chapter, we will focus on just these two views of government: (1) government serves to facilitate collective action; and (2) government enforces the rules that we all follow.

66. Ostrom, E. (1990). *Governing the Commons: The Evolution of Institutions for Collective Action.* New York: Cambridge University Press.

67. Calvert, R. L., M. D. McCubbins, and B. R. Weingast (1989). A Theory of Political Control and Agency Discretion. *American Journal of Political Science, 33*(3): 588–611.

68. Acemoglu, D., & Robinson, J. A. (2012). *Why Nations Fail: The Origins of Power, Prosperity, and Poverty.* Currency. Some of their most influential articles include: Acemoglu, D., Johnson, S., & Robinson, J. A. (2002). Reversal of Fortune: Geography and Institutions in the Making of the Modern World Income Distribution. *The Quarterly Journal of Economics, 117*(4), 1231–1294; Acemoglu, D., Johnson, S., & Robinson, J. (2005). The Rise of Europe: Atlantic Trade, Institutional Change, and Economic Growth. *American Economic Review, 95*(3), 546–579; Acemoglu, D., Johnson, S., & Robinson, J. A. (2001). The Colonial Origins of Comparative Development: An Empirical Investigation. *American Economic Review, 91*(5), 1369–1401.

69. Jensen, K. (2016). The Experiment: What Do Five Monkeys Have to Do with Negotiations? *Forbes*, October 31. https://www.forbes.com/sites

/keldjensen/2016/10/31/the-experiment-what-do-five-monkeys-have
-to-do-with-negotiations/#4c13280f498d.
70. Ginsburg, T., Z. Elkins, and J. Melton (2009). *The Endurance of National Constitutions*.
71. Xie, W., Ho, B., Meier, S., & Zhou, X. (2017). Rank Reversal Aversion Inhibits Redistribution Across Societies. *Nature Human Behaviour*, *1*(8): 1–5.

3. TRUST IN THE MODERN ECONOMY

1. U.S. Treasury Department. (n.d.). History of "In God We Trust." Retrieved January 4, 2020 from https://www.treasury.gov/about/education/Pages/in-god-we-trust.aspx.
2. "The Colour of Money." *99% Invisible*, January 1, 1970, 99percentinvisible.org/episode/episode-54-the-colour-of-money/.
3. We will see in the next section how we measure trust in currencies using interest rates. The United States tends to enjoy the lowest interest rates in the world as a consequence of that trust.
4. Benjamin, A., and A. Shore (2017). *Change Is Good! A History of Money*. British Museum Blog. Retrieved from https://blog.britishmuseum.org/change-is-good-a-history-of-money/.
5. Goldstein, J., and D. Kestenbaum (2010). The Island of Stone Money. NPR, December 10. Retrieved from https://www.npr.org/sections/money/2011/02/15/131934618/the-island-of-stone-money.
6. Federal Reserve Bank of St. Louis (n.d.). "Functions of Money—The Economic Lowdown Podcast Series." http://www.stlouisfed.org/education/economic-lowdown-podcast-series/episode-9-functions-of-money.
7. *GoldSilverCopper Standard* (n.d.). TV Tropes. Retrieved from https://tvtropes.org/pmwiki/pmwiki.php/Main/GoldSilverCopperStandard.
8. "Bryan's 'Cross of Gold' Speech: Mesmerizing the Masses" (n.d.). *History Matters—The U.S. Survey Course on the Web*. historymatters.gmu.edu/d/5354/.

Here's a fascinating (and ironic) footnote: Newton also spent much of his life on alchemy, trying to use chemistry to turn base metals into gold. He may have never figured out how to create gold using chemistry, but he was able to "create" gold through monetary policy as the central banker.

9. "Episode 421: The Birth of the Dollar Bill" (2012). NPR, December 7. Retrieved from https://www.npr.org/transcripts/166747693.
10. Fiat (n.d.). Dictionary.com. https://www.dictionary.com/browse/fiat?s=t.
11. Fontevecchia, A. (2012). How Many Olympic-Sized Swimming Pools Can We Fill with Billionaire Gold? *Forbes*, March 20. www.forbes.com /sites/afontevecchia/2010/11/19/how-many-olympic-sized-swimming -pools-can-we-fill-with-billionaire-gold/#37af2f2f69f1.
12. Neumann, M. J. (1992). Seigniorage in the United States: How Much Does the U.S. Government Make from Money Production? *Federal Reserve Bank of St. Louis Review*, 74(March/April). https://files.stlouisfed .org/files/htdocs/publications/review/92/03/Seigniorage_Mar _Apr1992.pdf.
13. Bernanke, B. (2000). *Essays on the Great Depression*. Princeton, NJ: Princeton University Press.
14. Krugman, P. R. (1994). *Peddling prosperity: Economic sense and nonsense in the age of diminished expectations*. New York: Norton.
15. Ramsden, D. (2004). *A Very Short History of Chinese Paper Money*. Financial Sense University. Retrieved from https://web.archive.org /web/20080609220821/http://www.financialsense.com/fsu/editorials /ramsden/2004/0617.html.
16. Everett (n.d.). *World War I Poster Showing Uncle Sam*. Fine Art America. Retrieved from https://fineartamerica.com/featured/world-war-i-poster -showing-uncle-sam-everett.html.
17. Roeder, O. (2014). *What the Next Generation of Economists Is Working On*. FiveThirtyEight, December 17. Retrieved from https://fivethirtyeight.com /features/what-the-next-generation-of-economists-are-working-on/.
18. Witko, C. (2019). "How Wall Street Became a Big Chunk of the U.S. Economy—and When the Democrats Signed On." *Washington Post*, Monkey Cage, April 18. Retrieved from https://www.washingtonpost .com/news/monkey-cage/wp/2016/03/29/how-wall-street-became -a-big-chunk-of-the-u-s-economy-and-when-the-democrats-signed -on/.
19. "Stuff" is just my way of explaining the concept of utility. When econo- mists say that we want to help people maximize utility, we just mean that we want to help give people what they want. The stuff that we want the economy to produce could be even more intangible than vaca-

tions or education, like dignity or identity, but that is something at the fringes of modern economics, which we will return to in chapter 6. Views of the importance of dignity and belonging and the creation of jobs are perhaps more in line with what many noneconomists want from the economy. We will touch on some of these topics, but they are mostly way beyond the scope of this book.

20. Malthus, T. R. (1986). *An Essay on the Principle of Population*. 1798. In *The Works of Thomas Robert Malthus, Vol. 1*, 1–139, London: Pickering & Chatto Publishers.

21. In an efficient market, the amount that they get paid should be equal to the value they create, but in an inefficient market, a monopolist could extract more.

22. Greif, A. (2006). *Institutions and the Path to the Modern Economy: Lessons from Medieval Trade*. New York: Cambridge University Press.

23. It is interesting to note that the potential for worker exploitation of capital is the opposite of what we might expect to be concerned about if we've read Karl Marx; in the Marxist view, it is capital that exploits labor. He was worried that if the owners of capital could monopolize that capital, then they would hold all the power in the capital-labor relationship. This problem is compounded if capitalists could use their power to bend government regulations to their benefit. The discussion in this chapter assumes an equal initial bargaining position between labor and capital, but it acknowledges that power dynamics would shift if one side or the other held monopoly power.

24. Yiin, W. (2019). Former Banks of NYC Repurposed into Drugstores, Ice Cream Parlors, and Pop-up Stores. *Untapped New York*, February 7. Retrieved from https://untappedcities.com/2013/08/02/former-banks-nyc-repurposed-into-drugstores-apartments-pop-up-stores/.

25. Chen, J. (2020). *Accredited Investor*. Investopedia, January 17. Retrieved from https://www.investopedia.com/terms/a/accreditedinvestor.asp.

26. Locke, M. (1989). Restaurant Issues Its Own "Deli Dollars." *LA Times*, November 19. Retrieved from https://www.latimes.com/archives/la-xpm-1989-11-19-mn-215-story.html.

27. Campbell, C. (2019). How China Is Using Big Data to Create a Social Credit Score. *Time*, August 14. Retrieved from https://time.com/collection/davos-2019/5502592/china-social-credit-score/.

28. Federal Reserve Bank of St. Louis (2020). 1-Month AA Financial Commercial Paper Rate. FRED Economic Data, January 17. Retrieved from https://fred.stlouisfed.org/series/DCPF1M.

29. National Bureau of Economic Research (n.d.). *The Global Financial Crisis: A Selective Review of Recent Research in the International Finance and Macroeconomics Program.* Retrieved from https://www.nber.org/programs/ifm/ifm09.html.

30. Irvine, Sol (2012). What Is It That A Lawyer Does That Takes So Many Hours? *Forbes*, May 21. Retrieved from https://www.forbes.com/sites/quora/2012/05/21/what-is-it-that-a-lawyer-does-that-takes-so-many-hours/#5047d986205b.

31. For a more thorough discussion of these questions, see B. Ho, and D. Huffman (2018), Trust and the Law, in *Research Handbook on Behavioral Law and Economics* (Cheltenham, UK: Edward Elgar).

32. Falk, A., and M. Kosfeld (2006). The Hidden Costs of Control. *American Economic Review, 96*(5): 1611–1630.

33. Halac, M. (2012). Relational Contracts and the Value of Relationships. *American Economic Review, 102*(2): 750–779.

34. Aghion, P., and J. Tirole (1997). Formal and Real Authority in Organizations. *Journal of Political Economy, 105*(1): 1–29.

35. Algan, Y., and P. Cahuc (2014). Trust, Growth, and Well-Being: New Evidence and Policy Implications. In *Handbook of Economic Growth* (Vol. 2, 49–120). New York: Elsevier.

36. Acemoglu, D., and J. A. Robinson (2005). *Economic Origins of Dictatorship and Democracy.* New York: Cambridge University Press.

37. Falk and Kosfeld, The Hidden Costs of Control.

38. Halac, Relational Contracts and the Value of Relationships.

39. Smith, A., and D. Stewart (1963). *An Inquiry into the Nature and Causes of the Wealth of Nations, Vol. 1.* Homewood, IL: Irwin.

40. Coase. R. H. The nature of the firm (1937). *The Nature of the Firm. Origins, Evolution, and Development.* (New York: Oxford University Press), 18–33.

41. Alchian, A. A., and H. Demsetz (1972). Production, Information Costs, and Economic Organization. *American Economic Review, 62*(5): 777–795. Coase, R. H. (2000). The Acquisition of Fisher Body by General Motors. *Journal of Law and Economics, 43*(1): 15–32.

42. Xie, W., B. Ho, S. Meier, and X. Zhou (2017). Rank Reversal Aversion Inhibits Redistribution Across Societies. *Nature Human Behaviour, 1*(8): 1–5.

43. Chwe, M. S. Y. (1990). Why Were Workers Whipped? Pain in a Principal-Agent Model. *Economic Journal*, *100*(403): 1109–1121.

44. Aghion, P., and J. Tirole (1997). Formal and Real Authority in Organizations. *Journal of Political Economy*, *105*(1): 1–29.

45. Bao, J. (2020). (How) Do Risky Perks Benefit Firms? The Case of Unlimited Vacation. In *Academy of Management Proceedings* (Vol. 2020, No. 1, p. 18308). Briarcliff Manor, NY: Academy of Management.

46. Lazear, E. P. (2000). Performance Pay and Productivity. *American Economic Review*, *90*(5): 1346–1361.

47. Fehr, E., S. Gächter, and G. Kirchsteiger (1997). Reciprocity as a Contract Enforcement Device: Experimental Evidence. *Econometrica: Journal of the Econometric Society:* 833–860.

48. See the summary of the gift exchange model of labor in S. DellaVigna, J. A. List, U. Malmendier, and G. Rao (2016), *Estimating Social Preferences and Gift Exchange at Work*, Working Paper 22043, National Bureau of Economic Research, https://www.nber.org/papers/w22043.

49. McAlister, A. R., and T. B. Cornwell (2010). Children's Brand Symbolism Understanding: Links to Theory of Mind and Executive Functioning. *Psychology & Marketing*, *27*(3): 203–228.

50. Kreps, D. M. (1990). Corporate Culture and Economic Theory. *Perspectives on Positive Political Economy*, *90:* 109–10.

51. Lewis, R. A., and D. H. Reiley (2014). Online Ads and Offline Sales: Measuring the Effect of Retail Advertising via a Controlled Experiment on Yahoo! *Quantitative Marketing and Economics*, *12*(3): 235–266.

52. Becker, G. S., and K. M. Murphy (1993). A Simple Theory of Advertising as a Good or Bad. *Quarterly Journal of Economics*, *108*(4): 941–964.

53. Wattenberg, L. (2015). *Was Freakonomics Right About Baby Names?* Baby-Name Wizard, July 30. Retrieved from https://www.babynamewizard.com/archives/2015/7/was-freakonomics-right-about-baby-names.

54. Berger, J. A., Ho, B., & Joshi, Y. V. (2011). Identity Signaling with Social Capital: A Model of Symbolic Consumption. *Marketing Science Institute Working Paper Series*. https://www.msi.org/working-papers/identity-signaling-with-social-capital-a-model-of-symbolic-consumption/.

55. Bertrand, M., and F. Kamenica (2018). *Coming Apart? Cultural Distances in the United States over Time* (No. w24771). National Bureau of Economic Research. https://www.nber.org/papers/w24771.

56. Berger, J. (2013). *Contagious: Why Things Catch On* New York: Simon and Schuster. Ho, B. (2017). How Hollywood Manipulates You by Using Your Childhood Memories. Quartz, October 24. Retrieved from https://qz.com/1108122/how-hollywood-manipulates-you-using-your -childhood-memories/.

57. Hsiaw, A. (2014). Learning Tastes Through Social Interaction. *Journal of Economic Behavior and Organization*, *107:* 64–85.

58. Farrell, H. (2020). *Dark Leviathan*. Aeon, January 23. Retrieved from https://aeon.co/essays/why-the-hidden-internet-can-t-be-a-libertarian -paradise.

59. Sabanoglu, T. (2019). *Amazon: Third-Party Seller Share 2020*. Statista, November 19. Retrieved from https://www.statista.com/statistics/259782 /third-party-seller-share-of-amazon-platform/.

60. Institutions of this kind have existed for a long time—they just are especially prominent in today's new economy, where the technology has given them greater scope.

61. Uber's market share in November 2019 was 69.7 percent.

62. Irwin, N. (2017). Tale of Two Janitors—Kodak vs. Apple—Dramatizes How Economy Has Changed. *Seattle Times*, September 9. Retrieved from https://www.seattletimes.com/business/economy/tale-of-two -janitors-kodak-vs-apple-dramatizes-how-economy-has-changed/.

63. Torpey, K. (2018). Study Suggests 25 Percent of Bitcoin Users Are Associated with Illegal Activity. *Bitcoin Magazine*, January 22. Retrieved from https://bitcoinmagazine.com/articles/study-suggests-25-percent -bitcoin-users-are-associated-illegal-activity1.

64. United States Money Supply Mo (n.d.). Trading Economics. Retrieved from https://tradingeconomics.com/united-states/money-supply-mo.

65. Purkey, H. (2010). The Art of Money Laundering. *Florida Journal of International Law*, *22:* 111.

66. Bloomberg (2017). Ethereum Bandits Stole $225 Million This Year. *Fortune*, August 28. Retrieved from https://fortune.com/2017/08/28 /ethereum-cryptocurrency-stolen-bitcoin/.

4. TRUSTING INSTITUTIONS WITH EXPERTISE

1. Pew Research Center (2019). Confidence in Leaders of the Military Has Gone Up; Confidence in Some Other Institutions Is Declining.

March 22. Retrieved from https://www.pewresearch.org/ft_19-03-21
_scienceconfidence_confidence-in-leaders-military-vs-others/.

2. Washington's Farewell Adress 1796, retrieved from https://avalon.law
.yale.edu/18th_century/washing.asp.

3. Lindgren, J. (2019). Science Study: Republicans Struggle with Evolution, Democrats Struggle with the Earth Going Around the Sun.
Washington Post, April 22. Retrieved from https://www.washingtonpost
.com/news/volokh-conspiracy/wp/2014/02/25/most-democrats
-dont-know-it-takes-a-year-for-the-earth-to-go-around-the-sun/.

4. Bullock, J. G., Gerber, A. S., Hill, S. J., & Huber, G. A. (2015). Partisan
Bias in Factual Beliefs about Politics. *Quarterly Journal of Political
Science, 10*(4), 519–578.

5. Lustgarten, A. (2018). Palm Oil Was Supposed to Help Save the Planet.
Instead It Unleashed a Catastrophe. *New York Times* magazine. https://
www.nytimes.com/2018/11/20/magazine/palm-oil-borneo-climate
-catastrophe.html.

6. Barbaro, M. (2019). *How the Democratic Debates Narrow the Field. New
York Times* podcast, August 2. Retrieved from https://www.nytimes
.com/2019/08/02/podcasts/the-daily/democratic-debates-2020-election
.html.

7. Benjamin, D. J., & Shapiro, J. M. (2009). Thin-slice forecasts of gubernatorial elections. *The review of economics and statistics, 91*(3), 523–536.

8. Bullock, J. G., A. S. Gerber, S. J. Hill, and G. A. Huber (2013). *Partisan
Bias in Factual Beliefs About Politics*. No. w19080. National Bureau of
Economic Research.

9. Cohen, G. L. (2003). Party over Policy: The Dominating Impact of
Group Influence on Political Beliefs. *Journal of Personality and Social
Psychology, 85*(5): 808–822.

10. Of course, as with any policy question, there is deep complexity within
abortion policy as well once you get into it—from the nuances of
biology, to ethics, to the economic impact of abortion laws, and the
impact on travel times. Famously, Steve Levitt showed that one benefit
that nobody anticipated of legalizing abortion was that there would be
less crime decades later.

11. Levitt, S. D. (1995). *Using Electoral Cycles in Police Hiring to Estimate
the Effect of Police on Crime*. No. w4991. National Bureau of Economic
Research.

12. Gawande, K., and U. Bandyopadhyay (2000). Is Protection for Sale? Evidence on the Grossman-Helpman Theory of Endogenous Protection. *Review of Economics and Statistics, 82*(1): 139–152.

13. Maskin, E., & Tirole, J. (2004). The Politician and the Judge: Accountability in Government. *American Economic Review, 94*(4), 1034–1054.

14. Murray, A., Smith, A. (1874). An Inquiry into the Nature and Causes of the Wealth of Nations . . . New edition, revised, corrected and improved. United Kingdom: A. Murray.

15. Silverman, C. (2016). *This Analysis Shows How Viral Fake Election News Stories Outperformed Real News on Facebook.* Buzzfeed, November 16. Retrieved from https://www.buzzfeednews.com/article/craigsilverman /viral-fake-election-news-outperformed-real-news-on-facebook.

16. Clark, D. J. (dir.) (2019). *Behind the Curve.* Retrieved from https://www .netflix.com/title/81015076.

17. Ho, B., and P. Liu (2015). Herd Journalism: Investment in Novelty and Popularity in Markets for News. *Information Economics and Policy, 31:* 33–46.

18. Hall, E. (2020). Here Are 20 Headlines Comparing Meghan Markle to Kate Middleton That Might Show Why She and Prince Harry Are Cutting off Royal Reporters. Buzzfeed, January 13. Retrieved from https://www.buzzfeednews.com/article/ellievhall/meghan-markle -kate-middleton-double-standards-royal.

19. Groseclose, T., & Milyo, J. (2005). A Measure of Media Bias. *The Quarterly Journal of Economics, 120*(4), 1191–1237; Gentzkow, M., & Shapiro, J. M. (2010). What Drives Media Slant? Evidence from US Daily Newspapers. *Econometrica, 78*(1), 35–71.

20. Gentzkow and Shapiro, Media Bias and Reputation.

21. Ho, B., and P. Liu (2015). Herd Journalism.

22. Formally, economists tend to use Bayes's rule to model information acquisition. New information comes in as a signal, and we use Bayes's rule to adjust our beliefs about the state of the world. So long as we are processing information correctly, more information can only move us (weakly) closer to the truth.

23. However, there is an interesting question about whether there is such a thing as *truth*, and if there is, whether it is ever knowable.

24. Berger, J., and K. L. Milkman (2012). What Makes Online Content Viral?. *Journal of Marketing Research, 49*(2): 192–205.

25. Cheng, I. H., and A. Hsiaw (2019). *Distrust in Experts and the Origins of Disagreement*. Tuck School of Business Working Paper, 2864563. Sethi, R., and M. Yildiz (2016). Communication with Unknown Perspectives. *Econometrica, 84*(6): 2029–2069.

26. Ortoleva, P., & Snowberg, E. (2015). Overconfidence in Political Behavior. *American Economic Review, 105*(2), 504–535; Stone, D. F. (2019). "Unmotivated Bias" and Partisan Hostility: Empirical Evidence. *Journal of Behavioral and Experimental Economics, 79*, 12–26; *Feelings About Partisans and the Parties* (2016). Pew Research Center, June 22. Retrieved from https://www.pewresearch.org/politics/2016/06/22/1 -feelings-about-partisans-and-the-parties/.

27. Krehbiel, K. (1993). Where's the Party? *British Journal of Political Science, 23*(2): 235–266.

28. Fiorina, M. P. (2016). The Political Parties Have Sorted. *A Hoover Institution Essay on Contemporary American Politics*, Series 3, 1–20.

29. Morris, S. (2001). Political Correctness. *Journal of Political Economy, 109*(2): 231–265.

30. Pew Research Center. (2018) Social media outpaces print newspapers in the U.S. as a news source. Retrieved from https://www.pewresearch .org/fact-tank/2018/12/10/social-media-outpaces-print-newspapers-in -the-u-s-as-a-news-source/

31. Oremus, W. (2019). These Startups Want to Protect You from Fake News. Can You Trust Them? *Slate*, January 25. Retrieved from https:// slate.com/technology/2019/01/newsguard-nuzzelrank-media-ratings -fake-news.html.

32. Eckles, D. R. F. Kizilcec, and E. Bakshy (2016). Peer Encouragement Designs. *Proceedings of the National Academy of Sciences, 113*(27), 7316–7322.

33. Bikhchandani, S., Hirshleifer, D., & Welch, I. (1992). A Theory of Fads, Fashion, Custom, and Cultural Change as Informational Cascades. *Journal of Political Economy, 100*(5), 992–1026; Banerjee, A. V. (1992). A Simple Model of Herd Behavior. *Quarterly Journal of Economics, 107*(3), 797–817.

34. Enns, P. (2014). *Presidential Campaigns Are Less Important Than Previously Thought in Influencing How People Vote*. LSE US Centre,

May 15. Retrieved from https://blogs.lse.ac.uk/usappblog/2013/09/05/presidential-campaigns-fundamentals/. Allcott, H., and M. Gentzkow (2017). Social Media and Fake News in the 2016 Election. *Journal of Economic Perspectives*, *31*(2): 211–236.

35. Schoenfeld, J. D., & Ioannidis, J. P. (2013). Is Everything We Eat Associated with Cancer? A Systematic Cookbook Review. *The American Journal of Clinical Nutrition*, *97*(1), 127–134.

36. Blendon, R. J., J. M. Benson, and J. O. Hero (2014). Public Trust in Physicians—US Medicine in International Perspective. *New England Journal of Medicine*, *371*(17): 1570–1572.

    While this trend persisted for much of the 2010's, there was a significant upswing in public trust for medicine in 2020 in response to the Covid-19 pandemic: https://www.pewresearch.org/science/2020/05/21/trust-in-medical-scientists-has-grown-in-u-s-but-mainly-among-democrats/.

37. Iuga, A. O., and M. J. McGuire (2014). Adherence and Health Care Costs. *Risk Management and Healthcare Policy*, *7*, 35–44.

38. Singer, N., and K. Thomas (2019). Drug Sites Upend Doctor-Patient Relations: "It's Restaurant-Menu Medicine." *New York Times*, April 2. Retrieved from https://www.nytimes.com/2019/04/02/technology/for-him-for-hers-get-roman.html.

39. Hall, A. J., J. E. Logan, R. L. Toblin, J. A. Kaplan, J. C. Kraner, D. Bixler, . . . , and L. J. Paulozzi (2008). Patterns of Abuse Among Unintentional Pharmaceutical Overdose Fatalities. *JAMA*, *300*(22): 2613–2620.

40. *Drug Overdose* (n.d.). Drug Policy Alliance. Retrieved from http://www.drugpolicy.org/issues/drug-overdose.

41. Okwo-Bele, J.-M. (2015). *Together We Can Close the Immunization Gap*. World Health Organization, April 22. Retrieved from https://www.who.int/mediacentre/commentaries/vaccine-preventable-diseases/en/.

42. O'Connor, C., and J. O. Weatherall (2019). *The Misinformation Age: How False Beliefs Spread*. New Haven, CT: Yale University Press.

43. Vinck, P., Pham, P. N., Bindu, K. K., Bedford, J., & Nilles, E. J. (2019). Institutional trust and misinformation in the response to the 2018–19 Ebola outbreak in North Kivu, DR Congo: a population-based survey. *The Lancet Infectious Diseases*, *19*(5), 529–536.

44. Hussain, R. S., McGarvey, S. T., & Fruzzetti, L. M. (2015). Partition and poliomyelitis: An investigation of the polio disparity affecting Muslims during India's eradication program. *PloS one, 10*(3), e0115628.

45. Mcneil, D. G. (2019). Polio Cases Surge in Pakistan and Afghanistan. *New York Times*, July 15. Retrieved from https://www.nytimes.com /2019/07/15/health/polio-pakistan-afghanistan.html.

46. Esposito, B. L., L. Rapaport, and D. Rauf (n.d.). *Fewer Disease Risk Factors, Yet More Fatal Heart Attacks.* EveryDay Health. Retrieved from https://www.everydayhealth.com/heart-health/1115/fewer-disease -risk-factors-yet-more-fatal-heart-attacks.aspx.

47. The most rewarding application of the placebo effect for new parents, of course, is convincing your children that kisses fix booboos.

48. Waber, R. L., B. Shiv, Z. Carmon, and D. Ariely (2008). Commercial Features of Placebo and Therapeutic. *JAMA, 299*(9): 1016–1017.

49. Zhou, X., K. D. Vohs, and R. F. Baumeister (2009). The Symbolic Power of Money: Reminders of Money Alter Social Distress and Physical Pain. *Psychological Science,* 20(6): 700–706.

50. Marchant, J. (2016). Placebos: Honest Fakery. *Nature, 535*(7611): S14–S15.

51. Kaptchuk, T. J., E. Friedlander, J. M. Kelley, M. N. Sanchez, E. Kokkotou, J. P. Singer, . . . , and A. J. Lembo (2010). Placebos Without Deception: A Randomized Controlled Trial in Irritable Bowel Syndrome. *PloS ONE, 5*(12): e15591.

52. Jabr, F. (2019). The Truth About Dentistry. *The Atlantic*, April 17. Retrieved from https://www.theatlantic.com/magazine/archive/2019/05 /the-trouble-with-dentistry/586039/.

53. Chandra, A., A. Finkelstein, A. Sacarny, and C. Syverson (2013). *Health-care Exceptionalism? Productivity and Allocation in the US Healthcare Sector.* No. w19200. National Bureau of Economic Research. https:// www.nber.org/papers/w19200.

54. Gottschalk, F. C., W. Mimra, and C. Waibel (2018). *Health Services as Credence Goods: A Field Experiment.* Available at SSRN 3036573.

55. Schneider, H. S. (2012). Agency Problems and Reputation in Expert Services: Evidence from Auto Repair. *Journal of Industrial Economics*, 60(3), 406–433.

56. Alsan, M., and M. Wanamaker (2018). Tuskegee and the Health of Black Men. *The Quarterly Journal of Economics, 133*(1): 407–455.

57. Hoffman, K. M., S. Trawalter, J. R. Axt, and M. N. Oliver (2016). Racial Bias in Pain Assessment and Treatment Recommendations, and False Beliefs about Biological Differences Between Blacks and Whites. *Proceedings of the National Academy of Sciences, 113*(16): 4296–4301.

58. Alsan, M., O. Garrick, and G. Graziani (2019). Does Diversity Matter for Health? Experimental Evidence from Oakland. *American Economic Review, 109*(12): 4071–4111.

59. Commonwealth Fund (2005). *Clinton and Obama Offer Bill to Encourage Disclosure of Medical Errors.* September 28. Retrieved from https://www.commonwealthfund.org/publications/newsletter-article/clinton-and-obama-offer-bill-encourage-disclosure-medical-errors.

60. https://med.stanford.edu/news/all-news/2012/09/little-evidence-of-health-benefits-from-organic-foods-study-finds.html; https://www.sciencemag.org/news/2016/05/once-again-us-expert-panel-says-genetically-engineered-crops-are-safe-eat; https://climate.nasa.gov/evidence/; https://www.cdc.gov/vaccinesafety/concerns/autism.html.

61. http://revisionisthistory.com/episodes/20-the-basement-tapes; https://www.hsph.harvard.edu/nutritionsource/what-should-you-eat/fats-and-cholesterol/cholesterol/.

62. https://www.mayoclinic.org/healthy-lifestyle/womens-health/in-depth/breast-implants/art-20045957.

63. https://www.healthline.com/nutrition/8-glasses-of-water-per-day.

64. Camerer, C. F., A. Dreber, E. Forsell, T. H. Ho, J. Huber, M. Johannesson, . . . , and E. Heikensten (2016). Evaluating Replicability of Laboratory Experiments in Economics. *Science, 351*(6280): 1433–1436; Open Science Collaboration (2015). Estimating the reproducibility of Psychological Science, 349. Begley, C. G., & Ellis, L. M. (2012). Raise standards for preclinical cancer research. *Nature, 483*(7391), 531–533.

65. For example, Benjamin et al. (2018) has proposed using a stricter standard of statistical significance while Olken (2015) and many others have suggested that researchers register their plan for doing research before they look at the data. Benjamin, D. J., Berger, J. O., Johannesson, M., Nosek, B. A., Wagenmakers, E. J., Berk, R., . . . and Cesarini, D. (2018). Redefine Statistical Significance. *Nature Human Behaviour, 2*(1), 6–10; Olken, B. A. (2015). Promises and Perils of Pre-analysis Plans. *Journal of Economic Perspectives, 29*(3), 61–80.

66. Berger and Milkman, What Makes Online Content Viral?

67. I am aware that formally the definition of confidence intervals is about the probability the true value is in the interval, which is not quite the same as the rate of false positives, hence the "more or less," but it is true more or less.

68. Morris, Political Correctness

69. See for example the Pulitzer Prize–winning book by Douglas Hofstadter for a very accessible treatment about Gödel's mathematics: Hofstadter, Douglas R., (1979). *Gödel, Escher, Bach: An Eternal Golden Braid*. New York: Basic Books.

70. Nordhaus, W. D. (2007). *The Challenge of Global Warming: Economic Models and Environmental Policy, Vol. 4*. New Haven, CT: Yale University Press.

71. Bó, P. D. (2005). Cooperation Under the Shadow of the Future: Experimental Evidence from Infinitely Repeated Games. *American Economic Review*, 95(5): 1591–1604.

72. Candelo, N., C. Eckel, and C. Johnson (2018). Social Distance Matters in Dictator Games: Evidence from 11 Mexican Villages. *Games*, 9(4): 77.

73. Frank, R. H. (1985). *Choosing the Right Pond: Human Behavior and the Quest for Status*. New York: Oxford University Press.

74. Rayo, L., and G. S. Becker (2007). Habits, Peers, and Happiness: An Evolutionary Perspective. *American Economic Review*, 97(2): 487–491.

75. Moore, F. C., N. Obradovich, F. Lehner, and P. Baylis (2019). Rapidly Declining Remarkability of Temperature Anomalies May Obscure Public Perception of Climate Change. *Proceedings of the National Academy of Sciences*, 116(11): 4905–4910.

76. Finnemore, M., and K. Sikkink (1998). International Norm Dynamics and Political Change. *International Organization*, 52(4): 887–917.

77. *Kyoto Protocol Fast Facts* (2018). CNN, March 21. Retrieved from https://www.cnn.com/2013/07/26/world/kyoto-protocol-fast-facts/index.html.

78. Technically, this vote was not on the protocol itself, but on the Byrd-Hagel Resolution, which basically nullified the protocol without mentioning it.

79. United Nations. (2020). *Paris Agreement*. https://unfccc.int/process-and-meetings/the-paris-agreement/the-paris-agreement/key-aspects-of-the-paris-agreement.

80. Improving No Child Left Behind (2011). *New York Times*, October 1. Retrieved from https://www.nytimes.com/2011/10/01/opinion/improving -no-child-left-behind.html.

5. TRUSTING ONE ANOTHER

1. Grossman, L. (2009). A *Watchmen* Fan's Notes. *Time*, March 5. Retrieved from http://content.time.com/time/magazine/article/0,9171,1883361,00 .html.

2. Friedman, T. L. (1999). The Lexus and the Olive Tree: Understanding Globalization. New York: Farrar, Straus, and Giroux.

3. Sturgis, P., and P. Smith (2010). Assessing the Validity of General-ized Trust Questions: What Kind of Trust Are We Measuring? *International Journal of Public Opinion Research, 22*(1): 74–92.

4. Pinker, S. (2008). The Moral Instinct. *The New York Times*, January 13. Retrieved from https://www.nytimes.com/2008/01/13/magazine /13Psychology-t.html.

5. Graham, J., J. Haidt, and B. A. Nosek (2009). Liberals and Conserva-tives Rely on Different Sets of Moral Foundations. *Journal of Personality and Social Psychology, 96*(5): 1029–1046; Haidt, J. (2012). *The Righteous Mind: Why Good People Are Divided By Politics and Religion*. New York: Pantheon Books.

6. Coughlan, S. (2014). *US Schools to have Non-white Majority*. BBC News, August 26. Retrieved from https://www.bbc.com/news/education -28937660.

7. Berger, J. A., C. Heath, and B. Ho (2005). Divergence in Cultural Practices: Tastes as Signals of Identity. Retrieved from https://repository .upenn.edu/marketing_papers/306.

8. Putnam, R. D. (2007). E pluribus unum: Diversity and community in the twenty-first century the 2006 Johan Skytte Prize Lecture. *Scandi-navian political studies, 30*(2), 137–174.

9. Abascal, M., & Baldassarri, D. (2015). Love thy neighbor? Ethnora-cial diversity and trust reexamined. *American Journal of Sociology, 121*(3), 722–782.

10. Falk, A., A. Becker, T. Dohmen, B. Enke, D. Huffman, and U. Sunde (2018). Global Evidence on Economic Preferences. *Quarterly Journal of Economics, 133*(4): 1645–1692.

11. Zhou, X., Y. Liu, and B. Ho (2015). The Cultural Transmission of Cooperative Norms. *Frontiers in Psychology, 6*, 1554.

12. Matsa, K. E., and E. Shearer (2018). News Use Across Social Media Platforms 2018. Pew Research Center, September 10. Retrieved from https://www.journalism.org/2018/09/10/news-use-across-social-media -platforms-2018/.

13. Dunbar, R. I., Arnaboldi, V., Conti, M., & Passarella, A. (2015). The structure of online social networks mirrors those in the offline world. *Social networks, 43*, 39–47.

14. Ortoleva, P., and E. Snowberg (2015). Overconfidence in Political Behavior. *American Economic Review, 105*(2): 504–535.

15. Enns, P. (2014). *Presidential Campaigns Are Less Important Than Previously Thought in Influencing How People Vote.* LSE US Centre, May 15. Retrieved from https://blogs.lse.ac.uk/usappblog/2013/09/05 /presidential-campaigns-fundamentals/.

16. Allcott, H., L. Braghieri, S. Eichmeyer, and M. Gentzkow (2019). *The Welfare Effects of Social Media.* No. w25514. National Bureau of Economic Research.

17. Boxell, L., M. Gentzkow, and J. M. Shapiro (2017). *Is the Internet Causing Political Polarization? Evidence from Demographics.* No. w23258. National Bureau of Economic Research.

18. Quoidbach, J., D. T. Gilbert, and T. D. Wilson (2013). The End of History Illusion. *Science, 339*(6115): 96–98.

19. Manson, M. (n.d.). *Why You Can't Trust Yourself.* Pocket. Retrieved from https://getpocket.com/explore/item/why-you-can-t-trust-yourself?utm _source=pocket-newtab.

20. O'Donoghue, T., and M. Rabin (1999). Doing It Now or Later. *American Economic Review, 89*(1): 103–124.

21. Centers for Disease Control and Prevention (CDC) (2020). *Smoking Cessation: Fast Facts.* May 21. Retrieved from https://www.cdc.gov /tobacco/data_statistics/fact_sheets/cessation/quitting/index.htm.

22. Chen, M. K. (2013). The Effect of Language on Economic Behavior: Evidence from Savings Rates, Health Behaviors, and Retirement Assets. *American Economic Review, 103*(2): 690–731.

23. In mathematical notation, economists often describe altruism as having Utility for yourself (x_i) plus some Greek letter alpha times the well-being of the Other, denoted by x_{-i}. Behavioral economists model the

trade-offs between your utility today and your utility tomorrow by saying that you have utility for yourself today (x_t) plus beta times your utility in the future (x_{t+1}).

24. Minsky, M. (1988). *Society of Mind*. New York: Simon and Schuster.
25. Ariely, D., G. Loewenstein, and D. Prelec (2003). "Coherent Arbitrariness": Stable Demand Curves Without Stable Preferences. *Quarterly Journal of Economics, 118*(1): 73–106.
26. Bénabou, R., & Tirole, J. (2011). Identity, Morals, and Taboos: Beliefs as Assets. *Quarterly Journal of Economics, 126*(2): 805–855.
27. This story is true but the details have been changed to protect the innocent.
28. Ho, B., & Liu, E. (2011). Does Sorry Work? The Impact of Apology Laws on Medical Malpractice. *Journal of Risk and Uncertainty, 43*(2), 141; Ho, B., & Liu, E. (2011). What's an Apology Worth? Decomposing the Effect of Apologies on Medical Malpractice Payments Using State Apology Laws. *Journal of Empirical Legal Studies, 8,* 179–199.

    An astute reader might note that earlier in the book I pointed out that statistics can only show correlation not causation. In our paper, we employed a number of econometric techniques to show causality using a differences-in-differences approach, including placebo tests, parallel trend tests, and testing alternate causes like tort reform and political party.
29. Tiedens, L. Z. (2001). Anger and Advancement Versus Sadness and Subjugation: The Effect of Negative Emotion Expressions on Social Status Conferral. *Journal of Personality and Social Psychology 80*(1): 86–94.
30. Cilliers, J., O. Dube, and B. Siddiqi (2018). Can the Wounds of War Be Healed? Experimental Evidence on Reconciliation in Sierra Leone. May. International Initiative for Impact Education.
31. Ho, B. (2012). Apologies as Signals: with Evidence from a Trust Game. *Management Science, 58*(1), 141–158.
32. Warner, G. (2018). A Case Study in How to Apologize for a War Crime. NPR. https://www.npr.org/2018/06/13/619447126/a-case-study-in-how-to-apologize-for-a-war-crime.
33. Glass, I. (2019). Get a Spine! *This American Life*. https://www.thisamericanlife.org/674/transcript. *This American Life* has actually had quite good coverage of many apologies over the years. I encourage you

to look them up. I've actually been a religious listener to the show since it came out in the 1990s.

34. Tavuchis, N. (1991). *Mea Culpa: A Sociology of Apology and Reconciliation*. Stanford, CA: Stanford University Press, 1991.

35. For example, see Fischbacher, U., and V. Utikal, V. (2013). On the Acceptance of Apologies. *Games and Economic Behavior, 82:* 592–608.

36. Minter, A. (2019). *Why Big Brother Doesn't Bother Most Chinese*. Bloomberg, January 24. Retrieved from https://www.bloomberg.com /opinion/articles/2019-01-24/why-china-s-social-credit-systems-are -surprisingly-popular.

37. *Social Credit System* (2020). Wikipedia, January 23. Retrieved from https://en.wikipedia.org/wiki/Social_Credit_System.

38. Anyone who has run a trust game experiment has likely seen gender effects in the data; I certainly have, and see also Innocenti, A., and M. G. Pazienza (2006). *Altruism and Gender in the Trust Game*. Labsi Working Paper No. 5/2006. https://ssrn.com/abstract=884378 or http:// dx.doi.org/10.2139/ssrn.884378.

39. Board of Governors of the Federal Reserve System (n.d.). Retrieved from https://www.federalreserve.gov/econres/notes/feds-notes/gender -related-differences-in-credit-use-and-credit-scores-20180622.html.

40. Darwall, S. (2008). Kant on Respect, Dignity, and the Duty of Respect.

41. Acquisti, A., C. Taylor, and L. Wagman (2016). The Economics of Privacy. *Journal of Economic Literature, 54*(2): 442–492.

42. Case, A., and A. Deaton (2020). *Deaths of Despair and the Future of Capitalism*. Princeton, NJ: Princeton University Press.

43. Sexton, S. E., and A. L. Sexton (2014). Conspicuous Conservation: The Prius Halo and Willingness to Pay for Environmental Bona Fides. *Journal of Environmental Economics and Management, 67*(3): 303–317.

44. Frank, R. H. (1984). Interdependent Preferences and the Competitive Wage Structure. *RAND Journal of Economics, 15*(4): 510–520.

45. Berger, J. A., B. Ho, and Y. V. Joshi (2011). *Identity Signaling with Social Capital: A Model of Symbolic Consumption*. Available at SSRN 1828848.

46. Buss, S., and A. Westlund (2018). Personal Autonomy. *Stanford Encyclopedia of Philosophy*, February 15. Retrieved from https://plato.stanford .edu/entries/personal-autonomy/#FourLessOverAccoPersAuto.

6. CONCLUSION

1. Ridley, M. (2010). *The Rational Optimist: How Prosperity Evolves.* New York: Harper.
2. Ehrlich, P. R., D. R. Parnell, and A. Silbowitz (1971). *The Population Bomb, Vol. 68.* New York: Ballantine.
3. Rosling, H., O. Rosling, and A. Rosling Rönnlund (2018). *Factfulness: Ten Reasons We're Wrong About the World—and Why Things Are Better Than You Think.* New York: Flatiron Books. Pinker, S. (2012). *The Better Angels of Our Nature: Why Violence Has Declined.* New York: Penguin.
4. Gates, B. (2018). Bill Gates: Why I Decided to Edit an Issue of TIME. *Time Magazine,* January 4. Retrieved from https://time.com/5086870/bill-gates-guest-editor-time/.

INDEX

Page numbers in *italics* represent figures or tables.